AMERICAN LABOR

FROM CONSPIRACY TO COLLECTIVE BARGAINING

ADVISORY EDITORS

Leon Stein *Philip Taft*

SPY OVERHEAD

THE STORY OF INDUSTRIAL ESPIONAGE

Clinch Calkins

ARNO & THE NEW YORK TIMES
NEW YORK   1971

HD
6508
.C17
1971

Reprint Edition 1971 by Arno Press Inc.

Copyright 1937 © 1965 by Clinch Calkins
Reprinted by permission of Harcourt Brace Jovanovich, Inc.

Reprinted from a copy in The State Historical Society of Wisconsin Library
LC# 70-156408
ISBN 0-405-02917-9

American Labor: From Conspiracy to Collective Bargaining—Series II
ISBN for complete set: 0-405-02910-1
See last pages for titles.

Manufactured in the United States of America

Spy Overhead

THE STORY OF INDUSTRIAL ESPIONAGE

by the same author

SOME FOLKS WON'T WORK

SPY OVERHEAD

THE STORY OF
INDUSTRIAL ESPIONAGE

Clinch Calkins

Harcourt, Brace and Company, New York

COPYRIGHT, 1937, BY

CLINCH CALKINS

All rights reserved, including the right to reproduce this book or portions thereof in any form.

first edition

PRINTED IN THE UNITED STATES OF AMERICA
BY QUINN & BODEN COMPANY, INC., RAHWAY, N. J.
Typography by Robert Josephy

TO MARK MERRELL

THOUGHT

Of obedience, faith, adhesiveness;
As I stand aloof and look there is to me something profoundly affecting in large masses of men following the lead of those who do not believe in men.
WALT WHITMAN

Contents

I.	THE VICTIM IS IDENTIFIED	3
II.	THE SENATE TURNS DETECTIVE	16
III.	SUPER-SLEUTHS	39
IV.	CONCERNING THEM THAT SEDUCE YOU	64
V.	SUBTERRANEAN LIFE	87
VI.	THE SMALL FRY OF VIOLENCE	130
VII.	IS GAS POLITER THAN GUNS?	168
VIII.	COLLECTIVE FIRING	223
IX.	THE FIELD OF HONOR	263
X.	THE PROUD HAVE HID SNARES	308
	INDEX	357

1. The Victim is Identified

WRITERS of detective fiction have an elementary rule: They must not arouse much feeling for the victim.

This is a good rule for a good reason. The author knows that, although he may number among his readers those vicarious detectives who smell out his best red herrings as fast as he can draw their fins across the page, to his average reader time spent upon a mystery is a period of suspended animation—so much muscular exercise of the eyes. When such a reader closes the book, sighing contentedly that his pleasure is over, he is unable to tell you who was murdered, why, or with what. The hour he spends with guns and cyanide is one of sheerest, delicious insignificance. Wiping his eye-glasses could not be of less emotional importance.

It is to preserve this enchantment of unreal, and therefore unimportant, violence that a mystery writer chooses his victim with such care. Regret must not retard the headlong progress of the action. He must dispose forever of the dear old lady who keeps her jewels in a secret drawer before she has time to win the reader's affection. His only other alternative is to guarantee the victim to be a brutal, felonious fellow in all his phases; one who has long since earned the murderous intention of every suspect, and for whose mysterious end the reader would, if he had time to linger on it, feel nothing but relief.

There has been unfolded before the United States Senate a true detective story whose main outlines I am giving here. The habitual readers of detective fiction must be forewarned that it can produce the same familiar tendency to rise above the meaning of the evidence, to float in excitement above the scene of the crime, forgetful of its implication. The reader is glued to the record long after the record has yielded up the clue for which he sought.

The story of *Spy Overhead* is the story of the American industrial worker caught in a trap of commercialized espionage and violence. An odd assortment of evidence in the files of the Sub-Committee on Education and Labor tells this story; secretly mailed requests to the President or the Department of Justice for bodily protection; income tax reports; testimony of industrialists; of labor organizers, detectives, union men turned traitors, or union men who have refused to turn traitor; the testimony of labor pimps, munition makers, sluggers, and ex-convicts. Together they make a decipherable and appallingly true story more like fiction than fiction is itself.

In the importance of the victim lies the fundamental difference between this true and the fictitious story. The victim of the American spy industry is neither a sentimental nonentity nor a felon, although it has been our custom to treat him alternately as one or the other. Instead he is a chief character in American life. Moreover, in the living story his fictitious role is changed. In fiction the victim is destroyed in order to create a mystery for the detective to solve. Here his destruction becomes the grim work of the detective's day.

The wage-earner in industry has played a tragic and curious part in American history. We are apt to look a little luminously upon the first days of the Republic when every worker was supposed to have his chance, could call the farmer and the merchant brother, could even call the local moneylender by a given name. Even then opportunity was a selective angel and left her mark on certain doorways only. The West, as we know, was not settled

THE VICTIM IS IDENTIFIED

alone by the adventurous. Hope, or the lack of it, could push as well as pull. Nor did those who stayed at home stretch and yawn in self-expansion. Our first recorded American strike, called by printers in the literate city of Boston, was in 1776, there being even in the first year of our political independence an awareness of the necessity of joining with others to make one's terms felt upon the labor market.

Even with our knowledge of the worker's early hardships, we must believe that the market had for the solitary bargainer more promise then than now. He was dignified by the size of the country into which he could disappear, but more than that he was dignified by the completeness of his craft; he could make a whole shoe or a whole house. At least so he appears to us in retrospect, a lone figure having some strength to strike a bargain with men who needed and respected him. If he could have foreseen the fabulous wells which were at his touch to gush forth from American ground, the fortunes to be made in forests, mines, and cattle-ranging, he would no doubt have believed that he and his children would be translated to the status of squires.

As a matter of fact just enough of them did obtain small property to fix their sympathies permanently on the side of their hope, which was to own big property. The volatile layer of American life which has stood like a blanket of fog between the wage-earner and his claim to a share in industrial government lies in the wide American group of small property owners and small business men, annually liquidated downward in great numbers, but occasionally vaporized to higher clouds of glory. It is in this group of the near-successful that hope springs like winter wheat. Later were added to them the small stockholders, salaried executives, and those white-collared workers who have only lately begun to suspect their economic identity with those who work for a wage. These mobile groups have prevented the labor movement from taking on the appearance of the class struggle which at base it has been.

To the man who lost out on that slight difference between a high wage and the successful business started on a shoestring, the wealth of America turned out to be not friend but enemy. It reduced his political stature and cheapened his economic price. The figure of the American worker has stood like a disappearing pigmy against a growing pile of riches. To understand how and why this has been accomplished is important to an understanding of the Senate's investigation into violation of constitutional rights in labor disputes.

At the beginning, many people looked on these findings as an indication of a pitched battle about to occur between capital and labor. The legislative committee of the American Federation of Labor in their convention of 1936 in Tampa so spoke of them in urging the Senate to pursue the inquiry, in the teeth of what they prophesied to be a million-dollar lobby against it, since it was clear even then that the first hearings had scarcely cracked the surface of industry's participation in labor espionage. Others believe that commercialized espionage is only a current manifestation of an unremitting war between capital and labor, now taking on especially ugly proportions as the process continues by which those who have little grow to be continuously more numerous and have less, while those who have much grow to be continuously fewer and have more.

If one subtracts from the 32,000,000 American wage-earners all those who are not immediately engaged in industrial occupations, there are approximately 19,000,000 workers in industry. Fifty-three billion dollars of the

THE VICTIM IS IDENTIFIED

national wealth is composed of, or invested in, manufacturing. This is nearly $2800 for every industrial worker, or, if you please, against him. Such a quotient carries little truth, and is purely literary. The worker may be considered separately; the money is indivisible. It cannot even be isolated from all other corporate wealth. The farm laborer has not yet learned how to combine with the industrial worker. Domestic and personal-service trades are too often casual to unite with others. White-collar earners have felt no economic kinship with any of them. But to separate one payroll from another in its ultimate pool of credit is like turning the cistern back into raindrops.

Even knowing what we do about the political power of money; money in the police courts; money in the press; money in the corridor; money in the college; money in the church; how it shapes governments, writes laws, conditions the air of courtrooms, commandeers the services of lawyers, it is impossible to escape the knowledge that since men created money, they can control it. Yet shut off from the aid of his fellows, disarmed by his own ignorance, the worker, always handicapped by pressing need, is in an awkward pinch battling with an adversary who brings on to the field the whole fighting paraphernalia of society; his detectives, his gas projectors and machine guns, his lawyers to second him, and the legislature right around the corner in a first-aid wagon.

To the outsider it seems evident that thirty-two million American wage-earners working intelligently together for what they separately want could lick even the apotheosis of money, polish up the seconds, and commandeer the wagon. It seems amply clear that their opponents fear the final implication of such preponderant numbers. But the lonely bargainer apparently is only learning this fact. After a century of effort to organize into mass formation there were, until the drive by the Committee for Industrial Organization in the winter and spring of 1937, estimated to be some 4,200,000 wage-earners who had been unionized. By the spring of 1937 the figure had been put between five and six million. The company union, which is little more than a customer's complaint box, and is an instrument to prevent rather than to further collective bargaining, claimed 2,500,000 more before the drive by C.I.O. Thus a huge majority of all wage-earners in the country are caught in the bargaining place alone, like one man with a shovel tunneling through a mountain.

This situation has been carefully arrived at by the foes of labor organization. The labor movement has sometimes been betrayed from within. It has sometimes been sold out by its own racketeering agents, usually for a price set high by those who would crush it. It has been intimidated and framed, gassed and shot down. Unions have been pronounced by law to be in restraint of trade. Picketing has been enjoined by the courts. Venal labor leaders have been encouraged. Vigilante committees have been spurred into action against it. The public has been cleverly instructed in the dangers of unionization. Too frequently labor organization, where it has taken shape, has taken shape acceptable to a management who, next to wishing it non-existent, would like to see it corrupt. The primary difficulty of the American labor movement is to stay organized, and while it stays unorganized it is impotent. Therefore management has concentrated on destroying the union before it came into being. The labor successes of 1936-1937 need set no one's mind at rest upon this matter. The temper which proposed to keep the union ineffectual is little changed.

Where it was possible labor has been kept from having any strength. Having strength, it has been kept from knowing it. The chief way of fostering its bargaining weakness has been to increase the number of contestants for the single job. The deafening roar of many voices for work at any price could be counted upon to drown out lonely protest against near-starvation earned in twelve-hour shifts.

Two agencies lent themselves superbly to this purpose. The ship's steerage could be counted on to teach gratitude to the complaining. So ships came in from Ireland, from Germany, from the Scandinavian north, from the European south. They even came from China. Seventy-five Chinese coolies were once brought into North Adams, Massachusetts, to break a strike.

The second agency was the family womb, generous to the poor. This has aided management in and out of season. It is only now, when it runs up the tax bill for unemployment relief, that it is cursed. Each new offspring made grist to the mill, the younger the cheaper. Like their mothers, the children could undercut their father. To the wage-earner's family this was inescapable arithmetic. The present status of the Child Labor Amendment demonstrates that this method of weakening the position of man labor has not been abandoned.

Other fuels, burning together through the nineteenth century and into the twentieth, boiled down the individual worker to his fullest economic helplessness. Many workers were put under one roof. Their crafts were divided into special tasks, so that no one man was indispensable to the completed product and no worker by himself could complete it. Next there was the honeymoon of money and machinery. Finally, mass production took over the field of creation, and the corporation took over human tasks of management and nullified human responsibilities of active ownership. What gains had been made by the limiting of immigration were more than offset by the increased mobility of workers who could descend like locusts where there was hope of work, and by the effect of technological improvements upon skills. The highly skilled craftsman except in narrowing circles became anomalous.

To say that this warfare has been from the first a contest of brute strength has the dangerous sound of a generalization. Documented by the battles between labor and management it still stands up as a statement. The apparently episodic quality of these battles; the facts that but a minority of them ever reaches public attention and that they are scattered over many fields and in many occupations tend to take the attention away from their real continuity or their united purpose.

The fight to keep labor legislation out of the federal jurisdiction has been but an attempt to keep in obscurity labor's common cause and to keep it from having self-knowledge of its strength. So far, money as a political instrument has been more effective than persons. Money is the only thing that labor does not have. To keep the legislative battle within the boundaries of the state is to multiply its money cost by forty-eight. But it does a further thing, perhaps more important. By keeping the issue local and under control of local political forces themselves well controlled by property, it tends to obscure the violation of constitutional right involved in the means of subjugation. Lest this, too, sound like a generality, may an instance in the long Colorado warfare of the 1900's be cited from a chapter entitled "Class War on a Grand Scale" in *History of Labor in the United States* by John R. Commons and Associates? After union miners had suffered glaring infringement upon their civil liberties, they undertook to publicize them in a way intended to draw attention to their status as American citizens.

In so doing, wittingly or unwittingly, they ran afoul of an ironical law. "On March 26 [1904], Charles H. Moyer, the president of the Western Federation of Miners, was arrested by the sheriff of Ouray County and charged with desecrating the flag. He was turned over to the militia and lodged in the Telluride bull pen. The charge was an outgrowth of a poster distributed by the Western Federation of Miners which showed an American flag with inscription in black ink on the stripes itemizing the forms of the violation of the miner's constitutional rights." This task of dispersing the forces of labor becomes easier and more important as management, taken out of the hands of the owners, is done (in the words of Edward R. Stettinius, Jr., Chairman of the Finance Committee of the United States Steel Corporation, speaking in the Harvard tercentenary celebrations on choosing executives) "like navigation, by instrument largely."

Business Week of February 27, 1937, in a study of migration of industry and trend toward decentralization of plant, admits the heightened impulse management feels to move its men advantageously across the states, checkerboarded with various labor and tax laws, into those positions in which the worker can make least claim upon his job and least claim upon the benefits of general social legislation. It says: "Any study of the migration of plants and industries will reveal that our manufacturing activities are in a state of flux probably never before approached in our history." Speaking of United States Steel's decision to expand further its production center in Birmingham, it says: "Existing capacity at Northern mills is considered ample to meet current and early future requirements, but the corporation is spending $29,000,000 for new capacity at a production center where its labor problems have so far been less complex, where state and local interests are sympathetic and where other advantages accrue."

Politically disillusioned, and forced to recognize that political and economic democracy are not necessarily either brothers or first cousins under the skin, labor has had no alternative but the economic weapon of the strike, often used as a lever to obtain political ends. The worker has been forced to learn that the warfare is one of commodities and not of human rights. His one commodity is service. Ergo, he will make his goods more dear by holding them back from the customer. The boycott is only an indirection of this. The strike and the boycott are the sanctions which they hold over their now legal right to bargain collectively. No political weapon the worker has ever found has matched the strike for effectiveness, it being the one vessel of defiance into which he may pour his stubborn intention and have it count. Although money can break strikes and has broken many of them, there is yet in this Croesian Age, something disconcerting, something terrifyingly bleak about the turned back of a displeased man who is willing to undertake suffering rather than to do business with you on your own terms. Human sensitivity, however, has little to do with its effectiveness. The determining factor is that without men, money cannot make materials, nor can materials make money.

Even in this administration in which labor has accomplished more for itself than in any dozen administrations preceding it and because of whose encouragement the ranks of workers have been swept by a triumphing will to succeed, the government's attitude toward strikes has been, in its most vernacular sense, middle class. Co-abiding with American tolerance of ruthlessness we have, as everyone knows, a fine humanitarian stream in our nature. We

THE VICTIM IS IDENTIFIED

can turn it on like a kitchen faucet of warm water whenever it seems useful to do so: the Boy Scout Good Deed; the American Red Cross Mother of all the World; the welfare period of American industrial relations; the Unknown Soldier; the Gold Star Mother. The list is long. In it must surely be included most of our governmental dealings with strikes. Alternating between exhortation and cruelty, the government has listened first to the property interests and second to a public opinion sometimes unpredictably on the side of the strikers, or to the sporadic protest of investigating bodies which have set forth conditions much prettier left unveiled. The shadowy periphery around class life in America, which has made so much more difficult the laborer's task of obtaining his part in industrial government, has accomplished a small thing in his favor. Class lines are broken by family relationships and neighborly dealings. One never knows who is related to whom. The policeman charged with attack upon striking workers may recognize his brother-in-law on the picket line, or his sister's children in the windrow area for gas. Storekeepers may be in sympathy with wage-earners from whom they get their living. Thus an employer who has just sent out an invitation for a strikebreakers' house party, who is putting cots in the plant and setting up a commissary for imported deputies, may find the enraged townsmen around his ears like yellow jackets. The strike thus cashes in on its second advantage. It is less negligible than the law, more conspicuous than a set of conditions.

The government is in a different predicament from that of the community. The public counts upon the government to see that its lettuce comes to the market and its coal to the bin. But government knows its family up to the last rich uncle, and boasts its separate obligations to all groups. Labor is one of these. Labor is weak. Labor is a brother. Labor is on a crusade. But isn't labor being a little inconsiderate? Especially now when we are at war. Or when business is just picking up. Or when everybody has just been given a Christmas bonus. Thus from the sending in of Federal troops down to the dilatory and reproachful tactics of NRA, the government has always run the scale in arpeggios from hatred and brutality to warning that "Mother must spank."

The strike is inconvenient. Indeed the strike is useful to labor only because it is inconvenient both to management and public. The more inconvenient, the better. That is why it is used in times of improving business when both management and public are impatient at being held back. In bad times, management can ignore the strike or even use it as an excuse for throwing off the responsibility of maintaining the worker.

The hardships to the strikers can scarcely be dismissed with the word inconvenient. To answer the strike call too often means suffering and want, perhaps permanent loss of livelihood, sickness and injury, or even violent death. It cannot be entered into lightly. Even in those instances when a specific provocation has seemed slight or silly to the outsider, it almost invariably bears real relevance to a history of oppression. Among highly organized laborers who enjoy good working conditions, old experience of deprivation, a smoldering sense of injustice, are like slow-burning black powder to a detonator. Their demands are apt not to be for material gains but for the principle of recognition. This insistence has tough roots in the American political idea.

How many thousands of workers have died to bring about united strength among them will never be known. No backward count can now be made. Most of them died obscurely. The necessary toughness and secularity of their fight has never made it susceptible to shrines or marble monuments. Theirs is, to people of comfort, an uncongenial kind of heroism. Once or twice before now the labor movement has reached towering proportions, only to be torn down. Yet those who have seen labor fail to consolidate their winnings, have seen them dispersed and fall back, have seen the public's interest in them flicker, flame, and go out, often forget that with each new cycle gains have been made. New permanent standards have been set in the public's mind by each temporary victory. Legislation has been written to protect the worker against certain forms of exploitation that once were commonplace. In other words, the wheel goes round from inflaming event to apathy. It turns, however, not like a revolving drum, but in an aspiring curve.

II. The Senate Turns Detective

THE Senate may command witnesses to appear before it, subpoena records, and take testimony under oath. It is for the purpose of obtaining information to help in shaping remedial legislation that the Senate uses these investigative powers. That, in the process of inquiring into some known or suspected evil, it hangs a very great deal of dirty linen on the public line to flap in the air is not the least of its ablutionary services. An indignant public can wash up exploitation more enthusiastically than the law, although to be sure it tires earlier. Much more important than its temporary indignation is—because it is later called upon to support the law—public understanding of what is being regulated.

Loud denunciations of "another Senate fishing trip" are always heard from the investigated quarter. As practical men, the denouncers and their silent fellow strategists, trying in cloakrooms to suppress an inquiry, are aware of the ephemeral quality of public temper. Nevertheless they know that publication of details gives the victim a good working knowledge of his victimizer. Some inquiries of great moment may involve technical matters hard to translate into popular terms. Even so the amount of newspaper space given to a Senate hearing may be a measure of its success as an educational instrument. It is not considered a fault if an investigation proves to be dramatic.

The Civil Liberties Investigation has been good theater. Hearings commence in the morning at ten and supposedly recess at noon when the Senate convenes, although if the matter is at a critical point the Committee sits until nearly one, and begins again at two. Fifteen or twenty minutes ahead of the hour the door is unlocked and the corridor empties a waiting audience into a small hearing room of the Senate Office Building, only half of which is available for spectators. Before proceedings are well under way every seat is taken. Day after day the same people appear like faithful attendants upon a movie serial, happy when the witness speaks out bold and clear, heads strained forward to catch the faint tone of the reluctant man under catechism. During noon recess, while Senators and staff are adding up the score on the morning's record and planning strategy for afternoon, the audience strolls down the corridor for lunch in the Senate Office dining room, or takes the subterranean trolley to the Capitol restaurant and whiles away the intermission.

In the other half of the room the play goes on. A magnet-shaped rostrum, raised three steps from the floor, supports on either side the veterans of the press, behind whom stand their footmen in uniform, the telegraph boys who fly in and out with yellow foolscap. Those who were not early enough to get seats squat down on the steps or occupy the two lengthwise press tables which form the orchestra.

Directly in the middle, at the curve of the horseshoe, sit the examiners, Senator La Follette of Wisconsin, chairman, and his fellow member, Senator Thomas of Utah. Senator Murphy of Iowa, the third member of the Committee, was killed in an accident during the first summer of the inquiry. Beside Senator La Follette sits his young lawyer John Abt. Abt is generally slated for a fine career.

Next to Senator Thomas sits Robert Wohlforth, the Committee's executive secretary, adroit and forceful manager of staff and agenda, usually characterized in the press as West Pointer turned pacifist, and the first employee to be hired by the Munitions Committee. To Wohlforth's skill in getting the committee's money's worth out of its slender funds must be attributed much of the success of the investigation. A little at one side, like the donor in a painting, sits Heber Blankenhorn of the National Labor Relations Board, his knowledge of espionage in industry guiding the course of the inquiry. Flanking these and in the rear of the choir are staff assistants, secretaries, and occasional distinguished guests.

The eyes of all these people are strained upon the pit below where enter, not from the wings, but from the startled audience, the witnesses under subpoena. I say startled, since an intent listener, his full attention strained to catch the drift of questioning about the perhaps nefarious goings on of some often-mentioned character, and the direction of his sympathies none too veiled, suddenly hears that character called by name, and sees the man beside him rise and go forward to the stand. Guarding the witness, if the witness happens to represent a corporation, sits his counsel, usually wearing a demeanor which seems to disclaim the faults and stupidities of all on hand. (In the stormy Harlan hearings when the lives of witnesses were threatened, many of the audience were searched for concealed weapons, and one witness, sentenced for dynamiting, came daily from jail in custody of a U. S. Marshal.)

The witness stands to be sworn by the chairman, then sits for questioning and resumes his pipe, his cigarette, or occasionally his gum, blinking helplessly as photographers like pyrotechnical buzzards swoop down upon him with their ceaseless explosions of light. Because this is an inquiry into a mystery story, and no single person carries its key in his head nor would willingly relinquish it if he did, as many as twelve witnesses have been called to the stand to testify at the same time, an unusual procedure. The story is thus unraveled rather than narrated.

What makes this such good theater? What could be said and done under Senate Resolution 266, calling for an investigation into violation of guaranteed rights of free speech and assemblage and the right of labor to organize for collective bargaining that would hold the same audience spellbound, hour after hour, day after day of frequently tiresome questioning?

Something more than the ingredients of a good newspaper story, the various concomitants of human interest, although it has these too. This investigation has been the reporters' darling. There has been no inquiry since Teapot Dome which has caused so many words to go upon the wire. Here is drama, not the illusion of conflict, but its reality, and conflict not on the scale of the theater, but on the gigantic scale of American society, people against property in its most intelligible terms of dollars, purchased violence and betrayal. The abstractions of learned assault upon the court are missing. Like actors the witnesses come, speak their pieces, and go. The voice varies in strength, gesture varies in expression; the story draws on new episode and embellishment. But for the moment of his appearance each witness becomes the apotheosis of his part, the embodied antagonist in a war of impersonal forces. Each brings into the hearing room the smell and roar of the battle that rages without. By the mere addition of conceded fact to the written record of human experience, suspicions that have long hung above like fantastic vapors are given shape, as if a fortress long concealed in mist had been unveiled upon a gentle landscape, and harsh light had shown scarred ground.

This audience, as in the theater, identifies itself with its favorite character. When it appears that the villain has been bested, it gloats over the villain, and rages visibly if he is unperturbed. La Follette grinds on, tireless, patient, shrewd, rephrasing each question until the eel-like witness can no longer wriggle through it. His method and the resistance to it furnish the suspense. In role of Greek, Senator Thomas interpolates the tragic meanings of the play, not afraid to state and restate for contemplation the moral situation which is set forth. As for the time element no dramatist could hope for more. The timelessness of the conflict, time out of mind, past and future, rob the show of cheap topicality, although its incidence upon the moment when labor is rising to unprecedented heights of daring makes it throb with excitement. All is there, even the comic relief of Senate turned detective, its ponderous monocle upon the spy.

It is not my intention in this book to tell the full story of any single case revealed upon the stand. The episodes with their vine-like roots have no beginning and their end is not conclusive. I hope rather to explain the functioning of espionage and strikebreaking in American industry as it is being currently disclosed.

First, it is important to know the Committee's objectives and methods as it operated under its first appropriation of $15,000 made in April of 1936. (In February, 1937, it received a second sum of $40,000 and could branch out slightly, although concurrently Congress passed a rider to the Deficiency bill, making it impossible for a Senate Committee to borrow personnel from government agencies whose funds are provided from relief appropriation, originally the source of a good share of its staff.)

The scope of any true inquiry into violations of constitutional rights of free speech and assemblage and into interference with the rights of labor must include racial discriminations, deprivations of court process, vigilante propaganda and violence, public and employer terrorism by racketeers in fake or seduced labor unions, implicit peonage of share-croppers and isolated cases of suppression of free speech, press, and assemblage. Such a scope was accepted by the Committee as its charge, to be taken up when Congress should make funds available. To match the almost fantastically small sum of $15,000 against such a scattered field or even against any sector of it, required narrowing the inquiry sharply into a first choice of subject matter, and dealing with that sector economically.

Gardner Jackson, tireless foe of injustice wherever it occurs, whose chief present interest is in the plight of share-croppers, brought about initial sponsorship of the Committee. It is no secret, however, that it has been almost from the beginning the child of the National Labor Relations Board. The Board's work of conducting elections under a law which legalizes unions has been constantly stalemated by espionage. Fragmentary but voluminous data presented by the Board at the preliminary hearings in April, 1936, charted the Committee's original course. It decided to go at once into the subject of labor espionage and strikebreaking.

For many years it has been clear, especially to men who have run afoul of them, that violations of constitutional rights have been losing their sporadic and accidental nature and have taken on the character of an institution. Most especially is this true in the field of employment. They have been conducted on a large scale, and have originated in high places. The employers responsible for them have made use of a shrewd, opportunistic group of enterprisers whose business methods run counter to accepted business practice.

Quick to see where their custom lies in the perennial feud between management hostile to unions and workers bent upon unionizing, these men have become an undercover supplier, furnishing to industry the goods and services of espionage, strikebreaking, and munitions. Their business structure, similar to that of the dope-ring whose wares are smuggled across the border, peddled mysteriously, and kept secret, has been pretty well concealed. The method is old, having been the right arm of the open shop movement throughout American labor history. It merely adapts itself to changing methods of production and changing organization, thriving best in times of labor upsurgence when workers, compelled and aided by political and economic forces of the moment, feel confidence in their strength to roll away a stone of any magnitude. It is then that spies introduced by management into the labor body multiply and move through it like maggots, corrupting its strength from within.

With only $15,000 in hand, and permission to borrow a limited number of aides for an uncertain time from various governmental agencies, while ahead of them lay the possibility of extinction at the hands of a heavy lobby, the Committee had no choice but to take the quickest route to the heart of the matter.

To examine labor as the victim would be a long and expensive process. It must be done by sample and not at random, because spies are known to have infiltrated every region and every trade. The since-proved extent of their operations has exceeded the previous suspicions of even the most seasoned labor investigators. Organized labor has been a stout ally of the Committee, eager to testify to that which it knows, and anxious to collaborate in getting to the bottom of that which workers merely suspect and cannot prove. But labor's knowledge of espionage is accidentally arrived at, indeed comes only when espionage breaks down at a given point and fails of that which it set out to do. Often workers experience its effects without knowing what has happened to them. The union is weakened or disbanded for no discernible reason. Union leaders are set upon and beaten by whom no one can prove. Strikes are broken by management's foreknowledge of them. Steady workers, possessed of skill in high degree, find themselves blacklisted into industrial vagrants, turned away from every employment office in their industry at the very moment when industry is complaining of a lack of skilled labor. Knowing themselves to be surrounded by spies, even over a period of years they cannot ascertain who is the trustworthy and who the treacherous one within their ranks. Arsenals slip by them into the factory without their knowing how. First intimation of their existence may come from the mouth of a machine gun or from physical convulsions induced by emetic gas.

Similarly it would be expensive and circuitous to examine industry until evidence should develop clues as to where espionage exists in its most concentrated form. As chief responsible party to transactions of doubtful odor, and still converted to their practicability as a means to an end long espoused, the open shop, industry might be expected to yield up their details reluctantly, an expectation that has been fulfilled. Skilled accountants would have to go over their books to extract expenditures well concealed under misleading entries. It was determined therefore to examine firms which cater to management, as being more vulnerable to scrutiny. These have tangible headquarters, if shifting ones, addresses, officers, payrolls, invoices, make out income tax returns.

There are some 300 detective agencies in the country,

known to be doing industrial work, admittedly the most profitable end of the detective business. There are a dozen systems having 150 substantial offices. Five of the largest of these were put under subpoena: Railway Audit and Inspection Company, Pinkerton's National Detective Agency, Corporations Auxiliary Company, International Corporation Service, and the William J. Burns International Detective Agency. The National Metal Trades Association, an employers organization, was also called. Three munitions companies who dominate the industrial market, the Lake Erie Chemical Company, Manville Manufacturing Company, and Federal Laboratories, Incorporated, were commanded to appear and open their records to Committee agents. Customers and labor have been brought in collaterally, as mentioned in evidence turned up by agents sent into the field to work upon subpoenaed records.

It could be expected that a business whose stock in trade is secrecy would make a contumacious witness. Not the static and ordinarily admired virtue of keeping a shut mouth, their secrecy is strenuous, elaborate, full of device and pretext. Secrecy is to the detective agency both means and end. If they divulge their means of doing business, they may warrantably expect repudiation by their customers. Agencies have lost much business since they, so unhappily, began to watch the Senate going over their affairs. Corporations Auxiliary Company are said to have closed up shop since their examination. Pinkerton's lost their largest account, that of General Motors, amounting in two years and seven months to $419,000, a few days before Pinkerton's went upon the stand in February for an exhaustive grilling and after General Motors had been subpoenaed. Secrecy is to the detective agency what good will is to an overt concern. In losing it, they lose not only their trade but their capital. To forestall disclosing the identity of their operatives, after the Social Security Act required registration of all employees by name, Pinkerton's changed their mode of doing business, dispensing with employer-employee relationship and entering into contract with their informers to purchase information.

Yet even accepting as a natural phenomenon the fact that agencies might fight what they considered a threat to their existence, the amount of defiance, evasiveness, and even perjury encountered by the examiners has shocked many followers of the inquiry. If impunity continues, the Senate's inquisitorial prestige must be diminished.

R A & I threw the challenge the first day of the hearing by not answering the subpoena, and by destroying their records. Showing their credentials to the building superintendents, according to instructions that the Committee's agents must from the outset make known their official capacity, the servers subpoenaed the waste paper. Maimed records were brought home to the Senate Office Building by the basketful, and, in a draftless room where pieces would not blow away, by the jigsaw-puzzle method and with pots of paste, they were reconstructed into telling evidence. The vice-president has since been sued for contempt of the Senate and has been acquitted.

William J. Burns International Detective Agency, Incorporated, tried a slightly different tack. Pretending full compliance, and answering personal subpoena, at least one of their branch offices destroyed subpoenaed records. Simultaneously, however, they floated misleading correspondence through the mails, bound to come under Senate scrutiny, which would indicate that destruction antedated the service of subpoena. A bale of reconstructed papers rescued from their trash was presented in the courtroom to refute them.

The means by which Pinkerton's strove to salvage their affairs from publicity's destructive fire was openly dramatic. The Pinkerton inquiry had been tentatively opened in September. During the ensuing months, Committee agents had been working on Pinkerton records, receiving little but pretended co-operation. On February 8 they came to hearing again, surrounded by Mr. Whitney, Mr. Bromley, and Mr. Blasier, counsel from Cravath, De Gersdorff, Swaine, and Wood of whose firm Carl De Gersdorff had served from 1930 to 1936 on Pinkerton's Board of Directors. The Committee met at ten in the morning. La Follette said: "The Committee will be in order. Mr. Brady."

Pinkerton's superintendent Brady from Cincinnati was intercepted, however, from coming forward. Instead a young man rose and addressed the room as follows: "Senator, my name is William D. Whitney. I am counsel for the Pinkerton Agency. At the last hearing, when Senator Thomas presided, he made a request of my partner, Mr. Bromley, that we produce today a witness able to testify to the names of certain secret operatives; and if you will allow me, I would just like to say a word in explanation of our position about that, so you will be informed. Mr. Pinkerton and I have given very careful consideration to that matter. We have certainly tried to co-operate with the Committee and have made all material available to the Committee that we could. But there is one point, and only one point, Senator, I am so informed, at which we feel that our co-operation will have to cease. We told that to the Committee representatives in the beginning, Mr. Wohlforth and his associates, and that is that we are unwilling, with the greatest respect, to break our faith with these secret informants of ours, and we feel that in loyalty to them we cannot disclose their names. Senator, may I say that the reason is that Mr. Pinkerton and his associates sincerely believe that to do that will lead to violence and even to murder. We have had that experience; we have tremendous records of violence in labor matters. Senator Thomas will recall that at the last hearing Mr. Burnside testified he was from the agency, and when he got home he received a letter saying, 'Scram, rat. Get out of Toledo and stay out.' Now, that happens to an officer of our concern who worked in the open, whose name is known to everyone. [Mr. Burnside appears in the record also under the aliases of Brunswick, Bronson, and Blackburn.] What will happen to men who work in secret and whom we know very well are regarded, rightly or wrongly, by the representatives of the unions as spies? Then Mr. Rigby testified here the last time, when the chairman of the Committee was not here—he said here on the witness stand, 'If it is the last thing I do I will get you.' That was one of the witnesses. He said, 'Senator, some tar and feathers would do some of these fellows good.' Now, under those circumstances, most reluctantly but most definitely and irrevocably, we feel we cannot go to the point of supplying the Committee with the names of these men; and if the Committee will permit me, may I say most respectfully that we suggest that the Committee, by its own efforts and the efforts of its investigators, without calling upon us—and they have been very considerate—without calling upon us to actually disclose the names of our men ourselves, that they ascertain the names of these undercover men. As to those whose names have been discovered, we, of course, are glad to co-operate with the Committee and give any information we have, because our only purpose is not for ourselves to expose them and disclose them when they are trusting in us, but if they disclose their own names then, of course, that will release us from that obligation. Although it is only submitted for your consideration—and we do earnestly submit it for your consideration—we would suggest that as a basis for your legislation you may not find it necessary to call upon us to disclose the names of comparatively unimportant individuals if there be other adequate information. We realize that one of your main purposes is to enact legislation to avoid just such violence, and we hope and submit to you Senators that it will be unnecessary in that work to call upon us ourselves to make disclosures which we sincerely feel will themselves lead to immediate violence. Also, although we do not put our request to you on that basis, we think it is our duty to say that we feel a pressure to that extent would raise the question as to whether there was an unlawful search and seizure under the fourth amendment to the Constitution."

It was truly an interesting situation. The brilliance and flashiness of the moment could not efface from the mind of the audience, so quick to communicate its thoughts, the memory of violence and betrayal in Pinkerton's participation in labor history.

What appeared to be an interminable search began for two things: the refused identity of the operatives and the nature of the relationship between Pinkerton and General Motors. Abt and La Follette were at their shrewdest. Pinkerton's were upon the stand for days, first one and then another of their men succumbing to amnesia, striving without avail to remember aught they had ever transacted in the way of business. One wondered how they could ever again pick up the snapped thread of memory and weave it into the intricacies of detective procedure, itself a feat in mnemonics. The immediate goal was to find exactly how Pinkerton's had collaborated with General Motors, their largest client, until a few days since.

How, for instance, after they had obtained, in addition to their separate contracts with its different plants, an overall espionage job for the executive offices in Detroit, had they set themselves up to take care of this important account? Written reports had ceased, by order of the employers, after service of the subpoena. Dangers of leakage, if telephonic reporting service were set up in the general office, appeared to be extreme. What did they do?

By rights, for the edification of the audience, a blueprint of their office elevation should have been passed about, as a map of the house of mystery is included in a novel. Without this aid the layout never became exactly clear. Roughly it appeared to be this. Pinkerton's had a large explicit office in Detroit; that is, the name of Pinkerton's was on its door. Next to this they rented a false-face office on the door of which was printed that catholic phrase, good to describe any operation at any time, the Acme Processing Company. When they feared that this arrangement had outworn its secrecy, rooms were rented on the other side, this time under the name of a non-existent Sales Representative, William B. Smith. Subsequently, a succession of apartment headquarters, lived in by two superintendents, were chosen for various strategic conveniences, chiefly to be within eavesdropping distance of union headquarters.

But with all this paraphernalia, the chief stir and bustle of secrecy to protect the General Motors spy system from the Cyclops eye of government occurred in the central Pinkerton office itself whose chief feature seemed to be a peephole or sliding door large enough for communication between the overt office where Pinkerton met the public and the side office where it met General Motors. It was in the official Pinkerton headquarters that the Committee agent put in his upsetting appearance. In the general scurry that ensued, someone had the forethought to telephone the side office, presided over by Mr. Peterson. "There is somebody in here representing himself to be a government man." But let us hear Mr. Peterson.

MR. PETERSON: Yes; that is all that was said to me then over the phone; yes, sir.

SENATOR LA FOLLETTE: What did you do then?

MR. PETERSON: Well, I did not do anything for a little while. I sat there at my desk for a little while.

SENATOR LA FOLLETTE: After you sat at your desk for a little while what did you do?

MR. PETERSON (*pause*): Well, we had—the chief clerk wanted to know what to do about the time sheets, and he said, "This fellow is running all over the office"; they did not know who he was or where he was from for sure, because he rushed in there, the superintendent was gone, and everybody got excited. So I said—

SENATOR LA FOLLETTE (*interrupting*): Where was the chief clerk when he said that to you?

MR. PETERSON: I think he just said that through the—

SENATOR LA FOLLETTE: Through the what?

MR. PETERSON: Through the door.

SENATOR LA FOLLETTE: Through the what?

MR. PETERSON: The door, the connecting door; through the connecting door.

SENATOR LA FOLLETTE: He opened the door?

MR. PETERSON: No, no. We have got a little cubbyhole through the door.

SENATOR LA FOLLETTE: What do you mean by "a little cubbyhole"?

MR. PETERSON: Well, just a little sliding door that you can raise and talk through there.

SENATOR LA FOLLETTE: What did he say?

MR. PETERSON (*long pause*): He said, "Here is a lot of personal papers of the superintendent's. What will we do with them?" I said, "Well, I'll hold them."
SENATOR LA FOLLETTE: Then what did he do?
MR. PETERSON: Well, he gave me some papers.
SENATOR LA FOLLETTE: How did he give them to you?
(No response.)
SENATOR LA FOLLETTE: Through this peephole in the door?
MR. PETERSON: Yes.
SENATOR LA FOLLETTE: How big is that?
MR. PETERSON: About a foot high by a half a foot wide, I should judge.
SENATOR LA FOLLETTE: How many papers did he give you?
MR. PETERSON: Well, I could not say now.
SENATOR LA FOLLETTE: Well, approximately how many papers did he give you?
MR. PETERSON: Oh, he gave me a few; but I could not really say, because I do not remember.
SENATOR LA FOLLETTE: Well, what did you do then?
MR. PETERSON (*pause*): Those are the ones that I put in my brief case and sent down—or was going to send them down to the car when the government man stopped us.
SENATOR LA FOLLETTE: Well, what else did you take?
MR. PETERSON: Well, I had all my personal file in there, and—
SENATOR LA FOLLETTE: What was in your personal file?
MR. PETERSON: Well, my personal letters, insurance papers, and things of that sort.
SENATOR LA FOLLETTE: Were there informants' reports in your personal file?
MR. PETERSON: Oh, no; no, sir.

SENATOR LA FOLLETTE: Just why were you apprehensive about the service of the subpoena with relation to your insurance papers?

MR. PETERSON: Well, I did not know who this man was myself.

SENATOR LA FOLLETTE: Did you make any effort to ascertain?

MR. PETERSON: Well, he came in there alone, you know, and I had to make sure who he was.

SENATOR LA FOLLETTE: Did you see the subpoena?

MR. PETERSON: Well, he held it up for me to see there, and he said it was for the Pinkerton Agency, and I asked him who he was and he said he represented the Senate Committee. I said, "Well," then he said, "Who are you?" I said, "Why, who are you?" And, so finally it developed that he just went on about his business over in the other office.

As the questioning continued, it appeared that Mr. Peterson's personal papers were reports from spies in General Motors which had been in transit when orders had come through for writing to cease. "I finally," he said, "took those down later on." His clerks seemed to bring him more during his indeterminate stay at home. For, by office instruction, Mr. Peterson went home to be sick. How long the illness lasted, whether it was four days or two weeks, Peterson could not remember though all aids were offered to his recollection. His compassionate office mates came there to see him and to delete the reports. Copies were furnished to the Committee, and the originals were forwarded to the New York office to the General Manager, Mr. Asher Rossetter. "Where are they?" asked the chairman. "The Committee has never seen an original report."

Then followed the game of who-has-the-thimble played

THE SENATE TURNS DETECTIVE

between counsel Blasier and La Follette who grew warmer and warmer on the trail.

SENATOR LA FOLLETTE: Did these original reports come into your possession?
MR. BLASIER: Yes, sir.
SENATOR LA FOLLETTE: Where are they?
MR. BLASIER: They are here in Washington.
SENATOR LA FOLLETTE: Produce them.
MR. BLASIER: I haven't got them.
SENATOR LA FOLLETTE: Leave the room and get them and come back as soon as you can.
MR. BLASIER: Senator, I think the reason the originals were not produced was because of the fact that they are in the handwriting of the men. As a matter of fact I think some of the originals at least bear the initials of Mr. Cranefield, who did see them and directed copies be made.
SENATOR LA FOLLETTE: Produce all of those originals at once.
MR. BLASIER: They are not in my possession, Senator.
SENATOR LA FOLLETTE: Who has them?
MR. BLASIER: They are locked up in a hotel room.
SENATOR LA FOLLETTE: Who has the key to the room?
MR. BLASIER: I don't know.
SENATOR LA FOLLETTE: Whose room is it?
MR. BLASIER: Whose room is it?
MR. ROSSETTER: What room are they in?
MR. BLASIER: They are in a trunk.
MR. ROSSETTER: What?
MR. BLASIER: They are in a trunk.
SENATOR LA FOLLETTE: What room are they in?
MR. BLASIER: I think the room is registered in the name of Mr. Lowe.

SENATOR LA FOLLETTE: Who is Mr. Lowe?
MR. BLASIER: He is a man from the New York office.
SENATOR LA FOLLETTE: What is his position?
MR. ROSSETTER: He is assistant superintendent of our New York office.
SENATOR LA FOLLETTE: Is Mr. Lowe in the room?
MR. ROSSETTER: No, sir.
SENATOR LA FOLLETTE: Where is he?
MR. ROSSETTER: He is staying with the records.
SENATOR LA FOLLETTE: I direct you, Mr. Pinkerton, to have these records produced before this Committee at once.

At this point, Mr. Pinkerton's counsel, Mr. Bromley, arose.

MR. BROMLEY: Senator, would you develop, please, that the Committee was furnished with Chinese or exact copies of the originals?
SENATOR LA FOLLETTE: I do not think the testimony so shows.
MR. BROMLEY: Not yet; but I am asking you, please, to develop that, sir.
SENATOR LA FOLLETTE: Mr. Mason has already testified that he indicated for deletion from these original reports all matters relating to labor things.
MR. BROMLEY: But he only drew a fine line through them, sir. They can be read.
SENATOR LA FOLLETTE: No one in this room has ever compared these reports?
MR. BLASIER: Senator, I think I can help you. There are about 52 or 53 original reports. In Detroit it was my understanding that some of the reports were copied exactly from the originals, with the exception that certain material, such as names of individuals who have

been talked to, times and places and so on which would tend to locate the writer of the report at a certain place and certain time were left out, x's put in to indicate that omission. On certain of the other reports only summaries were given; and when these reports were turned in to the Committee by the Detroit investigator those summaries did not prove satisfactory to the Committee. And it was for that reason that we directed, that the management on my instructions directed, that the reports be sent to New York.

When those reports got to New York I went over them. I had copies of the papers which had been given the Committee. I went through and compared them. I did not have anybody read them to me, but I compared them quite closely, and I discovered about sixteen of the reports were approximately exact copies, with the exception of the deletions. I have mentioned that the rest were merely summaries. Those reports I went through with a blue pencil and underlined such names of people and places that I felt if they stayed in the reports might give clues to the identity of the writer, and then I delivered those reports to stenographers in Mr. Rossetter's office, and they were copied, and I instructed the stenographers to make the copies as nearly like the exact originals as they could be.

The form we used was on the original report where lines were drawn through the written material, the written material in the original report would be copied in, and then a row of x's would be drawn in, and it could still be read. And where reports had been added to by certain handwriting for the purpose of editing the report that material would be put in above with a line underneath to indicate it was different material than had been written by the correspondent, and where anything was left out there would be a row of x's to indicate that.

SENATOR LA FOLLETTE: I direct you, Mr. Pinkerton, to furnish these original reports to this Committee at once.

MR. PINKERTON: Mr. Dudley will have to go himself to get those. Do you want him to go?

SENATOR LA FOLLETTE: Yes: I do.

MR. DUDLEY: Immediately?

SENATOR LA FOLLETTE: Immediately.

Mr. Pinkerton left with several of his men, followed at the chairman's request by an equal number of the Committee's agents, in a scene of dramatic tension. At the hotel, the Committee's agents were at first refused admittance to the room, but at last got in. At two, the witnesses reappeared with the reports, and flatly refused to hand them over in an announcement defended and counseled by Mr. Bruce Bromley of Cravath, De Gersdorff, Swaine, and Wood, alleging that the Committee was exceeding its constitutional powers and on the practical plea that should the identity of their operatives be known these men would be in danger of their lives. Even though their names should be deleted, the nature of the report might disclose their whereabouts and thereby their identity. His words were addressed to Mr. Pinkerton: "In my opinion, to compel the disclosure of these names, or other indicia of identity, would amount to unreasonable search and seizure, contrary to the provisions of the fourth amendment to the Constitution of the United States. I believe that the production of these records would tend to disclose the identity of secret operatives or correspondents of the agency. I understand that these persons have uniformly been contracted with on the basis of an agreement that their identity would remain secret, and that it is the unanimous opinion of everyone who is familiar with the situation that a disclosure of their identity at this time would subject them to very great danger, attack, injury, and even murder. In this connection the witness Letteer swore a few days ago that the disclosure of his identity resulted in attempts upon his life. Therefore, without intending any disrespect to the Senate, or this subcommittee, I advise you, in view of the offer which you have made to this subcommittee, you need not produce the records."

Since the General Motors sit-down strike was then in progress the implication was too clear. Once again that afternoon it was disclosed that Pinkerton's own sit-down strike was still in progress, with Mr. Lowe recumbent on still further documents. Mr. Pinkerton was sent out once again to get them. In elegant leather luggage, not unlocked but ripped open at the seam, the documents arrived. It was on this day of chicanery that Senator La Follette went to the unusual length of making counsel Bromley take the oath, to his visible affront.

Thus the bush is beaten and re-beaten. At last goes up one stupid bird, on the wing of a careless answer. Startled and unhappy, it catches the charge, falls, and is retrieved by the industrious dogs who have been waiting for the word, is presented in style and laid warm upon the record.

In whatever way the gross contumacy of such respondents is punished, it appears true, as it has no doubt appeared in previous investigations, that the greater the effort to conceal, the more guilt attaches in the public mind to the operations under concealment. Part of this is perhaps just baffled inquisitiveness. Yet what can be the nature of a business over which men will fence and spar and finally lie rather than to divulge their participation in it? What are the hidden reasons behind the cover of logic by which they justify open contempt? We shall see perhaps as the story progresses.

III. Super-Sleuths

ESPIONAGE is a service trade, and, like any other, one of its most important operations is that of merchandising. Before it attempts to canvass for customers, or advertise its wares, it surveys the field for potential business.

It is first as entrepreneur, the man who sees a doorway in the economic system into which he believes he can insert his foot, that it is interesting to study the detective, or more literally the detective agency, since we shall look only at the most successful detectives, those who have been able to achieve a syndicate, incorporation, stocks, dividends, boards of directors, and the other paraphernalia of size and ambition.

In looking over his market, the detective finds his problem one of adaptation only. Spying is an old, old business in a modern world. From time out of mind it has adapted itself to the task on hand. Where spying is profitable, there is the spy, although out of this generalization we must draw a further one that temptation of profit alone cannot make a spy. He must be born to his trade. Even the military spy, risking his life for his country without hope of monetary gain, must find it within himself to use treachery to gain his ends. Napoleon said, "The spy is a natural traitor." The spy comes first, his situation second.

This is equally true of the detective placed in service of law enforcement agencies, although his usefulness would be hard to deny even by those who find all espionage detestable. In a romantic history of the Pinkerton dynasty, Richard Wilmer Rowan traces the elaborate treacheries of famous detectives of that firm, among them its founder

Allen, his favorite henchman Timothy Webster, and James McParlan, spotter of the Molly McGuires. These men participated in the plots they were uprooting, became bosom friends, confidants—even inspirers—of those who plotted. Though often carried away by admiration of his heroes, Mr. Rowan says: "That a kind of ethical atrophy . . . accompanies success in crime detection most professional practitioners take for granted, and nearly all chroniclers of detective triumphs seem agreed to ignore. Gentlemen of benign ambition in America have undertaken to do many mundane things—to edit a newspaper for 'twenty-four hours,' to collect funds, promote sales of real estate and even conduct stock-exchange speculations according to the precepts of the saintly life. But none ever tried to apprehend criminals while manacled himself to rules of exemplary conduct or even good sportsmanship; and if the attempt were made it would fail. Allen Pinkerton was too instinctively expert a detective not to realize this, and hereafter, in relating whatever methods conformed to the need of his subordinates or himself, no question of principle or propriety will again be raised."

Arthur L. Pugmire, assistant Pinkerton Superintendent, on the stand in February of 1937, illuminated this point for Senator La Follette, in what was manifestly a sincere effort to establish his truthfulness concerning a discrepancy between his statement and that of another witness: "I wanted even at that late hour to have him know that I was truthful except when I was under pretext, and I think there is quite a line of deviation there. I really feel that if the Committee really understood just how important it is to tell what one might call 'white lies' for the sake of pretext—it is almost necessary. I do not think the Department of Justice could possibly have any success were they not able to use such pretexts as I have used."

If we accept without squeamishness Mr. Rowan's predication that the detective's work must very likely entail perfidious conduct, we can see why the successful detective, always the actor, always adroit and sometimes very brave, has often become a public hero, especially when he is engaged in what might be called his legitimate field of endeavor of catching public enemies. By legitimate, I mean that field acceptable to the public as being in its own interest. All fields, even that of labor espionage, are legitimate in the strictest sense of the word. The reader must divest himself of the notion that spying is illegal. Even when espionage becomes a tool of law-breaking as it does in present-day labor relations when the union is recognized by legislation, espionage is not itself against the law. Spying hardly aspires to be a committed act. It lays the scene for an act whose nature it determines. Yet with all its tortuous ramifications, it is scarcely more than a conspiratorial state of mind, an attitude hardened into gestures, the propped ear, the stance on tiptoe.

What jobs legitimately fall in the detective's bailiwick? Who could be called his rightful customer?

A lawyer's account would seem to be unexceptionable. The lawyer has missing heirs to locate, concealed assets and witnesses to find, legal papers to be served, patent infringements to be investigated. Public prosecutors, state and district attorneys, or private persons who do not want to take their search into the public eye, seek his help in apprehending breakers of the law, the escaped murderer out on the kill, the counterfeiter, blackmailer, dope smuggler, arson-plotter, the loft and jewel thief, the forger and embezzler. Bonding and surety companies use him, one might think with reason, to locate bond defaulters and investigate false claims for compensation. Business uses him to search out pay-roll irregularities, thefts, and frauds. How one feels about his aid to the suspicious marriage partner seeking evidence of adultery is a matter of taste. Though large and profitable to the apprehenders is the field of law-breaking, it is not indefinitely elastic, for where character fails, fear and discipline make honest men, or at least law-abiders, of the majority. As a market for the detective's wares, it has its saturation point. Furthermore, the detective catches only crumbs from the work of official secret police. He must either content himself with a modest livelihood or seek for greener fields.

If he is anxious for expansion, what factors must he take into account? First, that his is a personal-service trade, and as such deals with human beings. His staff, though perhaps perversely, is trained if at all in human relationships. He has nothing else to sell. Second: Who has the money? Not in little driblets, but in great bulk? Who finds the Great Consumer of anything? The weary peddler winding around the block or the salesman who after much persistence achieves the purchasing office of a national supplier? The question is rhetorical. Business has the money. Third: If business has the money, through what does it spend it in relationship to persons? Obviously through its employment office. Here is the very science of deduction, working for itself. His new customer is business as employer. But for what will it spend its money that a detective can supply? If the majority of men, and by the same token the majority of workers, are law-abiding, in what do workers indulge which to the employer is as reprehensible as crime and which, as a result, he will spend money to detect?

The answer to this emerges like invisible writing under

heat. Discontent. It is a curious answer when you stop to think of it. Accepted prod of the race in art and science, pedestal of freedom in the republic, discontent, when found in the worker, takes on such evil color that its possessor is known opprobriously as a "malcontent." The laboring man should have yielded up this human mortgage on divinity when he became a unit of the commodity labor, bought and sold on the market like coal or leather. That he shows no intention of doing so is his greatest drawback as a raw material of industry. The weight of a ton of coal is the same from year to year. Grades of hide can be anticipated. But it is because a laborer can sleep on a bed, or lacking it, a floor, can take love or leave it alone, that the labor cost is so vulnerable. For the same reason that you can count on a man to draw in his belt during famine he is apt to get notions, chief among them that life should be a good thing. For so long as it is tolerated, this expensive notion takes labor at once out of the list of inanimate commodities.

To stamp out discontent itself would be like trying to strain red corpuscles from the bloodstream. But fortunately for the control of the disease, you do not have to quarantine all those who own to it. Some men are carriers. Susceptible and articulate, they spread the notion. If you isolate the carrier you have the contagion in hand. Even under this selective process the number to be apprehended is legion.

The size of such a market could dazzle any enterpriser. Beside it the hard-earned profit of detecting the embezzler or even missing heirs pales into pin money. Here is a market for a millionaire. Out of it has risen a multimillionaire industry.

Such an analysis is misleading in one particular, that of time. The rise of the agency in the so-called legitimate operations of espionage and their branching out into the bulkier and more profitable traffic in labor-breaking, if not simultaneous were nearly so. Pinkerton's agency was founded by Allen Pinkerton in 1854. Only twelve years later they had moved into a strike in Braidwood, Illinois. By 1870 so great was the increase in demand for industrial service, they already had a competitor. By 1892 when the Carnegie Steel Company's contract with the Amalgamated Association of Iron, Steel, and Tin Workers expired, Henry Frick sent for Pinkerton's to break a strike in Homestead. Pinkerton sent three hundred armed men, recruited from New York and Chicago, up the river in a boat. A battle followed in which many men were killed. Testifying in the Congressional investigation that followed, a member of the United States Secret Service said of the forty Pinkerton men whom he had interviewed: "There is not one out of ten that would not commit murder; that you could not hire to commit murder or any other crime."

This was strikebreaking by violence, and not espionage, and of strikebreaking we shall hear more later. But the groundwork of those gory decades, the last two of the old century and the first of the new, was always laid by spies. Continuously forward into the 1930's, when Congress legalized the union, labor history is richly documented by illustrations of the agencies' working principle that where there is spying to do and money to pay for it, detectives will stick at nothing. Pinkerton's boast that they do no divorce work. Allen Pinkerton laid down that rule in the beginning. But a man struggling his way out of twelve hours a day in the mine or mill has from the first been as good prey as the man who has just squirmed his way out from behind penitentiary bars. As good, and more profitable. With such an outlook, how could the detective business do other than prosper in the first years after the depression? Resentment against misery had been banked through a long night. The morning seemed in order.

Out of such a market, detective agencies wheedled from General Motors $819,000 in the two years and seven months following January, 1933. Pinkerton alone got $419,000 out of it. Chrysler paid $211,000 to Corporations Auxiliary whose business in this period was $1,292,193. The combined known volume of business done by the four of the five big professional companies under subpoena in these thirty-one months amounted to $3,465,918, although these estimates are made from data known to be inconclusive.

An interesting guess as to the total volume of business done by the espionage industry was made by Heber Blankenhorn before the inquiry. Presented to the Committee in the preliminary hearings, as an evidence of how badly more factual data were needed, it is useful chiefly in showing the territory in which suspicion is active. It reads in part: "The labor detective is an inveterate liar. . . . The only time that detectives tell the truth about their finances is when they sue each other over contracts or when their receipted bills come to light. . . . A railroad labor leader of long experience has said he never 'knew of a gathering large enough to be called a meeting and small enough to exclude a spy.' There are over 41,000 locals. At the going rate of pay which seems to be $175 a month per stool pigeon, that would be over $80,000,000 a year paid by industry for stool pigeons. Supposing, of course, the stools were on the job throughout the year as are locals."

Testimony has revealed two of Mr. Blankenhorn's basic assumptions to be wrong. The pay varies widely. What the operative receives from the agency is no indication of what the employer pays the agency for his services. It is hard to get the facts on his daily or monthly cost to industry. The estimate as to the number of stool pigeons per meeting seems to be low; stool pigeons themselves on the stand have stated that most meetings have two or more, and that the stool pigeon himself rarely knows how many are present. His estimate, as to coverage and the time put in, may be large. Such a volume of business as Mr. Blankenhorn is talking about would be divided among the some three hundred agencies. We are looking at only five. Although Mr. Blankenhorn's estimate was admittedly a guess, nothing has been disclosed about the finances of espionage or strikebreaking which would necessarily depress such a general figure.

How are these five agencies geared up to do such a considerable business? Let us scrutinize them in order of their appearance before the Committee: Railway Audit, National Corporation Service, Corporations Auxiliary, Pinkerton's, and Burns. The National Metal Trades Association, whose affairs were opened just before those of Corporations Auxiliary, belongs in another category of such significance that it must be considered in a chapter by itself.

Railway Audit and Inspection Company, a Virginia corporation, chartered in November, 1903, with an authorized capital of $100,000, later increased to $250,000, succeeded to the business previously conducted by the Duplicate Transfer Rebate Company. With the characteristic flair for resounding names which detective agencies share with business, R A & I camouflages its subsidiaries, branches, and blinds under the title of the Pennsylvania Industrial Service, Central Industrial Service (this is the largest of its subsidiary operations—in the 1934 return of capital stock tax the value of the entire capital stock is given as $400,000), International Library Service, Forrest C. Pendleton, Inc., International Labor Bureau, New Jersey Engineering Corporation, and Eastern Engineering Company.

Its head office, a large suite presided over by Mr. L. D. Rice, Vice President and General Manager, is in the Sun Building in the 1600 block of Walnut Street, Philadelphia. Branch offices are in New York, Boston, Baltimore, Atlanta, St. Louis, Chicago, Pittsburgh, New Orleans, Cleveland, Detroit, Cincinnati, and San Francisco. It has four other officers than Mr. Rice.

Mr. W. W. Groves, some fifty odd years of age, worked himself up as employee to chairman of the board and has been president since 1933. His income from his various company stocks and salary is not recorded. His cousin, W. B. Groves, who in 1935 received $38,120, is vice-president. James E. Blair is treasurer and also in charge of the Pittsburgh office. W. G. Moore is assistant treasurer. It was he who made, or rather declined to make, the company's financial statement both in 1935 and 1936 on the ground that the business is professional and no credit is asked. He admitted a paid-in capital of $200,000 and that the company had good liquid assets. Banks reported the R A & I account as consisting of a five-figure balance. One bank reported twenty-five years of dealing, "prompt, regular and no accommodations asked." According to its own statement, it employs some three hundred accountants to do inspection work.

A partial list of companies utilizing the services of R A & I and its subsidiary, the Central Industrial Service Company, touches off the imagination as to what their volume may be. The list was assembled with difficulty from Labor Board cases and reconstructed records, testimony of operatives, and one salvaged list of fifteen hosiery manufacturers, among them Real Silk, Phoenixville Hosiery, and Reading Full Fashioned. The known clients are only sixty-seven in number, but volume and variety of the business are indicated by a few of their names: The Aluminum Company of America, Bendix Products Corporation, Borden Milk, Bush Terminal, Carnegie-Illinois Steel (subsidiary of United States Steel), Columbian Steamship Company, Consolidated Gas of New York City, Cushman Sons, Frigidaire Corporation, H. C. Frick Coal and Coke Company (subsidiary of United States Steel), Jewish Hospital of Brooklyn, New York, Kelvinator Sales Corporation, National Dairy Products, Pennsylvania Railroad, Truscon Steel, Western Union, Westinghouse, and the Woodward Iron and Coal Company. General Motors at the time of their co-examination with Pinkerton's, on January 31, 1937, had already dispensed with Pinkerton services but had not got around to firing R A & I, as yet more successfully obdurate against efforts to make them reveal the details of their business.

Next in order on the stand was the National Corporation Service, Inc., of Youngstown, Ohio. Testimony was likewise taken concerning their strikebreaking affiliate, the Allied Corporation Service, Inc., liquidated in 1934.

This is a much younger concern than any other under subpoena, having been organized only six years ago, in March, 1931, by previous employees of the R A & I— E. E. McGuffin, who became its president, and Forrest C. Pendleton, vice-president and originally equal stockholder with McGuffin. Its former accountant and secretary, A. E. Lawson, who left the company in April of 1935 to become a public accountant, was chief witness.

With short history and small capital this company, nevertheless, presents excellent background on two subjects salient in any study of espionage. In detail it gives a picture, in their dealings with each other, of the character of men attracted to this business, or what one might call detective ethics at home. After some rearrangement of the originally issued stock it came about that McGuffin and Pendleton were equal stockholders until February of 1935. By mutual agreement McGuffin in the home office was to receive $5,000 a year as salary. Pendleton in New Orleans was to receive a salary ranging between $2,400 and $6,000. Mr. Lawson's testimony was not specific as to how the equability should be arrived at. In 1934 the company held a meeting in New Orleans, where the two signed an agreement under which McGuffin was to settle salary rates for Youngstown and Pendleton for New Orleans.

According to Lawson, McGuffin returned to Youngstown and promptly raised his salary to $36,000 a year. In February he returned to New Orleans with the financial statement for 1934. Since he had absorbed the profit into his salary, there was small profit to show. Whereupon the discouraged Mr. Pendleton turned over his $10,000 of stock for the assets of the New Orleans office, and Mr. McGuffin returned to Youngstown as sole owner of the National Corporations service.

In the 143 names of its rather important clients, though only a few of them are stars of the first magnitude among American manufacturers, it illustrates the fact which emerges from almost every witness and record: espionage booms in times of labor trouble. In a turbulent period a new supplier does not find himself at a special disadvantage in competing with the prestige of an established firm, a character reference being then even more than ordinarily superfluous, if not actually embarrassing.

In 1931 and 1932 workers had no energy for militance or even organization. They were, as will be remembered, being widely and officially complimented for their supine patience. Until 1933, the National Corporation Service had to content itself with one solicitor for business. During that year, under a superintendent of sales, three or four other salesmen were sent abroad in Ohio and Western Pennsylvania with a proposition of business insurance. "Protect yourself and find out what is going on in your plant before trouble actually does occur." This, with a sideline offer to form company unions for employers, began in 1933 to bring real business. Since many employers hire several agencies at once, the file of National Service clients duplicates at points those of other companies. Among its 143 known customers are Goodrich Rubber Company, General Fireproofing, Greyhound Management, Midland Steel Products, Ohio Edison, Hazel Atlas Glass, American Fork and Hoe, Aetna Rubber, Republic Rubber, and Mahoning Steel.

The story of Corporations Auxiliary Company is a mixture of fantasia and super-realism. It unrolled before the astonished beholder like a scroll painting, full of pompous strutting figures doing indecipherable things upon an imaginary landscape. Torn between laughter and outrage, one had to pinch himself to believe that these comic-opera machinations, in which industry all but turned over its blank checks to the traveling gold-brick salesman, who took its money like candy from a child, had really to do with men's destinies, or the course of American history; determined who should be put in industrial quarantine or even whether men should eat or not.

Since the first of the investigation it has been clear that the truth about detectives is stranger than detective fiction. Of the personnel of Corporations Auxiliary it could be said even more than of the others that they looked more like detectives than imagination could desire. The president, James H. Smith of Cleveland, had, to be sure, been graduated into a kind of detective Valhalla where he could live upon his rewards and had acquired the snappy appearance of an elderly fop. He was president of five Corporations Auxiliary companies from each of which he was supposed to draw $15,000 as salary. His business was incorporated in 1905 under the laws of Ohio where it is known as the International Auxiliary Company and under which charter it did business in Buffalo and New York City. It was incorporated in Michigan and Delaware in 1917; in New Jersey in 1924 and 1927, under which charter it operated in Cincinnati and Cleveland. Under its West Virginia Charter of 1929, it operated in Chicago. Mr. Smith was also President of the Auxiliary Company of Canada and the Equitable Publishing Co. and belonged to the law firm of Smith and Weber. This was a legal firm which furnished stationery upon which to bill the client. After the Securities Exchange Commission Act made it necessary for business firms to show expenditures of more than $20,000 on certain reports to them, Chrysler and General Motors took advantage of Corporations' split-billing procedure. They arranged to have invoices rendered them, showing amounts just under $20,000. In 1933 Chrysler Corporation paid Corporations Auxiliary $61,627, and in 1934, $76,411. In 1935, although it had fallen back a little to $72,611, the total was divided into parts and paid to the Equitable Auditing and Publishing Company, Smith and Weber,

The Corporations Auxiliary Company, and the International Auxiliary Company.

While we are at it and to glance at the lighter side of his nature, Mr. Smith is also president of the Cincinnati Carousel Company, Youngstown Carousel Company, the Beehive Amusement Company, and the Kiddyland Company, the income from which is of course not included in the Senate records of Mr. Smith's annual income. In his detective business, in order not to have these bona-fide company names bandied about too lightly, Mr. Smith took recourse to the use of blind letterheads, among many others, the Allied Manufacturing Company and the Atlantic Production Company. These were used in writing to applicants who might come in, in answer to advertisements. They were, in the words of Mr. Smith, "not in business, they contracted no debts."

The gross income from his five Auxiliary Companies in 1933 was $284,847. In 1934, labor being on the march, it had increased by $204,284 to $489,131, and by 1935 had achieved $518,215, about 30 percent of which, or around $150,000, went as salaries to three or four officials.

The habitual attendant upon the hearings learns that examination almost invariably follows a given pattern. There is, among both agencies and industries, an indisposition to mention spies or unions too abruptly. Perhaps the witness is animated by the hope that the examiners can in some way be misled from the true object of the hunt, a hope of which one swift perusal of the deadly record would disabuse him. Perhaps he enjoys the ritual of delay. At any rate, preliminary to the chase, the anise bag is dragged off into the empyrean. For a full two-hour overture of good feeling and intellectual aspiration, the witnesses state their purpose in life. They are in business in a search for trends. They are educators. They want to learn employers' reaction to medical service. They want to strengthen familial ties between employer and worker by getting closer to their workers' thoughts. All is bland. Senator Thomas, blandest of all, encourages them to set their moral scaffold high. Suddenly the Senators are bored. The crack of the first direct question about their tattle-tale capacity sheers cleanly through this viscous nonsense like a whip of lightning in a humid summer calm. The air is cleared, and men can be about their business.

Mr. Smith's opening tactics were no exception to this rule. One look at Corporations Auxiliary purposes as stated in their second New Jersey articles of incorporation might lead the reader to expect a sickish prelude. "To create, foster and promote a better understanding between employers and employees, to promote among employees an insight into economic facts, a deeper sense of individual responsibility, and a spirit of co-operation in order . . . to reduce costs, to eliminate loss and waste and to diminish absenteeism and labor turnover through expert advice, recommendation analysis, inspections, and in general to conduct a business of welfare efficiency and consulting engineers."

Mr. Smith elucidated orally. His companies were engaged in the business of assisting manufacturers in increasing and improving their products both in quantity and quality, and in reducing their operating costs. It was a very simple process. "We feel that in order to get efficiency and to get a good product, the first thing you have to have is harmony, if you possibly can get it, because without harmony you get no efficiency or anything else, and therefore we sometimes say we assist in harmonizing conditions in a plant. That is all there is to it.

It is a very simple business. If you can keep everybody happy and contented, satisfied, everybody working shoulder to shoulder with a given purpose of increasing the production in quality and in quantity, and in reducing expenses as much as possible, consistent with good business, if they are all working that way, you have no trouble at all, you go right along. That is what we have been trying to do all our lives."

This apparently was not done by engineers since Mr. Smith could not recall whether they employed any. Nor, strangely enough, was it done by a system of revolving mirrors. For some time, "for possibly a couple of years," in order to accomplish their welfare work, according to Mr. Smith, they tried a poster service. This did not seem to be effective and then came the question-box and suggestion-box idea. They tried that out quite often in order to get some ideas that would be helpful. "In some cases," said Mr. Smith, "I think they are still using that now. In some cases they have eliminated it because, well, in certain ways it tends to promote discord to just have the suggestion box."

In looking over his years in the business, Mr. Smith felt his organization had realized its aims. In Michigan, for instance, he said, "Our clients have had a very small number of labor disturbances. We take some little credit for it."

It was two days after Mr. Smith's self-congratulation that Richard Truman Frankensteen of Detroit, Michigan, home of Mr. Smith's satisfied clients, sat at the witness table. At his right sat Mr. Smith and his general manager, Dan G. Ross, former Pinkerton man—large, of bluish cast, with a range of vision which seemed to take in three-quarters of the horizon, at so acute an angle could he turn his eyes. Mr. Ross's compensation in the great harmonizing enterprise was $50,000 a year salary with a ten percent bonus on results from all offices. At the right of Frankensteen sat the contented client, the slightly pursy but resolutely straight-gazed Mr. Herman L. Weckler, now vice-president and general manager of the DeSoto Motor Corporation, but previously to June, 1936—for two years—member of Chrysler general staff responsible for labor relations. Mr. Frankensteen, son of a Chrysler employee and himself a former worker in the trim division of Dodge—from which job he had been elected to be an officer of the Chrysler Corporation representative plan, was now member of the General Executive Board and organizational director for the United Automobile Workers. Conforming in no way to traditional pictures of the oppressed workers, either by Millet or Markham, Mr. Frankensteen was college bred, muscularly athletic, rosy cheeked, good looking, assertive, and mad clear through.

It was a time if ever to describe the workings of the poster system and the suggestion box. Instead, this story came out.

Frankensteen had had a fellow employee by the name of Johnnie Andrews with a wife and two children. "A nice clean chap," said Frankensteen. "I thought he was a very fine fellow." From the time when Andrews came up to Frankensteen at a union meeting which he had addressed and asked him if he played golf, their friendship developed. There was no golf, but Andrews cultivated him in other ways, drove him to and from meetings. One evening he and his wife invited the Frankensteens to go to a show. They came over. "It started to rain," said Mr. Frankensteen, "and we stayed at home. We sat down and spent a pleasant evening. My wife was from Dayton, Ohio, and did not have many friends in the city of Detroit. She rather liked Mrs. Andrews. They visited back and forth; they went downtown; they went to shows; they went shopping." During this time Andrews was very active in the union. The two spent five nights a week together working for it. He picketed during the Motor Products Strike. He sat in on meetings where strike strategy was discussed, used strong language, urged force and violence.

One day Andrews suggested to Frankensteen that they take their wives and their four children to Lake Orion for a vacation, dividing the expense. It would not cost much. It seemed a good idea. So they took a cottage together. After things were under way, Johnnie's uncle, Mr. Bath, turned up in Detroit and stayed at the Wardell Hotel where he had a suite of rooms. He was a retired theatrical producer—the record does not say of Broadway, but where else would he have made the million dollars to which he modestly admitted? "He appeared to be a millionaire. He looked as nice as Mr. Smith." Andrews asked Frankensteen would he mind if his uncle came out to the Lake. Not at all. So Mr. Bath came out. Mrs. Frankensteen was carrying a child. Mr. Bath was most solicitous of her well being. He put up at the hotel. He invited them out to dinner frequently. He gave them their first taste of champagne. He was a prince.

This vacation cost the Chrysler Corporation nearly $1,900, earned for Corporations Auxiliary Company by Andrews and Bath—a fill-in operative, now located in the Canada office beyond reach of subpoena. Johnnie has skipped the town, leaving a false address. How much the friendship, cultivated over a long period, on a weekly or per diem basis cost the Chrysler Corporation was never added up by the Committee. The name of the account was "The R. F. Special" and was considered of sufficient importance to warrant a long-distance personal call, which appeared in the expense account for $2.45, to Mr. W. P. Chrysler himself. Frankensteen did not know, until he was apprised in Detroit by a staff investigator of the Committee, that Johnnie was other than the friend he claimed to be.

When Frankensteen was through with his narrative, he addressed the Chrysler official in terms later denounced in the press as "a strike threat made in a Senate hearing." Within six weeks Chrysler was on strike. "Mr. Weckler yesterday made the statement that they had to have the espionage so as to develop a firm basis for industrial relationship. I want Mr. Weckler to know and I want the Chrysler managers to know—and I speak for a majority of his employees and I feel that he knows we are willing to prove it—I want him to know we are not going to work in any of their plants with that type of individual. They are either going to get out or our people will not work in their plants."

Corporations Auxiliary, according to their former client, the Akron Employers Association, went out of business on February 1, 1937.

In February (they had been upon the stand briefly in September), Pinkerton's were examined first alone and then in conjunction with their newly lost client, General Motors. This oldest and most renowned of the firms, eighty-three years of age and for seventy-one years the hated foe of the American Labor movement, has its headquarters on the sixteenth floor of the old Tribune Building in New York City. In addition to its secret offices which open and close as the demand for them arises, it has twenty-six or -seven branches in the principal American cities, and one in Canada. The gross income of this company from agency service in 1934 was $1,745,475, from patrol services $441,765, a total of about $2,100,000. For 1935 the gross income from agency services was $1,922,910, the income from patrol services $395,128, or approximately $2,300,000. For the first seven months of 1936 agency services, the total was $1,037,351 of which $231,792 came from patrol. As has been said before, the net income of the Pinkerton agency, after taxes before dividends, leapt, in the two busy years of labor organization, from $76,760 in 1933 to $268,703 in 1934 and $243,351 for 1935.

The present head of the business, great grandson of the founder, is Robert A. Pinkerton, by the press said to be of Groton and Harvard and thirty-two years of age. He is variously described by those who beheld him in his hour of business ordeal as: a cool customer; a nice young man dragged by circumstance into a filthy business of whose nature he had been kept unaware; romantic; appealing; rather brave; very weak; gallant toward his workers; contumacious toward the Committee. In other words, he puzzled the audience who felt that his polite education should have improved his critical powers, and that a man is not wholly absolved from an unquestioning attitude toward the faith of his forefathers if, as a reward for their efforts, he has been pushed upward in the social scale to a place where he can at leisure examine it. Wellmannered even in his contempt of the Senate, he nevertheless gave the appearance of being constantly nauseated, and was in apparent uncertainty over the cogent advice of counsel that he had ground that would hold under him if he should refuse to hand over certain information. The only opinion about him that all observers seem to hold in common was that, before the subpoena was served, this young man, owner of 70 percent of the 1,000 shares of Pinkerton common stock, the other 30 belonging to his two aunts, knew nothing about the detail of his business. With all charity his stand had to be interpreted in the light of the fact that, although it might be an unpleasant business, he had much to lose through its collapse. His income from dividends was, in 1935, $129,500. His chief stock in trade, and the thing which he so fought against relinquishing, was the concealed identity of the supposed six hundred operatives who made this money for him.

His top man and obviously devoted friend and protector, for whose comfort under the strain he appeared solicitous, drew $12,000 a year as salary and bonus. This was Asher Rossetter, vice-president and general manager of Pinkerton's, who, since the day fifty years ago upon which he joined the Pinkerton staff as office boy, has worked for the firm in every capacity. Looking the part of a greens chairman, with a decoration in his buttonhole, a man of intelligence and open character, he was the man to whom looked for orders an outfit of employees, so amazingly involved in their own camouflage that one wondered if they knew who they were when they woke up in the morning.

The last detective agency to appear was William J. Burns International Detective Agency, Inc., now represented by the brothers Raymond J., president, and W. Sherman, secretary-treasurer, both of whom had the look of success and quiet respectability as befitted top men in their business, rivaled in prestige only by Robert Pinkerton, their name in copper tablets on innumerable American business doorways, as psychological protection. Mr. Raymond had something of the air of a former tennis player keeping in condition, or an enthusiastic horseman. Their business, held completely in the family, was founded in 1909 and has its headquarters at 370 Lexington Avenue, New York City. Lewis Carroll seemed not too far in the background as these brothers responded to La Follette's statement of their business. Their strong resemblance to each other also gave them an end-man quality. La Follette read:

"According to this statement the gross income of the full agency for these years was as follows: for 1933, $418,335.73 of which $62,490.69 was gross income from industrial espionage and guard work; for 1934, the gross income was $502,733.50, of which $109,842.63 was gross income from industrial espionage and guard work; for 1935, the gross income was $505,025.62 of which $85,651.77 was gross income from industrial espionage and guard work. . . .

"Your agency has submitted a statement for the first six months of the year 1936, showing a gross income from industrial undercover and guard work, aggregating $129,194.64. Can you tell us approximately what your gross income from all sources was during that period?"

MR. W. SHERMAN BURNS: Not without referring to the books.

MR. RAYMOND J. BURNS: No; not without referring to the record.

SENATOR LA FOLLETTE: Have you any records with you that you could refer to?

MR. RAYMOND J. BURNS: Senator, this does not include expenses, this statement here?

SENATOR LA FOLLETTE: It is gross income.

MR. W. SHERMAN BURNS: That is right.

MR. RAYMOND J. BURNS: Yes, sir.

SENATOR LA FOLLETTE: I stated that. It is not net; it is gross.

MR. W. SHERMAN BURNS: It does not include expenses. This is not the total billing to the client.
SENATOR LA FOLLETTE: You mean it does not include expenses which you have charged the clients?
MR. W. SHERMAN BURNS: That is correct.
SENATOR LA FOLLETTE: Yes. Thank you. . . . Now, Mr. Burns, the rate of profit on industrial undercover and guard work is higher than that on any other phase of your business, is it not? . . . As a general rule is it not a more profitable, better type of business than the other types of business that you do?
MR. W. SHERMAN BURNS: No.
SENATOR LA FOLLETTE: Is not the overhead expense low on this business, this industrial undercover work and guard work?
MR. W. SHERMAN BURNS: Well, it is very difficult to divide the overhead expense.
SENATOR LA FOLLETTE: I offer for the record your "All Office Letter" No. 587, dated August 1, 1933, headed "Prospective Business Industrial Work." The entire letter may be printed as an exhibit. I read one sentence from it:

"This work is very profitable inasmuch as it does not entail any substantial overhead expense." . . .

I offer for the record another "All Office Letter," dated May 18, 1936, headed, "Prospective Business Industrial and Strike Work." It is signed by W. Sherman Burns, but I read a sentence only from the first paragraph:

"The principals feel that a number of the offices are not giving this potential business the proper attention, notwithstanding the fact that this type of business is most lucrative in our line."

You are the persons referred to in that sentence, are you not?

MR. W. SHERMAN BURNS: Correct.

SENATOR LA FOLLETTE: Now, on the industrial work, both undercover and guard work, it is your practice, is it not, to pay your operatives from 40 to 50 percent of the charge made to the clients?

MR. W. SHERMAN BURNS: That is about right.

MR. RAYMOND J. BURNS: Correct.

SENATOR LA FOLLETTE: This means, does it not, that usually your gross profits from industrial business are about 50 percent of your gross income, is that correct?

MR. RAYMOND J. BURNS: Except on long-term contracts, Senator; the rate of pay would be a little higher on industrial work.

SENATOR LA FOLLETTE: Now, when you take that into consideration in connection with these two statements I have read, that this work does not entail any substantial overhead, and that it is one of the most lucrative lines of business that you are in, it would be true, would it not, your net profit from industrial business is about 50 percent of your gross income from that business?

MR. W. SHERMAN BURNS: Except on long-term contracts; yes.

The Senator's figuring was upheld in the Burns' work for the New York elevator strike of March, 1936, and the strike at Remington Rand. During the New York elevator strike Burns furnished guards to 160 clients at a charge of $93,491 and a cost of $47,629 for guard wages. Its charge to Remington Rand from May to September was $28,317 and the cost $12,328.

The agency has branch offices in Atlanta, Baltimore,

Boston, Buffalo, Chicago, Cleveland, Dallas, Denver, Detroit, Houston, Kansas City, Los Angeles, Miami, Minneapolis, New Orleans, New York, Philadelphia, Pittsburgh, Portland, Oregon, Richmond, Virginia, St. Louis, San Francisco, Salt Lake, Seattle, Spokane, and Washington, D. C. As its territorial spread would indicate, it takes in a wide range of industrial activities. Among its something less than three hundred customers (more than half of whom bought undercover work—and another large fraction surveillance, guards, or prevention of sabotage), we find lumber, oil, stevedoring, canning, shipping, and fishing industries; movies, flour mills, breweries, furniture, leather, paper, cereal, shoe, clothing and cotton manufacturers. We find stores: Woolworth, the A & P, and American stores. We find Mt. Sinai Hospital.

In all of these agencies, gradations of respectability were manifest. The farther away from the bottom layer of dirty work the officers and proprietors had managed to escape through its rewards, the more did they assume the demeanor of honor and open dealing. Pinkerton's general manager, Rossetter, colonel of a regiment of men whose profit to their company lay in the depth of the pitfall they could dig under their pretended friends in the unions which they were instructed to join, was clearly appalled in the hearing room at the bleak and repulsive details of how this was accomplished. Perhaps he had forgotten. The employers themselves drew their coats a little closer as a woman draws away her skirts in distaste, when they were forced to sit at the stand beside the parade of spies. But they admitted they had ordered the goods and paid the bills.

iv. Concerning Them That Seduce You

STORY-BOOK detectives are called in by their clients. Artists that they are, they rarely hang out shingles. The industrial spy is much more active. Day in, day out, he peddles his gifts of intrigue. If he is as well known as Pinkerton or Burns the client sometimes comes to him, but without promotion this does not happen frequently enough.

What is his sales talk? What are the goods he can promise to deliver? He answers these questions by posing several others to himself. For what will the employer spend his money and how can the spending process be prolonged? Which does the employer consider to be more expedient, to destroy the union after it has been accomplished, or to abort it?

Experience has demonstrated that once the union is born and has grown strong, it is hard to kill, although not of course impossible. (Pinkerton's entered a Lansing union and when they got through five members only were left, all of them officers and all of them Pinkerton spies.) Usually it is much simpler, cheaper to management, not to say less disquieting to the public, if the union's attempts to organize continuously miscarry. The doctor who can promise to bring about union mortality by abortion has something to sell to the worried employer. If the employer is serenely unconscious of his prospective trouble, especially if no trouble is in prospect, the malpractitioner need not be above stirring up malicious rumor, or even stirring up trouble itself. It is a slow, tedious job, but if the employer is properly coached, he can become accustomed to paying for abstractions. After a while, he hands out money as if he were under a spell.

The sales campaign, like any other, is laid out carefully in the home office, and given elaboration and tone by salesmen in the field. Some of these espionage salesmen are very good, having in addition to the requisite promotor's talents, two other qualities, an uncritical admiration of their wares—they apparently could push butter and eggs or electric chairs with equal enthusiasm—and a deep-seated love of indirection for its own sake.

Lacking the stimulus of personal contact with challenging individual situations, the sales managers in the home office have to base their strategy upon a principle. This principle is merely a restatement of the detective's law of demand, that where there is trouble, or the prospect of it, there is a market. The detective agency thus studies the industrial map of the country, its finances and its employment problems, in order to superimpose upon it a second map which it is constantly constructing, a map of labor hotspots. Most agencies operate what approximates a library or clipping service which follows labor events. The labor press and journals of liberal opinion are carefully watched and clipped. Information is fed out to canvassers who in turn pass back to headquarters the rumblings of labor dissatisfaction heard in employers' offices. Spies' reports are used in making general summaries. An ear is kept to the ground for both state and federal legislation. If some regulatory measure seems to have a chance of passage, its oppressive character is drawn to the notice of manufacturers who are also warned of the contagiousness of distant strikes. The rise and fall of NRA, and the threat and passage of the Wagner Disputes Act as well as its subsequent violation under legal advice, were made to order for such purposes.

Already in 1933 W. Sherman Burns was on his toes, and was writing President Dumaine of the Amoskeag Mills:

"My Dear Sir: If, as we all hope the deflationary forces have been arrested and the measures adopted by the present administration result in an inflationary commodity price level, we will of necessity pass through a period of industrial unrest, due to the failure of wages to keep pace with the cost of living. This period will continue until industry is sufficiently revived to enable it to increase the wage scale all along the line.

"Faced with this labor unrest, individual companies must do one of two things—either their cash and surplus position is such that it will enable them to immediately meet the increased wage demands, or they must take the necessary steps to convince their employees that a short period of disparity between prices and wages is essential to the recovery of prosperity.

"The success of this latter undertaking will largely depend upon the methods used to accomplish it. It is quite obvious that statements or addresses by the officers of corporations or the heads of welfare departments or any round-table discussion will not be effective. Companies will again have to contend with the professional agitator, sincere or otherwise. It is a simple, but none the less true fact that all individuals are more readily and thoroughly convinced of the justice of a position taken on a controversial subject if the arguments advanced emanate from a sympathetic source; in this instance, from a fellow employee.

"If executives will anticipate this condition of unrest and meet the work of these professional agitators by a counter undercover propaganda, they will probably avoid serious labor disturbances, with its usual heavy losses. It is, of course, highly important that this work be intelligently supervised and handled with discretion.

"We are equipped to install and carry on this important work for your company on an economical basis in a confidential and efficient manner. If interested, I would appreciate a personal interview."

International Auxiliary was writing hopefully, during NRA:

"Dear Sir: No matter how much you are occupied with other affairs, you will probably agree it is important for you as an employer to make a positive effort to stop the campaign of misrepresentation now being waged by organized labor to the extent it may affect your interests. Employees are continually being told by trained exhorters that the Government is behind them in Section 7-A of the NRA. Truths are often concealed or distorted. Organized labor misleaders have found a rare opportunity . . ."

By May of 1935, perhaps urged on by competition, or perhaps only aware of the great potentialities of this new market, W. Sherman Burns again took his pen in hand and wrote "All Office Letter No. 696":

"To All Officers:

"There has recently been and no doubt will continue to be considerable industrial unrest, and although this Agency does not furnish strikebreakers, we do handle undercover and guard work. The Principals feel that a number of the offices are not giving this potential business the proper attention, notwithstanding the fact that this type of business is the most lucrative in our line.

"Each manager should make the proper contacts that will enable him to be advised of agitation and possible strikes involving any concern or industry in his territory and should follow up this information by doing the necessary soliciting in order to secure undercover work, or in the case of strikes, the guard work. If a strike is contemplated in a manager's territory outside of his city, he should contact with this prospect by long distance telephone. If the *Daily Worker*, which is the official Communist organ, is available on his newsstands, he should purchase same daily. If he can establish some contacts through informants that will keep him advised on the industrial situation, he should do so. In order to keep the Principals advised of what efforts are made to secure strike work, we request that a soliciting report be rendered to the New York office on all calls covering efforts to secure strike work.

"Recently there has been some agitation among State legislatures and even in Congressional circles—a movement to legislate against detective agencies and limit their activities in industrial work, and so that every manager will be familiar with the policy of the Principals with reference to this work, it is desirable to set forth here the fact that in the first place the Agency, as I have stated before, does not furnish strikebreakers. We will not take an investigation the purpose of which is to deliberately disrupt a labor union. We will, however, furnish employers with undercover service for the purpose of ascertaining what agitation is taking place among their employees, whether this be radical or otherwise, and of course for the purpose of ferreting out thefts, sabotage, etc. We will also furnish guards, both uniformed and plainclothes, for the purpose of protecting life and property at all times and during a strike.

"The opportunities for securing this type of business have been on the increase and will continue, but only that

CONCERNING THEM THAT SEDUCE YOU

agency will secure the business whose representatives plan an intelligent sales campaign. A solicitor, whether he be a manager or any other employee, must not only cover the ground properly and promptly but must be familiar with the problems of the particular industry he is soliciting. The Principals earnestly request that each manager give this prospective business his immediate and close attention.

"Kindly acknowledge receipt of this letter."

More fruitful of alarm perhaps than any other tocsin that can be sounded by the espionage salesman is that of Communism. Once an employer becomes known as living in fear of the red menace, he is honey to the bees. E. D. LeMay, assistant to the president of the Tennessee Coal and Iron Railroad, a subsidiary of U. S. Steel, and J. H. Eddy, president of the Kaul Lumber Company, also of Birmingham, had this attractiveness to the Pinkerton canvasser Carleton, who wrote his chief Littlejohn in Atlanta: "As you know this organization [T C & I] has their own secret service and while there is no indication that we are going to break in on them, I do feel that we have established a very favorable contact with Mr. LeMay. . . . As matters now stand I do not want anyone but yourself to see Mr. LeMay. He is deeply interested in communistic activity, so bring that subject up. . . . [Eddy] like Mr. LeMay is deeply interested in the Communist situation and works with LeMay on it. Obviously the main purpose in seeing Mr. Eddy is to assist in cultivating Mr. LeMay." It is interesting to note that not one of six Pinkerton officials examined upon the subject had the haziest notion as to what constitutes a Communist.

Although Pinkerton's strove to give the impression that

they accept industrial work only when the employer is anxious to stamp out Communism, the record reveals profusely that the agency never refused to spy on unions affiliated with the American Federation of Labor. In practice the name Communist, radical, and agitator, or more popularly, outside agitator, is applied to any person having any sympathy with an independent union. The peppery sauce of Red Scare is put on to make the anti-union drive more palatable to the public. The epithet is also useful in alarming hesitant candidates who stand upon the brink of union membership, it being well known that many ardent union men hate the very word of Communism.

The biggest industrial client warrants greater strategy than can be expected of the small-time canvasser. For these, scouts are cultivated by agency officials. That there is a mutual desire to do business and that frequently the client may take the initiative, is implied in the following instruction sheet as to what the Corporation Auxiliary salesman must procure in way of information when writing a contract for new business:

"1. What are the duties our operative will be required to perform?
2. What other qualifications must he have such as religion, nationality, etc.?
3. How many men in the plant? How many women? How many men in the department? How many women?
4. What is the pay system used in the department (hourly, group bonus, Bedeaus, etc.)?
5. When is payday and how much is held back? Pay is by (cash) (check).
6. How many hours a day does the plant operate?

CONCERNING THEM THAT SEDUCE YOU

How many hours per week? How many hours on Saturday?
7. Will our operative work the above hours? If not, what hours will he work?
8. What is considered overtime? How much overtime is generally worked in the department where our operative will be?
9. What is the shop rate for the class of work our operative will do? What is the overtime rate? Average weekly earnings are how much?
10. Is there to be a "guaranteed rate" for the operative? What is it? Does the client understand how this is to be billed?
11. What organizations are active in the plant? In the department? In the city? Must operative have card when applying for work? What organization? Is he to join? Which one? How soon?
12. Is there an "employees representation" plan? How does it operate?
13. Does the company publish a set of rules? Get a copy from the client.
14. Does the company publish a set of safety rules? Get a copy from the client.
15. What is the client particularly interested in having our operative cover?
16. Who are the officials (with titles) who will know the identity of our operative?
17. How is our operative to get his job?
18. Name of man who gets reports? Street address? City? Envelope to be "Personal"? Double envelope? Is this the office? Residence?
19. Same information for any others who get them. Name? Street address? City? Envelope to be "Per-

sonal"? Double envelope? Is this the office? Residence?
20. Name of man who gets bills? Street address? City? Is this the office? Residence? Are bills to be on Company bill heads? Are they to be on S & W bill heads? If on S & W, is itemized bill to accompany? On what kind of stationery? Did you explain S & W billing to client? (The accounting department prefers to do all billing on Company bill heads and S & W bills are only sent to accommodate clients.) Did you explain to client that envelopes used for both bills and reports show a box number only?"

Practical aids are given to routine canvassers, like the indefatigable William Gray, perhaps the most accomplished of all small-time canvassers, hookers, and spies in the business. His Atlanta Chief, Mr. Ivey, Railway Audit's general manager in Philadelphia, gives us a closer view of the education of a solicitor for business. In this letter we catch a suggestion of the characteristic love of detail, the total recall which so enthralls the reader of detective reports. These hew to the theory advanced by Thomas Mann that nothing but the truly exhaustive is interesting. The detective's love of item and his ability to remember it photographically make his complete amnesia on the witness stand even the more phenomenal. Let me quote verbatim:

"At 8 A.M. Mr. Gray called the office, and I told him to come up. I gave him a January, 1935, edition of the textile book and marked therein all of our present clients. I went over the entire Carolina and Tennessee territory with him. I advised him to buy a map of the territory and to draw concentric circles through the states and to follow his itineraries. I then told him that after he had covered the entire states and made notations on the map where good prospects were located that he could then cover them with a great deal more ease and with less expense than if he worked the territory haphazard.

"I went over with him every possible question that could be asked by the textile men. I made him give me a sales talk. I corrected certain misunderstandings and filled in his lack of information and knowledge by detailed descriptions and advices. I spent about two and one-half hours with Mr. Gray. I then advised him to leave Atlanta and go by way of Athens and Anderson, S. C., into South Carolina. I told him to work every little mill along the road, as well as the big ones. I told him to put our name before every possible person he could think of. I told him to further keep me advised of his itinerary day by day. I told him to send his representative reports at the end of each day, original to you P. O. Box 793, Philadelphia, and a copy to me P. O. Box 957, Atlanta. After I finished my conference with Mr. Gray I made him ask me any questions he could think of concerning the rates and the business. I grounded him as best I could, and he left here at the same time I did, which was approximately 11 A.M."

As this letter indicates, small business is not to be sneezed at. Even with General Motors in the bag to the tune of well over a hundred thousand a year, Pinkerton's had four or five canvassers in the Carolinas and Tennessee in the year of 1935. Among them they made some 175 calls on large and small manufacturers, most of them unfruitful of results. Mr. Gray, covering simultaneously the same territory for Railway Audit, would probably have sympathized with them if he recognized them when he crossed their paths. "This labor situation is very quite," Mr. Gray wrote to his chief. "Mr. Adams could not stir their Hosiery Mill workers up in this section & the Cotton Mills are closing down, as you have probably noted in the papers & the workers are scared to death about this thing & are very quite & I find that a number of them are losing confidence in the Administration as well as the Mill owners & officials. The Mill owners are only interested in one thing now that is getting this process tax off their neck & about all we can do with them is visit with them and sympathize with them & otherwise get into their good graces, as they will not spend any money for service."

Pinkerton reports on prospects, on the other hand, are laconic and monotonous. The employer's disposition and receptivity are noted, the number of his employees, their state of loyalty and any hope or likelihood of trouble. They read similarly, for the most part, to this one:

"Shelby, N. C.
"Jan. 21, 1935.

"Eton Mills Co., A. B. Quinn, secy. & asst. treas.; cotton mills: Stated the labor situation was very good in their plants now. That he saw no need for our service at the present. He was familiar with our service as he had been quoted rates by some of the officials in the past. Stated he would call on us if our service was desired in the future."

There are ways and ways of overcoming apathy. Who could fail to admire Mr. Gray's ingenuity when faced with a poser? Let us read him for his inimitably chatty prose, if for nothing else, as he addresses himself in May of 1935 to his chief, Mr. Ivey, more familiarly known to his operative as No. 700:

"I hope that the office will not go into a nervous prostration when you receive this order for an operative, but

CONCERNING THEM THAT SEDUCE YOU 75

I tell you truthfully that I never tried so hard to make good on one job, as I have this one, and I certainly appreciate the patitence that you all have had with me, but it has been tough, but I think that I have hit on the vital spot now and here it is these cotton mill 'boys' want to chisel on the code, and they are scared to do it because of labor trouble, and I have hit on the solution, and that is to place undercover men in the mill and then start to slip the word out in an effective manner that in order for the Mill to stay in operation the management is going to have to make some adjustments in prices on the work, and then let the operatives pick up the reaction, and then follow right along with the gen, propanganda, this has caused more concern than any thing that I have used yet, and I am going to play along those lines I know that this is a ticklish angle to work on but I got a good approach all worked before I spring it on them, and then I carry it on as far as I can. I hope that you have a good all around man for this job at the Holt Mill, and I think that I will get another one for the Tarvora Mill in Graham, boy when you said that these southern boys were smarter than I was you knew whart you were talking about, and you can not high pressure them, but I am getting them to warm up to me and I feel that unless that the Gov. does something to straighten these codes out, that I am going to get some business, as these Southern Mill men see now that they got to get busy and that the Gov. do'nt give a damn about nothing but politics, and if they are going to stay in business they have got to do so on their own initiative, and fight, and I am playing on that and have been for some time, I had to be careful who I talked to, but I got it across to them directly and in-directly, and I can see that it is takeing hold, and I look for plenty trouble when they start chiseling on the code. I am going to get around Charloote the first of next week working Thru H. P. and then on down, and then get back in Durham, the latter part of next week, as I want that job there, and the only way I am going to get it, is to keep it hot, and believe me if I ever get that job, I am going to keep that Labor proposition hot there, as that is the best spot in the N. C."

Later, his enthusiasm unabated—for as Mr. Gray often says, "I have Confidence in myself and that is all that it takes to do this work"—he writes:

"Do not misunderstand my set up, that I am introducing, as I know that it is dynamite, but boy I got to get some business, and they are falling for it and I am sincere about, and warned them as to how careful they must be, and they realize it, but they are up against the gun, and they have got to do something."

The proposition, of course, once the susceptible employer has been found, is that the agency will aid him to keep the union impotent by spotting its sympathizers. The detective has alternative services to offer, according to the delicacy of the situation, the immediate objective being, of course, to keep the client informed as to labor developments within his plant. The first method is to find bona-fide employees in the plant who are susceptible to bribe. These will be put on the pay roll of the agency as informers, and the client will be charged for their reporting services, plus profit for the idea, for procurement, and for supervision. If no vulnerable employees can be found, the agency will volunteer to bring in outside spies.

Time is necessary to nurse along either of these operations, as both of them are delicate and dangerous. The danger in the first method lies in the fact that, if the approached employee should unfortunately prove to be loyal to his fellow workers, he might be shocked if the true nature of his task were told him too abruptly. If his sense of decency were too outraged, he very likely would tell them what he knew and the cat would be out of the bag. Resentment against the management would be thus intensified and efforts to organize become stronger and more secretive. The agency, whose stock in trade is its adroitness, would be accused of fumbling and would lose a profitable job. Therefore the potential traitor must lose his innocence by imperceptible degrees. Not until he is caught in the trap beyond self-extrication must he be allowed to learn what he is really doing. This is likewise the reason for attempting to keep a man employed after he has been completely hired. Mr. Rice deprecated the necessity for leading a man to believe he had a job when none was to be forthcoming. "Little things like this don't help us any," he wrote, "as this man can go out and do a lot of talking about us."

This tender operation of getting a worker on the line is known as hooking. A man well hooked in time becomes invaluable. If he is finally suspected and exposed by his fellow workers he can become a professional hooker, or perhaps be transferred to other plants under the same management. In a new place he becomes the ideal candidate for the second method of procedure, the insertion into the ranks of an unknown worker, who goes upon the employer's pay roll as a bona-fide mechanic, weaver, plumber, watchman, or electrician, and draws wages as both worker and spy. This method is slow because he must overcome the native workers' initial distrust of a stranger and overcome it, if possible, to a point where he can become president of their union. If he can become its financial officer that is as good, for from either of these vantage points he can report to his employer the full roster of union-minded workers and the union's financial status, can control its policies (we shall see later that to make the union quiescent is not always, from the agency's point of view, the most profitable end), and last (and why should we be shocked at this?) perhaps run off with the money.

Before revealing the later workings of the game, let us watch the opening round, starting with the man who is about to be hooked. Both physically and in sympathy he is the nearest to the victim of all the participants.

First, and most important, let us not try to make out too much of a case for him. He has his price, and according to the standards of the cause it is a low one. The real price of his sell-out cannot be measured in terms of money. Although a worker may be accustomed to low wages, and the size of the bribe be very tempting indeed, no such low estimate is placed upon his sell-out by his union which has a collective amount at stake, as well as its principles. United strength in labor, as well as in any other cause, depends upon trust between individuals and separate bravery to undergo sacrifice for immediate gains.

The pay of the informer varies widely. There seems to be no average. The green spy hooked from among the workers is paid according to his quickwittedness and strategical position. He sometimes is started off as low as twenty-five dollars a month, this sum being supplementary to his plant wages. The outside informer placed in the plant may add his plant wages to his salary from the agency. If the two combined bring his income above the amount fixed upon by the agency in the employment contract, the wages are deducted by the proper amount from his agency pay. Good operatives are paid as high as three hundred a month, but not often. Expenses are added;

union dues, camouflaged on the itemized account as entertainment, concert or dance tickets (one correspondence noted "an arrearage in entertainment"), telephone, liquor, strike donations, and such other odds and ends as will lubricate the work of the sleuth.

The temptation to the hooked man in this price lies in the need he may have for such a sum. Consequently we must not find it strange if the hooker at large is in receipt of instructions from his own agency to locate a candidate who is in acute financial distress or at least one who is in bad want of money for some specific purpose.

Red Kuhl is a reformed hooker of twenty years' experience, chiefly with Railway Audit, who came into this work via the railroad, the army, and the International Correspondence School. He left it a few years ago in disgust because it was too dirty, and has since been very active as a sort of free-lance agent in nullifying spy work among the unions. We shall be indebted to him frequently for practical explanations of the organic nature of espionage and strikebreaking. Upon this subject of hooking he has to say: "Well, first you look your prospect over and if he is married, that is preferable. If he is financially hard up, that is number two. If his wife wants more money or he hasn't got a car, that all counts." The wish to save is prominently stressed. Sam Brady of Pinkerton's in writing a heartening talk to his new operative No. 260, Jones:

"The money of course is yours as you may see fit to dispose of it; but please permit me to make a little suggestion:

" 'Lay it aside' it as you know amounts to $720.00 per year without or not counting any interest in 5 yrs. time. You will have enough sand to invest in a nice comfortable home, and I have seen any number of my co-workers do this little trick."

The ideal candidate is a union leader who is laboring under a conspiracy of inauspicious stars, sick children, discontented wife, and anxiety to save. If the client has taken the initiative in calling in the agency, he may have already eased the task of the prospecter by having on hand a list of workers with such assets. The Republic Rubber Company composed a hookers' list containing the names of their employees who, they hoped, might be susceptible. All names upon it were those of strictly union men. If there stands out conspicuously among the other workers a union man who has desirable talents but who is making a go of it within his wages, it is not unknown for the employer to shift him from regular to irregular employment, thus artificially inducing a tempting stringency of funds.

The worker's financial circumstances thus having been ascertained as carefully as if he were an applicant for credit, which in a way he is, since he is putting up his future as collateral for secrecy, he is approached under subterfuge. Two men shrewd enough to look beyond these subterfuges will tell us in their own words how this process works. The first speaker is Mr. John J. Mullen, then chairman of Employees' Representatives of Clairton Plant of the Carnegie Illinois Steel Corporation, who told his story to the La Follette Committee in April, 1936:

"On Saturday morning of January 4 I was approached at home by a man who represented himself as Mr. Walter Sears of the Fidelity Bonding Co., Empire State Building, New York City, and he told me that his company controlled quite a block of stock in the corporation, that is, the United States Steel Corporation, and they were very much aware that there was dissension among employees and lack of harmony between management and employees, which in turn cut into production and profits, that they were interested in rectifying that condition as much as possible, and he said they knew in order to rectify it they had to get somebody who was down in the ranks and could give them first-hand information. He was very flattering when he approached me. He said I had been investigated from several angles and proved very desirable. He told me that for reports on favoritism by the bosses they were willing to pay me $50 a month and expenses.

"Well, shortly before that I had been reading a condensed review of a book in which some of the evidence presented here was referred to. I was interested in this man's proposition. I told him I hated to be asked to act as an informer on the men who were employing me, that it did not seem much of a display of loyalty. He said, 'Mr. Mullen, who do you really owe loyalty to? To the stockholders of the corporation who are actually paying your salary or to the bosses and officials down here who are driving you and your buddies?' I said, 'That sounds logical enough. I guess I do owe loyalty there.'"

Mullen accompanied Sears to McKeesport where they met a Mr. Henning. The deal was negotiated and Mullen signed a receipt for a five-dollar advance, and over a period of time earned two twenties and a ten.

Meantime, Mr. George A. Patterson, president of a sister organization among employees of the Carnegie Illinois in Chicago also found himself attractive to the stockholders of big business. Said Mr. Patterson, who followed Mr. Mullen on the stand:

"On Lincoln's Birthday I returned from work and I found a heavy, burly man in my home. I was quite upset about it. I wanted to know how this man got in my home. It so happened that I have an invalid sister who is at home at all times, and she happened to allow this man in. I felt rather mad to find this stranger in my house. So I asked him what his business was. He said that he had a proposition to make to me. I could not understand what he had to do with me. So he took me aside into my little kitchenette in the apartment and started a very fluent salesmanship talk. He said that he represented the Fidelity Bond Co. of the Empire State Building, New York, and he went on to state how interested they were in trying to increase the profits of the stockholders, and that he believed that there was trouble between employees and managers, and that he thought I could help. . . .

"In fact, he knew almost as much about myself as I did. When he got through he said, 'How would you like to do this for us? We will not ask you to do anything for us that will get you into trouble. Just go about your business in the usual way and make reports.' By this time I thought this was a very peculiar situation, and I felt kind of peculiar. He sort of repulsed me, because I had never been approached in any way by anybody like him before. He could tell me I was a good church member, that I was general superintendent of the Sunday school where I attended, and so on. The man evidently had investigated my character.

"I began to find out he was offering money, but he did not state just how much money he would give me. He said he had a friend outside in a car. . . .

"By the way, this man said to me that his name was Sears, Mr. Sears.

"I said, 'How do I know your name is Sears?' He pulled

out a letter and showed me credentials. It was written 'Fidelity Bond Co., Empire State Building, New York. To whom it may concern,' and so on, and 'This should only be produced upon request.' So I had requested him, and he showed me his name was on there, 'Sears.'

"We went outside into this car and I met a man by the name of Mr. Henning."

Already the story to us has a familiar ring. But not to Mr. Mullen and to Mr. Patterson. Fishy, perhaps, but not familiar. Mr. Patterson was sent to Pittsburgh for a convention which, he learned there, had been postponed. As he sat in the station wondering what to do he remembered a name that had occurred in the convention correspondence, J. J. Mullen of Clairton, and found it in the telephone directory. Mullen came downtown. They exchanged union talk and found themselves en rapport. "In the course of the conversation," said Mr. Patterson, "I noticed he looked at me kind of peculiarly. He said to me, 'Have you ever been approached in any way by a man?' He just needed to say that much. I said, 'Well, what do you know about that?'" It had not taken an exchange of confidences to put them on their guard, however. Already Mullen had impounded his money with Clinton Golden, regional director of the National Labor Relations Board. It paid his expenses to Washington to tell his story to the Committee. Patterson had already confided in the police. A Mr. Macklin, introduced at one interview as the big boss from New York was later identified as an officer of the H. C. Frick Coal Company.

The interested stockholder is a very favorite pretext. Sam Brady on occasions used a variation of it, although he too, like Sears and Henning, underestimated his adversary, William Jones. Jones in connivance with Phil

Ziegler, secretary and treasurer of the Brotherhood of Railway Clerks, had secreted a stenographer in the closet just before Mr. Brady came to see him. Brady, alias Bradley for the moment, said he represented a "group of philanthropists and public-spirited men who collected data in all parts of the country about wages, about the conditions under which men worked, and that this information was collected and made available to organizations who were interested in promoting the general welfare of workers, and which had been made particularly helpful to labor unions when they were engaged in wage cases." These words are from Mr. Ziegler's testimony.

The next words belong to Mr. Brady as they were taken down by the closeted recorder. "On our Executive Board we have fifty men. We have certain State Senators, Congressmen and many prominent men such as Charles Evans Hughes, Henry Ford, John D. Rockefeller, Dr. Park S. Cadman, Father Ryan, Dr. Finley, the great surgeon, and other people in the movement."

The hooking device can be simple or elaborate, depending upon the mood of the hooker, or the simplicity of his dupe. Pinkerton's operative Frenchy Dubuc, himself somewhat confused about his true nature, since he attempted to play straight with both Pinkerton, whom he swore he never led astray, and his union, to whom he revealed their secrets, described the involution of their identity. Dubuc had been hired by Arthur Pugmire, using the alias Palmer. In answer to La Follette's question as to whether others than Palmer-Pugmire had ever received his telephonic reports, Dubuc said: "Well, to start with it was Pugmire and than a man by the name of Mathews, but since then I know is Mason. Of course, that might be a different alias, but I know him as Mason now. Then Parker, but now I know he is Peterson. Then

Sullivan came in the picture and then after Sullivan there was a man by the name of—no, Roberts came in the picture and then Sullivan came and finally a man by the name of O'Riley, but Pugmire told me that it was O'Riley and to call him Ed, that his real name was John, and after that he did not know who O'Riley was, but it was O'Riley, so I think it was a fictitious name."

One stool amazingly describes his employment by Corporation Auxiliary who wrote him under the letter head of the Atlantic Production Company. "I was interviewed by a Mr. J. C. Carter of that office who stated his was a firm of consulting engineers and that if they placed me on a job I would have to report as to the conditions existing in their plant. I was also given a literacy test."

Opinions differ as to the original sin of the hooked man. Red Kuhl believes that "70 percent or next to it" from the start know what they are really doing, and that "in no time at all, say 90 percent know within two or three months." Frankensteen named, as much for the benefit of Mr. Weckler in the chair beside him as for the Senators, good men of long work and labor record who had been innocently taken on the line, been exposed, and cast out.

Another labor organizer was less charitable, refusing to believe that hooked men are ever really fooled. Certainly the worker turned informer was at no time on the stand a prepossessing moral spectacle. Full of rationalization, long and involved stories about why he had continued with his spying once he had got caught, he invariably failed to impress the hearers with his innocence or his integrity of motive, anxious though they might be to believe him an unwitting victim. A few have undoubtedly been deceived over a long period. A few have fought their way back into union confidence with great effort and self-sacrifice. Frenchy Dubuc, a Pinkerton informant in General Motors, completely retrieved himself by the aid which he gave to the union. So useful to the union can be a man who knows about detective operations in its plant that when a loyal union member is approached by a hooker and so reports to his union officer, he is invariably advised to accept the job. False information is thus fed the agency, as it is also done through bona-fide stools who do not know their presence to be suspected. This device was used in the General Motors strike, when two strike committees were chosen, one with known stools upon it to whom one set of plans was given, the other of trusted men to whom the real strategy was revealed.

To give a hooked man his due, let it be said that once a man has been hooked, he is often threatened with blackmail if he attempts to withdraw. The agency very carefully keeps proof against him. Red Kuhl says, "You have his receipts, and probably he will sign a receipt with only a number, and he says, 'Aw, hell, that don't mean anything. That is only a number,' but still you have his handwriting where he wrote in his original reports. . . . If he comes right out and says, 'I am done with this,' why, he can be done with it." One such pleasant example turned up in the person of Harold Lewis, hooked for the Chevrolet plant in Janesville, Wisconsin. This man's uprightness of character made him a wasteful outlay to Pinkerton, for when he realized the turn affairs were taking he terminated his reports. In vain did his hooker expostulate. He refused politely, like a stalled car. It was as simple as Kuhl had said, "They can get out of it, if they want to, but they don't know it."

v. Subterranean Life

ALL that is unpleasant in the theory of spying is even more unpleasant in its practice; unpleasant, but interesting—by the same token that a malicious scandalmonger can always find an ear. In iconography, the informant would surely be symbolized by an ant-eater, ranging a long snout greedily and inquisitively over the ground.

After a session of reading reports, one speculates idly about the literary habits of the spy. In spite of his bad spelling and engagingly broken constructions, he apparently feels an elation at turning author. One can see him at night carefully testing the privacy of his boarding-house bedroom, or in his home sequestering himself from the inquisitive eyes of the children. He gets out his pencil or his pen, and sits down at this new kind of manual labor, his tool clutched stubbily in his hand, his tongue between his teeth. This is a double release; a release from the shut mouth of his peeking, prying, snooping, eavesdropping day, and a release into an expression of his self-importance. In his humble way he is helping to swerve the destinies of business. He is two of the Fates. He spins and cuts the thread. At a word from him a man is mowed down. His tedious garrulity can also be explained by a universal though not amiable human weakness. He loves to make his work seem hard: He got up very early. He had a blow-out. It was zero weather. He went back three times and the man wasn't there. In other words, this work was worth the money.

Of the stances and positions he assumes on his research he leaves us in no doubt, for there is the proud record of his ingenuity: He stood in a dark doorway and counted the union members going up the stairs. He sat behind a curtained window and beckoned to a confederate to take the numbers on departing cars. He went up to the pump room and chatted with the boys. He took a man out for a drink or went fishing with him. He drew near some men who were talking in undertones. He slapped people on the back. He found out what mail so and so was getting. He learned that Smith and Jones were seeing each other very often. He dodged into telephone booths. He took out a union card, or better still presented evidence, often faked, of union activity in some distant town, although if he were a member in good standing this delay was obviated. He made himself popular, as per instructions. He became union treasurer, or maybe even president, and had access to the files, or failing this, he got a key and had it duplicated, or so frequently hung around the union office that when the janitor caught him there alone his presence gave no occasion for suspicion. He got on the strike committee and learned its strategy. If his agency was in the double business of providing strike-breakers, he served on the picket line, urging violence. Or if the employer's spending mood could better be protracted without milking the cow too dry, he counseled inactivity. Then he went home and wrote his report, signed it with his number, sealed it in an envelope with no return address, sought out one of his several favorite mailing stations, and sent it to whichever name and box number his superior officer was using currently. And then the laborer in the vineyard laid down his pruning shears and went to bed, that he might rest his wits until the morrow.

Let us read some one piece of this contemporaneous literature. It was hard to make a selection from the many others by that bright prolific pen. The number 765 by which he is designated gives a clue to his identity. It is Andy Anderson of Railway Audit, writing in October, 1936, a week or so after the Committee had opened its inquiry. His letter was rescued from a bale of waste:

"OPR. 765:

"This morning Bull Huey told me when I made my rounds be sure and go in the bath house. I said, Bull, why do you want me to be sure to go in the bath house? He said because I think somebody put some communist hand bills in there last night. I said, Did you see any of those bills? He said, Yes I got one and gave it to Mr. White. Mr. White said he was going to give it to Mr. Merrill, the plant superintendent. Bull said, They put out some of those communist bills on this W. P. A. job here in front of the By-Product Plant. I said Bull who do you reckon put those things out? Bull said dam if I know. When I made my rounds last night I saw several of the bills in the bath house. Today see if you can find any of them. Then Bull said, I'll be back in a few minutes. He left the watchman's office and walked down on this W. P. A. job and talked with three different men. Then he came on back up to the watchman's office and sat on top of the desk and waited for Herman Newborn to check out so he could ride home with him. Bull and Newborn left the plant around seven o'clock. When Bull left I went straight to the bath house and went in the negroes side first. I didn't see anything in the negros side and came out and went in the white side. I didn't see any literature at all. If you remember I reported in one of my reports what Bull said about Hurd and Beddows asking him if they could come to the by-product plant and put out some literature on his shift. Bull said he told Hurd and Beddows that they couldn't put out any literature on his shift, that he wouldn't stand for anything like that. And now Bull says he found some literature on his shift. I always have believed that Bull's in line with this outfit. He had guilty this morning written all over his face. While we was talking about it Bull couldn't look me in the face. I believe he gave that piece of literature to Mr. White, is that he's trying to keep himself in the clear. The reason he told me about it he thought I would find some of it anyway. I went in all departments looking for some of it but didn't find any of it. The fellows must have it in their pockets. I came on back to the watchman's office and made some notes. Then went over to the Pig Plant. I didn't say anything to anybody. I just hung around there for a few minutes then put out for the corn field looking for Mr. Bass. I went all over that corn field looking for Bass but didn't find him. I left and went back to the By-Product Plant then went around by the ovens on by the coal washer. I haven't seen much loafing around the coal washer since Gunn left. Gunn seemed to be a draw back for every man on the job. But now things seems to be getting along much better. I left the coal washer and went to McWilliams store, and bought something to eat and a coca cola. I finished eating and drinking and came on back to the plant and went back to Mr. Basses corn field again. This time I went through the corn field and on up to his home. I found Mr. Bass at his pig pen sitting on a fence watching his pigs. He saw me coming and got down off the fence and asked me if I wanted a drink of ice water. I said I wouldn't mind having a good drink of ice water. He said come on up to the house. I wouldn't mind having a cool drink myself. We walked up to his house together talking about nothing that amounted to anything. After we got to his house his little girl came out with a picture of ice water. We both had a glass of water, then I asked him if he had missed any more corn. He said, No, it's just like I said the other day. They won't bother it any more until it gets good and hard. Then they'll take my field away. I said, Well the Woodward Iron Company don't want anybody working for them that will steal everything they get their hands on. I made him believe that the Company wanted to know who's stealing his corn. By telling him that, it made him feel more friendly towards the company. After I told him the Company wanted to know who got his corn he said, That's mighty nice of the Company being willing to help catch the devil. Then I said Mr. Bass, the T. C. I. troubles are all settled, isn't it? He said Yes I think they are. You know that was all foolishness. Those fellows didn't gain one dam thing by pulling that strike. They went back to work loosers. Didn't gain anything in the world. They lost nine or ten week's work just by listening to some radical person. I said Well that's the way all the strikes turn out. The Company always wins. He said that's right. The Company always gets the best of it every time. Now I know a old man who the company's been keeping up for several years came in my front yard the other day and stood right where you are sitting now. And told me that he had a real good job now with the union. He said he was making fifteen dollars every week and driving a automobile every day with the gas bought for him. He's working for the Company and the union on the side. I said Mr. Bass, How long has Mr. Holloway been working for the Company and the Union? He said, Did I say his name was Holloway? I meant to say Ole Man D. Earley, Mr. Bass said. D. Earley or B. Earley. I said what kind of work does he do for the company? He said the old man don't do anything much. He just piddles around on the job. The company don't want to lay him off on account of him being an old man. And here he is all lined up with the union doing all he can against the Company. Man like him ought to be ashamed of his self. One of my friends told me not to pay any attention to Old Man Earley. He said he just hung around a bunch of bootleggers all the time. I said Mr. Bass in what department does Mr. Earley work in at the By-Product Plant? He said Why he don't work for the Woodward Iron Co. He works for the T. C. I. I said I thought you said he worked for Woodward. He said No, not this old man. But there's some working for Woodward Iron Company doing the same thing, old man Earley's doing. Old man Earley was laughing and talking the other day about how the union had men working in all of these Plants right under the Company's nose and the companys couldn't find out a dam thing about it. I said I wonder who's working at the By-Product Plant. He said Well I wouldn't know. Early didn't say but I know there's somebody's working for the union in there. But I don't know who he is. Then Mr. Bass began talking about fox hunting. I stayed around and listened to his talk about fox hunting for about forty minutes, then left. I saw he had mind oct on hunting so I didn't hang around any longer. I came on back to the Plant.

"After I got home this afternoon I heard Mrs. W. H. Whare the lady I room with giving Mr. Kemp the devil for searching her brother's place of business for pig iron that was stolen from the Woodward Iron Company. Mrs. Whare said Mr. Kemp searched her brother's place of business without a warrant or permission and the Woodward Iron Co. can be sued for that. These people are red hot about that. They say Mr. Kemp's overstepping his rights when he comes up here in Brighton and searches people's place of business. They didn't have very much to say about it but they did say something about sueing the Woodward Iron Company. I'll try to learn more about it tonight.

"765"

By the time such a report reaches the final upperling of the firm which put in the order for it, it will have been reduced to pemmican by men in his own office who have been told that the executive is too busy to read more than a digest. But long before it reaches the customer, a superintendent of the agency, either at home in the head office or roaming to hook or canvass, will have extracted the salient facts from where they nestle in cozy irrelevancies. For the ideal report must be studded with certain stars; the names of union leaders, the names of union members, the state of the union treasury, and the plans, if any, for striking.

In other words, the agency has a first-rate editing job on its hands. The employer is not going to continue to pay to learn about trouble if he never hears of any. Neither is he interested in the joyful excursions of an ego as it junkets through the pump-room in search of literary material. The superintendent, a man of parts, who perhaps landed the client and who therefore knows his needs, will be responsible for toning up or down the reports of the whole shoal of his hooked informers. He receives their mail and with the aid of a typist puts it into salable shape.

The sooner the superintendent can make a good operative out of the man he has hooked, the less arduous will be his own literary labors. The educational process, therefore, is important and immediate. The employer may have been taught that the apprentice period for one of his own workers turned informer will be unfruitful. It is to his own advantage as much as to the agency's that the worker's innocence should not be taken away too abruptly. Even so, it is expensive business; one cannot know how long his patience will hold out while the operative laboriously follows out his first instructions, and reports his views on fire hazards, employees' reactions to the medical service, and the nepotism of foremen.

This must be a trying period in other ways for the employer, if and when he is ever allowed to read the unabridged account, for thus he sees how his workers would like to run his business. An excellent example of the conscientiousness with which a new man may undertake his reporting duties is found in the letters of Harold Lewis, mentioned before, hooked by Pinkerton for the Chevrolet plant in Janesville, Wisconsin. They are the letters of a just and intelligent man suddenly given a chance to right his small world: The hose was old and unsafe. The aisles were too narrow for efficiency. Loading was badly done. Some man, a good man, had got a raw deal. The seniority rights of certain fellow workers had been ignored. He expressed temperate indignation at arbitrary methods. The thoroughness and thoughtfulness of this and certain other reports rather sadly comment on the results of the modern divorce of ownership from management.

Pinkerton informer AX for Chevrolet in Saginaw bore witness to this. His report was one of those deleted in Peterson's home into what counsel referred to as a "true or Chinese copy" for Committee consumption. Therefore the word "Badge" should be followed by a missing payroll number:

"Resumed at 7 A.M.
"Discontinued at 3:30 P.M.
"Badge remarked that there was hisself and many other of the boys in the maintenance department who could

offer valuable suggestions as to cut repair costs or improve the job, but due to the manner in which the foremen receive such suggestions the men have to remain silent as they are given the impression they are paid to do as told and not to try to run the job.

"The entire chain on No. 4 overhead conveyor was removed, much to the surprise of most all the men working on the job just to change the trolleys and the men feel that a lot of unnecessary work was done as it all could have been done without removing the chain."

The worker removed to an impersonal distance from both employer and consumer is still animated, as he has perhaps been from the beginning of time, by pride in work, and this has as its prerequisite a critical sense as to how it should be done. When a ray of light singles him out for his advice and help, it is not surprising that he should feel a slight giddiness as he receives the stigmata.

Men like Mr. Lewis, however, are rare in the hooking business. The novice period usually wears away as fast as the color of snow. The hooker begins to nudge. He himself may be getting an important call from headquarters. Rice of Railway Audit wrote to one of his roving superintendents, "the reports of No. 3250 do not contain very much information. It might be advisable to see him and coach him a little bit, so there will be no complaint from the client." Red Kuhl told how he had put the heat on while he was with Corporation Service. "For instance, an operative was falling back in his work, or this client does not seem to think he is receiving enough information, why you go out and get hold of these ops and tell them, come right out and tell them flat turkey. 'It is your job, too, so maybe you better use your imagination a little and write something in here that is of interest to the client.' " Littlejohn, Pinkerton man for Atlanta, calls this putting "more meat in them."

Meantime, granted the worker has become willing, or is willing from the start to furnish full union information, he may not have an impressive amount to tell. Brady, for the moment alias Bradley, got around this difficulty as have many others by preparing the first two weeks' reports for his operative Jones No. 260 to sign, with the understanding that Jones would soon begin preparing his own. These first reports were very general in nature. Then instructions began to tighten up, Brady still giving support in the shape of printed materials and suggestions:

"DEAR SIR:—I was informed by a friend that at the last meeting of the local held last Thursday a number of new applications for membership were received. As names are published in the monthly magazine as per the article enclosed, it occurred you may be in a position to furnish the names of the applicants and refer to same if it was a result of a drive for members on any particular road, or terminal point.

"This information is as a matter of record, and will show that some progress is being made, etc. In fact it would make up a very good letter, and I refer to this to assist you.

"For your information, the organizers at Columbus are making a drive for shop craft members, and to drive out of existence the shop craft ass'n, or so called 'Hump Union' on the P. R. R."

and later:

"Incidentally, would suggest that you submit a report relative to the men you met last Saturday. One of them if I recall was a chairman of the Big Four going to N. Y. His mission there I believe is in connection with some adjustment that will apply to Freight Handlers and Express men."

Meanwhile he urged Jones, who was a night watchman with access to all rooms, to get at the files. As will be remembered, Jones was working for Brady with full knowledge of his union treasurer, Ziegler, who arranged a faked file for him to show to Brady. Wearying of having to do all the work, Brady wrote: "At this moment I am at loss to assist you; in fact, I am kept so busy jumping from one place to another and crowded with details, that at times I am unusually busy." Not wanting to discourage his man, however, he continued a month later, "it behooves us to try to dig up information as referred to and hold on to the thing which compensates us for our efforts." Later Jones had to be discontinued. Brady wrote him his regret in the following words:

"Broadminded and fair as you are, I am sure you will agree that I fulfilled my 'contract' with you and assisted you in every way to prolong the work in question because it was a pleasure to be associated with you, and only for the lack of information and reducing expenses, did matters come to an end which was to be expected.

"In due time there will be a 'Turning Point' when things may cut loose. Thus, perhaps we can re-affiliate; in any event you will be given the preference."

Lawson, ex-accountant for National Corporation, was most affirmative as to the custom of build-up. Reports "can be and are always built up: Cut out the things that were unsatisfactory and put in a little something that would be a little more satisfactory." Miller of Railway

Audit justified the build-up on the ground that "some of these people are not of average intelligence."

Spy life is illuminatingly set forth in the examination of an ex-Pinkerton spy, Lyle Letteer, working in the Chevrolet plant in Atlanta, from May, 1934, up to the time of his exposure in August, 1935. This exposure came, he said, through William Bannister, another Pinkerton man "during the time I was working in the labor office and getting some of the most vital reports, I do not know whether it was through a spirit of jealousy or through a spirit of the other man just being yellow, but in order to save his own hide."

Letteer was an eager witness. The fullness of his testimony may be perhaps explained by the fact that his father, formerly the assistant superintendent for Pinkerton in Atlanta, now works for the federal government. Obviously Letteer, Jr., brought up in the trade, would be able to skip the hooking stage. Already on a part-time job in the trim division of the Chevrolet plant, he obtained the Pinkerton job through his own efforts, which necessitated some correspondence between the New York and Atlanta office since there is a Pinkerton law "that no two members of the same family can work in the same office." The exemption may have been made because Pinkerton sold Chevrolet their service during the slack season of the year when men were being laid off and Pinkerton could not get men into the plant through regular channels. In spite of the fact that young Letteer was knowledgeable, he was put through a preliminary period in which he was to deal with fire hazard and medical service. Told at first that reports were expected of him at the rate of six a month, he soon was making thirteen or fourteen, for which he was to be paid $4 a report and expenses. His expense account included besides the usual union dues and assessments, "anything that was half-way legitimate such as street car fare and buying a little drink or anything that the men would enjoy." This privilege of incorporating his liquor expense into his expense account was exploited as follows: "To start with, the liquor was non-tax-paid liquor, and I bought it through the business secretary of the union, and I took it to my home; and if there was something special I wanted to find out from any of the men, I would invite them to the house and set the liquor out before them, and the general run of the men drink pretty heavily, and under the influence of the liquor you can ask them point-blank questions and get your answer."

About thirty days after he had started rendering the general report, Littlejohn, his chief in Atlanta, gave him new instructions. Labor, in Mr. Littlejohn's words, was beginning to get "hot," and it looked as if a strike might break. Moreover, Mr. Littlejohn informed Letteer, the Pinkerton Agency now had a general contract with General Motors Corporation to get information on labor. "They wanted to know what was the financial condition of the labor organization, that is, the A F of L organization, and they wanted to know the number of members that were paid up, the number in good standing and the approximate percentage of the members that were working in the plant. . . . They asked me to get all the names I could possibly get together."

This new contract was to be taken care of from Detroit where, as we have learned, a special office had been set up under the name of the Acme Processing Company, and later under the anonymous aegis of Mr. William B. Smith, Sales Representative. Letteer was asked to work on Sundays, to visit as many union leaders in the area as possible, "to get their viewpoint." His reports were to be lengthened to at least four typewritten pages. He was beginning to have to make them as often as twice or three times a day. Littlejohn said he wanted to "pull the investigation along," to prolong it. "If I made the reports longer and put more meat into them, the Detroit office would carry them along quite a while longer than they ordinarily would run." At this time Letteer was raised to a flat $4 a day and expenses. With three reports a day at $4 each, piecework was becoming too expensive for Pinkerton's and General Motors.

Letteer was instructed to "nose around in the labor hall and get some one to vote him in." In the meantime, when the lay-offs came for the other men, Letteer was affected. Reinstated in the capacity of truck driver, his new mobility enabled him to wander through the whole grounds and plant. Instigated by pressure from above, he got himself elected to the office of union guide, a petty honor, but one which enabled him to tend the door, and to take minutes if the secretary were out. He was by now sending in different types of reports. One entitled general report carried "little odd pieces of conversation I might pick up in the plant." The reports on meetings "carried a very thorough source of news all the way from the opening prayer until adjournment, every detail. . . . I turned in the same report to Pinkerton's as the corresponding secretary of the local put on the minutes of the books."

Not all of this was memory, although as Mr. Letteer admitted, he made mental notes, presumably while tending door. Later when he was put in charge of the local office, he had access to all records. In the early summer of 1935, all officials who were free to do so went to a convention in Detroit, leaving him in sole charge of the books, a situation of which as Mr. Letteer admitted to Senator La Follette: "I took advantage to this extent, that after asking Littlejohn what he wanted to know and receiving his answer, I went to the labor office and as I was going to close up for the night I would take all the records, including the ledger and everything, whatever he called for for that day, take it to the office, and we would make copies that night."

SENATOR LA FOLLETTE: You mean the Pinkerton office?
MR. LETTEER: Yes, sir.
SENATOR LA FOLLETTE: Then you returned the records to the office the next morning?
MR. LETTEER: Returned the records to the office next morning.

After his exposure, the union went through no formal procedure. In fact, he was apprised of how matters stood one night after he had attended a "pretty hot labor meeting. . . . I went directly to my home and was sitting by a desk by my window making a report and all of a sudden a gun went off in back and a bullet struck the window jamb about 14 inches from where my head was. I passed it by. Of course, it caused me some little concern. Then at other times in dark places on the road while visiting in Atlanta, going to or from labor meetings, my car was almost forced off of the road." Twice again he was shot at, but he began to throw suspicion away from him by offering to do as many jobs as he could for the union. His union position was greatly strengthened by his being "laid off from the Chevrolet plant with a cry of discrimination 'against me.'" So far as he knew none of the officials of the Chevrolet plant knew he was a Pinkerton man, his work being for the overall contract.

Here the elaboration of duplicity becomes a little hard to follow. After stating that his lay-off was a clear cut case of union discrimination, and that every case of discrimination was covered by some "half-way definite reason," he thus explained: "It was the policy of the drivers as they took the cars out all the time on the O.K. line, in the back of the plant, to void the tickets that were on them, and I voided one of those tickets by tearing it in half and placing it on a truck. I do not know who it was, but when I came back into the plant the first thing that happened was that the foreman of this section came to me about it, and, of course, I was laid off after that."

SENATOR LA FOLLETTE: Did the union make any effort to have you reinstated?

MR. LETTEER: Yes, sir.

SENATOR LA FOLLETTE: Describe what was done as a result.

MR. LETTEER: When I was laid off it was the policy of the company to give you what they call a quit slip, which had to have the O.K. of the tool crib in the plant, on which the tools were to be turned in before you could get your money, so after my tool slip was O.K.'d I carried the slip down to the union office and they in turn carried to to the courthouse in Atlanta and had photostatic copies of it made, and those photostatic copies were brought back to the union office, and placed on file, where they were going to make a test case out of it. Along with that test case I also carried a copy to Mr. Littlejohn, my superintendent, and he said, "As long as the union is going to make a test case out of it we will make another one to see how strong the union is."

SENATOR LA FOLLETTE: Did you continue to report on the union activities for Pinkerton after you were laid off by Chevrolet?

MR. LETTEER: I continued for quite a while.

SUBTERRANEAN LIFE

SENATOR LA FOLLETTE: How did you get your information on union affairs after you were laid off?
MR. LETTEER: It was the policy to hang around the plant. I could not stand around the plant without getting someone suspicious, without getting some suspicions thrown around me, so I bought a truck, and this truck I carried to the union building, and during one of their meetings I asked the president for permission to make a little talk during the meeting; and during the course of this meeting, when I made my talk, I asked if there were any union members that were planning to move in the near future and if so to give their work to me . . . ; and I was given permission to stay in the union hall and take my calls over their phone, and as a result I got quite a few jobs from it."

Thus as entrepreneur compelled by the sad exigencies of union life to go into a shoestring business for himself, he kept in touch with union members who were fighting his case for him, and was enabled to continue his reports for the overall General Motors-Pinkerton contract. After every meeting he called the Pinkerton office on the telephone (these reports were later verified in writing) which they had installed in his home for the purpose. That out of this rhomboid situation, Mr. Letteer should not know exactly upon which side he was standing at a given moment and put his ultimate faith in some circumstance yet to come is not queer. Unknown to the agency, he made a duplicate of every report he ever sent to Pinkerton. These he was commanded to give to the Committee. That his final refuge would lie in state's evidence never crossed his mind, yet he offered himself as willingly upon the stand as he apparently had offered his trucking services to the union members.

Closing this pretty tale, let us take up the busy days of Mr. William Coates of Pittsburgh, since 1909 an undercover man for the W. J. Burns Detective Agency. Like Mr. Letteer he was not a hooked man, although unlike Mr. Letteer he never worked in the client's plant as a wage-earner. Nor has it been his practice apparently to purchase information from men he had hooked. By cultivating friendship with union men and exchanging information, he in his own words "got it gratuitously." Much of his work was done among the miners of Colorado, West Virginia, and Pennsylvania where he claimed to be chiefly interested in Communist activities, although, running true to form, names of any union members were chief grist to the mill. One of his reports on Communists is interesting for its wide sweep into the NRA, an inclusion which brought from Senator La Follette the question, "Do you regard President Roosevelt as a Communist?"

Dated in April of 1935 from Connellsville, Pennsylvania, Mr. Coates' report to Burns read:

"Continuing on the above investigation, I arose at 11:30 A.M. and had lunch with my informant and after doing so went to Uniontown, Pa.

"Arriving there, I learned the Amalgamated Clothing Workers of America have an account in a local bank and that the officers of the Union Local are Marie Bowden, President, Laddy Karl, Secretary and Treasurer.

"The Amalgamated Clothing Workers of America contribute to the Soviet Government in Russia through their bank connections, which in turn is controlled by Sidney Hillman who organized the Amalgamated Clothing Workers of America and is Chairman of the Board of the Amalgamated Bank of New York, director in the Amalgamated

Trust and Savings Banks of Chicago, and their other Communistic connections are as follows:
> Director Garland Fund 1922-23.
> Committeemen on Defense Committee of IWW.
> President Amalgamated Clothing Workers since 1914.
> President and Organizer Russian Amer. Ind. Corp. from 1922 on.
> Connected with Legal Mutual Aid. Author 'Reconstruction of Russia and the district of Labor.'
> Honorary president in national and labor funds.
> Member Quill Joint Committee on Employment.
> Builder Call-Operative House in New York City.
> Member Berger Funds.
> Member Conference for Progressive Political Action.
> Roosevelt appointee to labor Advisory Board of NRA 1933.

"It appears quite evident from the famed threat McGlaughlin made to Mr. Brown that his strike against the industries in Connellsville arose through the Pro-Soviet Amalgamated Clothing Workers of America and unless close watch is kept on the whole by not only the client but your industries as well, it will not be no time until the entire district is organized under a Pro-Soviet affiliated Union.

"It was impossible for me to interview another informant until 5:30 P.M. and in doing so I learned that he is contacted with an official of the Communist Party in this district and also has a list of all the Communists in Fayette County but when I considered the list I discovered the list did not contain all the sheets.

"Paid information one and a half days, $5.25."

The informant, as he explained, was not the man to whom he was indebted for this information, but another Burns operative whom he had employed because he could attend union meetings in eight languages. This letter from Mr. Coates describes routine and easy work. Such information as he enclosed would have been free to any searcher in a public library. As undercover man in the Haller Baking Co. in 1933 and 1934, he had better occasion to display his talents. This job later enlarged to include espionage for the Ward Baking Company, National Biscuit, Liberty Baking Company, Seven Baker Brothers, Stocklein Brothers, and the Brown Baking Company, joined into a Master Bakers Association of which Fred Haller was president. Here as so frequently happens in the best detective circles, Mr. Coates had to watch his step not alone lest the union should discover him, but because he was not certain how many detectives were on the job watching each other. Of the presence of two Burns confederates he was fairly certain, though his memory bogged down concerning the identity of one of them. Of other Burns' stools, he said he "didn't know. There might have been somebody there checking on me for all I know," it being, as he admitted, not an unknown practice for Burns men to check on Burns men. He listed five stool pigeons present to his certain knowledge who were working not for any agency, but who had probably been employed by the Master Bakers themselves.

For the purposes of the Master Bakers, Mr. Coates was a truck driver, newly, and he feared temporarily, employed. He was interested in unions. His first visit to the union hall was reported on July 15. His paid-in membership was reported a week later.

Typically full of detail, though shorn of the novice's meandering design, his report begins:

"I was instructed to accompany Investigator D-1 to the vicinity of the McGeagh Building where those identified with the bakery industry were to have a meeting. I was instructed to endeavor to be admitted to the meeting and ascertain what transpired.

"At 7:30 p.m. I left the Agency Office accompanied by Pittsburgh Investigator D-1 and when at an appropriate distance from the McGeagh, we separated.

"Approaching the McGeagh Building, I observed several men who were no doubt active in unionism, closely observing all those who were entering the building. Watching my opportunity I managed to go into the building immediately in the rear of three other men who had inquired if there was a meeting in the building. The watcher at the front of the building advised us the meeting was in the room in the rear of the third floor of the building.

"I followed up the stairs to the third floor and observed several men in the third floor hall closely observing all men that entered the rear room where the meeting was to be held."

This precautionary activity at the front door was to see if the Master Bakers had the arrivals spotted; on the third floor it was undertaken for fear stools were entering the meeting, the principal reason for small attendance being that men were afraid they would lose their jobs if they were seen congregating. Well practiced in avoiding their suspicion by acting green and frightened, Coates was able to disarm them. A little farther on he says, "When Sam [the business agent of the union] saw that this was going over so well he again came to my chair and asked me for my application and I advised him of my financial circumstances, pointing out to him that as I had just been employed at Hallers' Bakery only eight days ago and did not know all the men and was afraid there might be someone spotting in the room, I would rather mail my application in. I advised Sam there was no doubt in my mind that several others felt just like I did and Sam then went on to declare to all the men that another good point had been brought up and that while arrangements had been made to stop any spotters coming to the meeting and he was confident there were none present, it was possible there were men in the room who desired to join and were afraid they might lose their jobs but if they desired to do so they could fill out their own application blank and mail it to him and he assured all those present that he and no one else would know who joined until the organization was complete, and the records then turned over to their secretary, to be elected later by them."

Coates' expressed fear that other spotters were present, as he explained, was based on certitude. In his words, "Senator, in my experience for the past twenty some years I have found out there are stools in every organization. . . . There was a number of men there on that particular night that I knew they were stools, because I had seen them contact master bakers in this association."

By the end of the evening Coates had made himself pretty solid with the men. His social gifts were standing him in stead. "I took this opportunity to properly introduce myself and compliment Sam in his masterful manner in handling his subject tonight, but while Sam shook hands with me he stated he was 'Sam' and desired to see me at the next meeting. I told him that I expected to be present if I was still working, and hoped he had success in securing 100-percent organization."

So good was the work he was turning in that Principal Raymond Burns himself, wrote in answer to the manager's weekly letter from Pittsburgh:

"My only suggestion in connection with this work is that you be extremely careful of your reports; I suggest you keep the operatives' original reports and the typewritten copies of reports in the safe and not keep them in the regular files, as under no circumstances must we take any chances on the undercover man's identity being disclosed."

The case dragged on without especial drama. In the classical words of spy William Gray "one day protracts itself into another." "At one meeting, for instance," says Mr. Coates, describing his foes the other spies and their puzzling buzzing about, "there was one man that was very active in the meeting, professing unionism, and he would go to the front window, where I knew there were some Master Bakers' employees across the street parked in a parking lot, and he would signal to the men across the street in the parking lot that certain men were leaving the meeting room. I didn't want to be tipped off, so I went out the backway." The operative allowed, as a possibility, in one report, that some of these numbers and names which he was enclosing "were merely visitors to other homes in the neighborhood, but it is suggested that all members of the association check over all the names for the ascertaining if they have any of these men on their pay roll."

He makes further suggestions. The union leaders mention late hours. Master Bakers in each plant should ascertain if their men are being picketed; if so, organizers should be placed under surveillance. And, "I wish to suggest that in the future I think it would be a much better plan for all the active heads of the different bakery companies to remain in the background as much as possible. The new legislation under which the men are organizing has some very dangerous features in it that are somewhat ambiguous and especially Section 7 of the Industrial Recovery Act. It is too early at this time to predict what the labor unions might capitalize from this section but with the present trend of times the courts would certainly favor a labor union that complained about any coercion being used to preclude them from organizing under this Act."

Soon Mr. Drake, manager of the Ward Baking Company, like another small boy playing Indian, gets drawn into the fun. One can see him thinking up his participation. "He had arranged a signal that he would draw the shade in the office once when he wished me to follow an employee as they left the building, and would draw the shade twice when he wished me to visit a small lunch room run by a man called Jerry, which is located at right of the bridge . . . it was thought that some valuable information might be picked up there."

Still things were not coming fast enough. They never did, as a matter of fact. After a while Coates was satisfied that they had gotten "wise" to him, and he was off to less knowing fields. But not until he had given us a stereopticon glimpse of the Sleuth at Evening:

"When I went to the McGeagh Building at 5:00 P.M. I met Sam Wehofer, who appeared in much better spirits. [Sam had been sad at the slow progress of his organization.] He was working in Room 310 . . . in which there is a small safe. I have made it a point to frequent his office as much as I could so that anyone else would know that Sam and I were friends, and not cause any suspicion if I were seen there alone. The telephone is in Room 310. . . . I remained about the office, pretending I wished to write a letter until 9:30 P.M. when Sam finished with his work and watched him placing his records back in the desk which he locked, and he counted some cash, which I would estimate as being around $25.00, which he placed in the safe. He does not carry a portfolio but usually bundles the records up in one bundle and places them in the large drawer in the desk to the right hand side."

On the next night, it was late July, 1933, and just before prohibition was over, "I then went to the McGeagh Building and went to Room 310 where I observed the door was open and an Italian was reading an Italian paper at the desk. When I was about to make myself comfortable the Italian janitor requested me to go across the hall to another room as he had to lock up the Bakers office. The Italian suggested that I take some medicine he had in a bottle not unlike an Italian drink called Fernet Branca. I asked him if it was not Fernet and he replied it was. I inquired what it cost and he replied that he could get it for $1.75 a bottle. I gave him $2.00 and requested him to get me a bottle and while he was gone I tried the door at Room 310 but found he had locked it. I then told him I did not care to carry the bottle with me and asked him to take care of the bottle for me, which would give me the opportunity to cultivate him further. After remaining away from the union headquarters until 5:30 I again went to the McGeagh Building where I met my new acquaintance, the Italian. I inquired if Sam or Metchett was about and learned they were not. We both went to the third floor where he secured the Fernet and we both took a small drink. I inquired when he left the building and learned he sleeps on the top floor. I inquired if there were any others that sleep in the building and he stated that he usually has from two to as many as ten or more that sleep in the building when they are out of work and just landed in town waiting for something to do as there are a number of other unions in the building and he has orders from the different unions to let the men have a place to sleep in case they had no money. This complicated matters as I learned that across the hall from where the Bakers Union offices are located on the third floor, there is usually one or two that sleep there every night. In fact one fellow has his trunk in the steamfitters' room. There are no cots or beds in the room but they very likely sleep on the floor."

But let us leave the unemployed bakers asleep on the floor in the steamfitters' room. Coates is squirming out of town, and presumably Raymond Burns has the goods in the safe. It was only a few months later that he was writing:

"All-Office Letter No. 617
Re: Labor and Industrial Disturbance

To All Officers:

"Inasmuch as these seems to be considerable labor unrest and industrial disturbances throughout the country at the present time, our managers should make a concerted effort to obtain a volume of work in this connection, and should solicit not only guard work but also undercover service.

"Managers should arrange to receive daily the Communist publication known as 'The Daily Worker,' which is published in New York City but can be obtained at almost any newsstand. This will keep you informed of not only labor disturbances but also Communistic activities throughout the labor world.

"Managers should also arrange contact with the office of the Regional Labor Board, as the Regional Labor Board is approached and consulted on all labor disputes. If our managers are in close touch with the office of the Regional Labor Board they will be in a position to solicit the guard work before the strikes have actually been declared.

"A number of our competitors are also making a concerted drive for this business. We feel, however, that we are better equipped and have the facilities for handling this work much more efficiently than any of our competitors, but in order to obtain the work it is necessary to put forth your best efforts."

Mr. William Earl Hemphill, operative No. 3550 for Railway Audit and Inspection, would bear out the contention of a famous war correspondent that spies are lazy men though prone to throw off an emanation of busyness. Formerly an electrician by trade and hooked in Atlanta as such to work temporarily as elevator inspector, he was six months later sent over into Birmingham to check up on the activities of the union. On the stand Hemphill could not remember whom he talked to there. "I couldn't recall offhand the names I have talked to; it would be impossible for one man to memorize every man he talked to." His memory was refreshed, however, to the extent of bringing forth some recollection of Mr. Mitch, head of the coal miners' association, Mr. Googe, southern representative of the American Federation of Labor, and Mr. Beddow, organizer and chairman for the CIO of whom he solicited employment as an organizer.

Some of Mr. Hemphill's reports, salvaged from the trash to which they had been so fittingly assigned, give a picture of how a man if he has imagination can collect for time put in. One cannot escape the observation that, in espionage, at some time or other everyone plays the gull. This time it was the agency.

Senator La Follette read Hemphill's report to Hemphill:

"I contacted Mr. Beddow today and talked with him for sometime, in which he was saying how they expect to organize the southern workers one hundred percent.

"Beddow said that the ones which they would start first would be as follows:

> Gulf States Steel Co.; Tennessee Coal, Iron & Railroad Company; American Steel & Wire Company; Woodward Iron Company, Bessemer, Alabama; then they are planning on taking the others as they come to them."

"Did Mr. Beddow make any such statement to you?"

The ensuing dialogue between them is interesting.

MR. HEMPHILL: Mr. Beddow talked quite a while.

SENATOR LA FOLLETTE: Did he make any such statement? Answer my question. Did he make any such statement? Did he make any such statement as you have made in your report?

MR. HEMPHILL: I am trying to answer the question. It is not possible to remember everything—

SENATOR LA FOLLETTE (*interposing*): Did he make any such statement?

MR. HEMPHILL: Mr. Beddow told me several places they were going to try to organize. Others have also told me places they were going to try to.

SENATOR LA FOLLETTE: Did Mr. Beddow make the statement that you made in your report he made to you, in which you said Mr. Beddow said 'That the ones which they would start first would be as follows,' and then gave the list of companies which I have read?

MR. HEMPHILL: He didn't give me that whole list; no.

SENATOR LA FOLLETTE: Why did you attribute that statement to him then?

MR. HEMPHILL: Because others I got came in line with them.

La Follette read on:

"Beddow said they were going to try and plant undercover men in each plant and as many of them as they were able to, so that they would be in a place where the mill company had been in the past, and in place of the company knowing what the union was doing the union would know what the mill was planning on.

"These men will be workers and some are new in this part of the country. Will try and get a list of them in a few days.

"Note: Please be very careful with information in next paragraph. This only going to you and Pittsburgh.

"The writer will have a desk in the CIO office and it will be much easier to get the dope than it has been in the past, due to their being scared of everyone and they are very careful who they are putting on."

"Did you get a desk in their office?" asked the Senator, to which Mr. Hemphill answered, "I have not yet; no."

SENATOR LA FOLLETTE (*reading*):

"Contacted Mitch and Beddow this A.M. and had a long talk with both, in which time they were getting things ready to meet Moor and then meet the mill officials on rejecting the workers from their homes. Beddow told me later that they were able to get the matter adjusted which was a big gane on the labor side."

Did Mr. Beddow tell you that?
MR. HEMPHILL: He did.

SENATOR LA FOLLETTE (*reading*):

"Talked with them about the trouble at Talladega, and which Mitch said that he had been looking for it some time. And there would be plenty more of the same or worse if they, the heads, didn't listen to the workers and the heads of organizers. He said that he was going to see that the workers organized in the South, that they had worked for nothing long enough. And that the companys heads had said that he would never organize the coal miners be [sic] he showed them what he could do, and that he would show them again just how strong he did stand with the workers."

Did Mr. Mitch tell you that?

MR. HEMPHILL: He didn't only tell that to me. He made that in a meeting. He made that talk in a meeting.

SENATOR LA FOLLETTE: I understand that; but did he tell that to you?

MR. HEMPHILL: I was in the meeting, and I heard him make that statement.

SENATOR LA FOLLETTE: As a matter of fact, was it not also in the newspapers?

MR. HEMPHILL: Yes, sir.

SENATOR LA FOLLETTE: And you sent it in this report, however, as if you got this information out of him personally?

MR. HEMPHILL: No; I sent that in on the meeting.

SENATOR LA FOLLETTE: Oh, no. You do not mention the meeting in here. You say you talked with these two gentlemen, Mitch and Beddow, and, as a matter of fact, you got that information from the meeting and from the newspapers, didn't you?

MR. HEMPHILL: I was at the meeting; yes, sir.

SENATOR LA FOLLETTE: That is where you got it, wasn't it?
MR. HEMPHILL: I read the newspaper, too. I got it from both places.
SENATOR LA FOLLETTE: And you did not, as a matter of fact, get it from them in private conversation with you?

"Things will start Monday in a big way as to the organizing drive. Will have a list of all the organizers and their district, as they will assign each to his post Monday, and a list will be given to each."

Did you get such a list?
MR. HEMPHILL: No.
SENATOR LA FOLLETTE: Why not?
MR. HEMPHILL: I couldn't say.
SENATOR LA FOLLETTE: Don't you know why you could not get it?
MR. HEMPHILL: It was never given to me; that is all I know.
SENATOR LA FOLLETTE: Had it been promised to you?
MR. HEMPHILL: I was told I would know who they were.
SENATOR LA FOLLETTE: Who told you that?
MR. HEMPHILL: Mitch—I mean Beddow.

In about a fortnight, Mr. Hemphill is recording:

"Mitch, Beddow, V. C. Finch, Carlton, and several others had a conference in the office of the CIO, third floor of the Steiner Building, Birmingham, today. Telephone 3-3937."

To which Senator La Follette, knowing the end of the story, pressed:

"How did you know those gentlemen had a conference there on that day?"

MR. HEMPHILL: Well, I talked with them.
SENATOR LA FOLLETTE: Were you present?
MR. HEMPHILL: No; I wasn't present at the convention— I mean at the meeting; no.
SENATOR LA FOLLETTE: Who told you they had been in conference?
MR. HEMPHILL: They told me in the office.
SENATOR LA FOLLETTE: Who told you?
MR. HEMPHILL: When I went in there to see Beddow, they told me they was in conference.
SENATOR LA FOLLETTE: How did you know who was in there? Were they in the same room where you could see them?
MR. HEMPHILL: I could see them.
SENATOR LA FOLLETTE: You mean they were in the same room with you?
MR. HEMPHILL: They wasn't in the same room, but an adjoining room, and the door was open.
SENATOR LA FOLLETTE: And you saw those men and recognized them there?
MR. HEMPHILL: Well, I know them all.

The matter goes on for some length, and has its denouement in a letter from William Mitch:

"Mr. CLINTON S. GOLDEN,
Steel Workers Organizing Committee,
3600 Grand Bldg.,
Pittsburgh, Pa.

"FRIEND GOLDEN: Relative to the matter you talked to me about, of someone spying and reporting our actions, I assure you that we have found the individual. He never was on our pay roll, and never received a cent from us, but Mr. Beddow had talked to him a few times and I have some copies of reports that he made to the Railway Audit & Inspection Co. In these reports, he filled in a great deal that never happened or never was said. In fact, he reported that he had contacted Beddow on days that Beddow was not even in the city of Birmingham.

"However, I am glad to furnish you the information that we have caught the 'rat.' His name is W. E. Hemphill.

"We have a letter from Steve Nance, who is president of the Georgia State Federation of Labor, stating that George Googe, himself, and others got this 'bird' in the office and gave him a good grilling, and finally got out of him an admission that he had been reporting."

Whether Hemphill informed his agency of his exposure is not recorded. We can make our deductions from his hopeful statement, "he hadn't got a desk in the CIO office yet."

In the middle of March, 1937, Pinkerton's prepared a list without identification of their 303 secret sources of information carried on under arbitrary or secret designations. Of this number, 132 are members of trade unions: six of these are presidents of the union; 5 are vice-presidents; one holds office as treasurer; 3 hold office as secretary; 9 are recording secretaries; 6 are trustees; one is a business agent; 3 are organizers; 3 are delegates to the central labor union; one is chairman of the shop committee; 4 are committee men; one is financial secretary; 3 are members of the executive board; one is division chairman. Forty-three are spies in company unions, but only 6 of these held office.

Brought out to lie on the cold wet pavement like angleworms in rain, exposed spies are repellent but not alarming. It is only by glimpses into the dark subterranean of

National Corporation Service, Inc, Officers, Employees, and Operatives

Identified by E. E. MacGuffin	Identified by A. E. Lawson	Operative Number	Name	Address	Position and Assignments	Compensation	Time of Service
			OFFICERS, SOLICITORS, ETC.—con.				
(?)		516	C. J. M				Mar. & Apr. 1934.
	(*)		"Old Bill" (last name unknown). C. E. O'Neil.	Mineral Ridge, Ohio. 93 E. Northwood Ave., Columbus, Ohio.	Stool pigeon on behalf of the Mahoning Valley Steel Co., Niles, Ohio, July 1933 to April 1934. Salesman and superintendent of operatives. Did street work during the Johnson Bronze Co. strike, New Castle, Pa. and operated during the Val Decker Packing Co. strike, Piqua, Ohio.		July, 1933 to Apr. 1934. July, 1934 to July, 1936
(?)		337	Unknown	1117 No. Garland St., Youngstown, Ohio.		$5 per day	Aug. to Oct. 1934.
(?)		602	John Palaios		Street operative on behalf of the Republic Rubber Co., Youngstown, Ohio and in connection with the "Phantom Killer" case on behalf of the Wheeling Steel Co., Steubenville, O.		Aug. 1933 to Nov. 1933 and Aug. 1934 to Nov. 1934.
(?)		602	Unknown		Operated on behalf of the Lake Erie Power & Light Co., Bellevue, Ohio.	Paid by A. E. Wheat $5 per day.	Jan. to March, 1935.
(?)		603	Unknown		Operated on behalf of the Lake Erie Power & Light Co., Bellevue, Ohio.	Paid by A. E. Wheat $5 per day.	Jan. to March, 1935.
(?)		604	Unknown		Operated on behalf of the Lake Erie Power & Light Co., Bellevue, Ohio.	Paid by A. E. Wheat $5 per day.	Jan. to Oct. 1935.
(?)		610	Unknown			$50 per mo. and $10 exp.	Aug. 1933 to Nov. 1933.
(?)		610	Unknown			$40 per mo. & $5 exp.	Jan. and Feb. 1935.
(?)		611	Unknown	Youngstown, Ohio.	Operated during the Val Decker Packing Co. strike, Piqua, Ohio in 1934. Did propaganda work in 1935 on behalf of the Youngstown Auto Dealers Association, Youngstown, Ohio, and in 1936 on behalf of the Dayton, Ohio Auto Dealers Association.	$100 per mo.	Part of 1934, March, 1935 to Feb. 1936.
	(*)	98	Barbara Parnell.				
	(*)	509	Carl Parshall		Former inside stool pigeon on behalf of the Commercial Shearing Co., Youngstown, Ohio, who was killed in an auto accident in 1936.		Jan. to Mar. 1934.

(*)	551 ²¹	Harry Phillips	1752 Logan Ave., Youngstown, Ohio.	Street operative on behalf of the Commercial Shearing Co., Youngstown, Ohio, in 1933.		Aug. 1933 to Oct. 1933.
(*)	514 ⁸	William Pope		Operative on behalf of the Brainard Steel Co., Warren, Ohio.	$30 per mo	Aug. 1933 to June, 1934.
(?)	515	Unknown			$10 per mo	Aug. 1933 to Aug. 1935.
(?)	71 ˢ	C. P				Jan. 1934 to Sept. 1934.
(?)	72	Unknown				All of 1932.
(?)	792	Quigley			1935: $60 per mo. 1936: Jan. $33.34, Feb. $50, June $47 & $5, July $10.	Nov. 1935 to date.
(?)	793	Unknown			Jan. 1936: $18.33, Feb. $50.	1936.
(?)	638	George Redden	Cleveland, Ohio	Street operative on behalf of the Newton Steel Co., Newton Falls, Ohio, and operated during the Columbus Rail and Light Co. strike, Columbus, O. Also acted as fink on several jobs.		Feb. to Apr. 1934.
(*)	677	Frank Reiggleman			$40 per mo. and $5 exp	July, 1934 to Aug. 1935.
(?)	701	Unknown	641 Marshall St., New Castle, Pa. and 946 E. Hazel St., New Castle, Pa.	Stool pigeon operative on behalf of the Johnson Bronze Co., New Castle, Pa. before and during the strike in 1934. Also operated during the Columbus Rail and Light Co. strike, Columbus, Ohio.	$50 per mo	Mar. & Apr. 1935.
(*)	543	Frank Reiter			$40 per mo. and $5 exp	April 1934 to June 1935.
(*)	625	Arthur D. Root.	3421 Fortune St., Cleveland, Ohio.	Stool pigeon operative still employed by the Otis Steel Co., Cleveland, Ohio.	$40 per mo. through 1935, 1936: Jan. $40, Feb. $48.62, Mar. $41.63, Apr. $42, May $42, June $43.	Sept. 1933 to 1936.
(?)	626	Unknown			$40 per mo	Feb. 1934.
(?)	630	Unknown				Oct. 1933 to July, 1934.
(?)	631	Unknown				Oct. to Dec. 1933.
(?)	375	Rubadur			$35 per mo. & $5 exp	June and July, 1934.
(*)	554	Sanberg		Operative on behalf of the Hazel-Atlas Glass Co., Washington, Pa. in 1934.	$40 per mo	Apr. to June, 1934.
(*)	65	Lewis Saunders.	Akron, Ohio	Undercover operative employed by the Akron Transportation Co.	Aug. 1932–Dec. 1935 was paid $50 per mo. & expenses. Actual payments in 1936 by month were: Jan. $55.50; Feb., unknown; Mar. $50; Apr. $50; May $38; June $54.	August, 1932 to date.

⁸ Number probably reassigned.
²¹ Alias Barbara Palmer.
¹¹ Nephew of E. E. MacGuffin.

NATIONAL CORPORATION SERVICE, INC, OFFICERS, EMPLOYEES, AND OPERATIVES—Continued

Identified by E. E. MacGuffin	Identified by A. E. Lawson	Operative Number	Name	Address	Position and Assignments	Compensation	Time of Service
		OFFICERS, SOLICITORS, ETC.—con.	E. C. Schultz	Detroit Mich	Investigator and solicitor. Undercover operative Youngstown Municipal Railway, Youngstown, Ohio. Solicitor in Detroit, Michigan Office. Seen by Earl B. Trombley, at Terre Haute, Ind., during Columbian Enameling and Stamping Co. strike, Nov. or Dec. 1935. Schultz said he was selling insurance. (See No. 635.)		June 1935 to June 1936.
	(*)	635	Ed. C. Schultz	Detroit Mich	Salesman and superintendent of operatives in the Detroit office, who formerly operated as stool pigeon for the Youngstown Municipal Railroad, Youngstown, Ohio; in the Portsmouth plant of the Wheeling Steel Co., and during the Columbian Stamping & Enameling Co. strike, Terre Haute, Ind.	$40 per mo	Jan. to Aug. 1934.
(?)		303	Schwartz		Stool pigeon operating on behalf of the Cleveland Tanning Co., Cleveland, Ohio. Also operated prior to the strike on behalf of the Wheeling Steel Co., Portsmouth, Ohio; now operating in the vicinity of Detroit, Mich.	$30 per mo. and $5 exp. 1936; $20 in Jan.	Aug. 1934 to Dec. 1935 and Jan. 1936.
(?)		304	Unknown				July to Oct. 1934.
(?)		552	Seibert		Operative on behalf of the Hazel-Atlas Glass Co., Washington, Pa., in 1934.	$30 per mo. and $5 exp.	April to June, 1934.
		790	Ray Shilling		Solicitor and superintendent of office. Advanced money May 10, 1934, to operatives no. 620, 551, 556, 309, 34-340, 559, 34F, 630; on June 8 to 518 and 542 and on July 3 to 640.	$200 per mo	April to Nov. 1934.
			Bill Shanholtz	Girard, Ohio	Stool pigeon in the plant of the Ohio Leather Co., Girard, Ohio, during part of 1933 and 1934 and possibly later.		Various months in 1933 and 1934.
(?)		512	Smith	Youngstown, Ohio	Street and undercover operative. Operated on behalf of the Newton Steel Co., Newton Falls, Ohio in 1934; the Lake Erie Power & Light Co., Bellevue, Ohio, in 1934; the Wilson Rubber Co., Canton, Ohio, in 1934 during the strike, and the Wheeling Steel Co. plant, Portsmouth, Ohio, in late 1935.	$35 per mo. and $5 exp. $35 per mo.; $40 and $5 exp.	April to June, 1934. Feb. 1934 to Nov. 1935.
(?)		538	Earl A. Smith				
(?)		540	Unknown			8/1/35 $40 & $5 exp.; 10/16/35 $50. $40 per mo	Feb. 1934 to Nov. 1935.
(?)		385	L. Smith				July and Aug. 1934.
(?)		428	Unknown			Jan., Mar., Apr., & May, 1936; $50 per mo.	1936.

No.	Name	Address	Description	Pay	Dates
(*)	520	J. P. South	Youngstown, Ohio, moving frequently into other cities.	Undercover and street operative and superintendent. Worked on behalf of the Pennsylvania Power and Light Co., New Castle, Pa. In 1934; the Ralston Steel Door Co., Columbus, Ohio; the Dayton, Ohio, Auto Dealers Association during the strike in 1936; and the Wheeling Steel Co., Portsmouth, Ohio; Columbian Stamping & Enameling Co., Terre Haute, Ind. etc. This man's criminal record includes a sentence of a year and a day in the U. S. Penitentiary, Atlanta, Ga., beginning Apr. 9, 1919, for stealing Govt. property; his federal penitentiary number being 9393; also a sentence of 3 to 6 mos. in the Allegheny County Workhouse, Blawnox, Pa. for larceny. His sentence began Dec. 24, 1932; his number was 33093. Arrests in Pittsburgh, Pa., where his number is 21630 and in Akron, O., where he gave the name of John L. Rollins and where his number is 25036, did not result in convictions or jail sentences.	$150 per mo. and $5 exp.	May 1934 to Dec. 1935, Dec. 1935 to July, 1936.
(?)	70 [1]	L. B. Sparks	859 Langer Street, Massillon, Ohio.	Undercover operative in the plant of the Reliance Mfg. Co., Massillon, Ohio.		Apr. 1934 to July 1934.
(?)	71	(Unknown) V. Stockdale.				Nov. 1932 to Nov. 1933. Apr. to Aug. 1934.
(?)	553					
(*)	84	Mrs. Hazel Strothers.	1276 W. 112 St., Cleveland, Ohio.	Operative on behalf of the Hazel Atlas Glass Co., Washington, Pa., in 1934. Street operative on behalf of American Fork & Hoe Co., Ashtabula Hide & Leather Co., American Bow Socket Co. and the Aetna Rubber Co., all in Ashtabula, Ohio, in 1934; also on behalf of the Val Decker Packing Co., Piqua, Ohio, during a strike there in 1934; also worked to prevent a strike said to break up the union for the Hazel-Atlas Glass Co., Washington, Pa. In the spring of 1934, worked to prevent growth of the auto mechanics union in Youngstown, Ohio in the spring of 1935, on behalf of the Youngstown Auto Dealers Association, Youngstown, Ohio. She was employed as an undercover operative in 1934 on behalf of the Cleveland Railway Co., Cleveland, Ohio, securing information from her husband, an employee of that company.	Special daily rate	Sept. 1932 to Nov. 1935.
(*)	84 X					Sept. 1932 to Mar. 1933.
	550 and 57	Robert Strothers.[22] R. S.[22]		Operative who received advances in pay from W. H. Gray and R. G. Milton in 1934. Worked two days with C. E. O'Neil in 1936, receiving $12.	$6 per day	April & May 1934, and May 1936.
(?)	57 and 550	R. S. (name unknown).		Undercover operative.		February to April 1934.
(?)	57 [23]	Roy Taylor	Fremont and Bellevue, Ohio.	Stool pigeon operative in the plant of the Lake Erie Power and Light Co., Bellevue, Ohio. He was secretary of the United Brotherhood of Electrical Workers of Joint Union Power House and Traction Line Maintenance Men.	$50 per mo. up to 1936. 1936: Jan. $52, Feb. $52, Mar. $27.	Oct 1934 to Dec. 1935 and part of 1936.
(*)	560					

[1] Number probably reassigned.
[22] Son of Hazel Strothers #84.
[23] Attempt to reassign # 57 to a new operative, whose initials are V. F. The attempt to book apparently failed. A booking attempt was made by # 310 in Feb. 1935 and a charge is shown in the books of $25—advanced to V. F. However, op. # 310, who was B. Dentino, was discharged in Feb. 1935.

NATIONAL CORPORATION SERVICE, INC., OFFICERS, EMPLOYEES, AND OPERATIVES—Continued

Identified by E. E. MacGuffin	Identified by A. E. Lawson	Operative Number	Name	Address	Position and Assignments	Compensation	Time of Service
			OFFICERS, SOLICITORS, ETC.—con.				
....	(*)......	98......	Dorothy Timlin ⁴......	63 Fernwood Ave., Youngstown, Ohio.	She operated during the Johnson Bronze Co. strike New Castle, Pa. in 1934 as well as on behalf of the Stevens Metal Products Co., Niles, Ohio, during part of 1934. Also assisted in spreading propaganda on behalf of the Ohio Power and Light Co., Oberlin, Ohio, in 1934, working among the school teachers and others against a municipal light plant. Also checked stores and did other "legitimate" work.	$6 a day and exp......	Feb. 1933 to August, 1934.
....	(*)......	59......	Frank Timlin.	63 Fernwood Ave., Youngstown, Ohio.	Undercover operative employed at the Falcon Bronze Co., Youngstown, Ohio, whose last pay, shown openly in the books of Natl. Corp. Ser., was for work done in Apr. 1932. In May and June 1933, the Falcon Bronze Co. was billed for service in the amount of $200 during those months. Timlin is now corresponding representative of the Molders Union, Local #196, in Youngstown.	Special......	Book entries end Apr. 1932.
....	(*)......	93 ⁵......	Thomas E. Owens.	Cleveland, Ohio....	Stool pigeon in the plant of the Otis Steel Corporation, Cleveland, O.	....	June, 1936.
(?)......	(*)......	510......	Earl Trombley	333 Oak Knoll, Newton Falls, Ohio—home address. Lived at 1111 Second St., Moundsville, W. Va., up to Sept. 2, 1936.	Undercover, street and stool pigeon operative. Did undercover work in 1933 on behalf of the Paterson Foundry & Products Co., East Liverpool, O. Gathering information as to thefts in the plant; was assigned to the Newton Steel Co. in 1934, where he became secretary of Lodge 184, Amalgamated Association of Iron, Steel & Tin Workers of America (which position he still held in Sept., 1936; and used in issuing union cards to other undercover operatives working within the Amalgamated Assn. of Iron, Steel and Tin Workers for Natl. Corp. Service, Ind.); did undercover work in 1934 & 1935 for the American Fork & Hoe Co., Ashtabula Hide & Leather Co., American Bow Socket Co., Aetna Rubber Co., all in Ashtabula, Ohio; operated on the streets in 1935 on behalf of the Columbian Enameling & Stamping Co., Terre Haute, Ind.; and up to Sept. 2, 1936 did stool pigeon work as a heater in the Moundsville, W. Va., plant of the U.S. Stamping and Enameling Co., Moundsville, W. Va. At Moundsville, W. Va., he was instructed by A. E. Wheat "to check on Charles Newby, President of the Union, in the	$90 a mo. and $17.50 exp. in Ashtabula; $135 per mo. in Terre Haute; $75 per mo. in Moundsville, W. Va., $35 per mo. and $5 exp. in Newton Falls, Ohio	Sept. 1933 to July, 1936.

	Number	Name	Address	Assignment	Compensation	Dates
(?)	641	H. E. Tucker [23]	Park Ave., Niles, Ohio.	U. S. Stamping & Enameling Co. plant, and see if there is any possible way to get him in out of town." On this assignment he met F. S. Earnshaw, Gen. Mgr. of the plant, who arranged at this meeting to provide money for the purpose of taking Chas. Newby for a joy ride to the City of Detroit, whenever Trombley became sufficiently acquainted with Chas. Newby to arrange it.	$125 per mo. and $15	Feb. to Dec. 1934.
				Street operative on behalf of the Newton Steel Co., Newton Falls, O., 1934; the Reeves Mfg. Co. New Philadelphia, O., 1934; also operated on behalf of the American Fork & Hoe Co., the Ashtabula Hide and Leather Co., the American Bow Socket Co., the Aetna Rubber Co., all in Ashtabula, O., 1934.		
(?)	638 [24]	Unknown				June and July, 1935.
	640	W. T. Tucker	20 Vermont St., Wheeling, W. Va.	Street operative on behalf of the Newton Steel Co., Newton Falls, Ohio, 1934; the Reeves Mfg. Co. New Philadelphia, O., 1934; the Val Decker Packing Co., Piqua, O., 1934; several clay and sewer pipe companies, names not identified, Urichville, O., 1934; the Wilson Rubber Co. Canton, O., 1934; the Hazel-Atlas Glass Co., Washington, Pa., 1934.	$165 per mo	Feb. 1934 to Apr. 1935.
(?)	590	Tyger				July and Sept. 1935.
(?)	93	S. T.				Mar. to Sept. 1933.
	216 M	Charles T. Vanderwall			1936: $40 per mo. Jan. through April; $45 May through July.	1936.
(?)	218	Unknown			$45 per mo	March and April, 1935.
	222	Unknown			$6 per day	April and May, 1935.
	224	Unknown			$50 per mo	Apr. and May, 1935.
	227	Unknown			$50 per mo	Sept. to Dec. 1935.
	228	Unknown			$60 per mo. in Jan., Feb., and March, 1936.	Oct. to Dec. 1935.
	228 M [25]	Unknown				Part of 1935 and into 1936.
(?)	229	Unknown			$50 per mo., Jan. through Apr. 1935; May $60; June $75; July $75.	Nov. and Dec. 1935.
(?)	229 M [25]	Unknown				Part of 1935 and into 1936.
(?)	230 M [25]	Unknown			Jan. 1936: $41.67; Feb. through July $50.	Part of 1935 and into 1936.
(?)	231 M [25]	Unknown			Jan. 1936: $45; Feb. through July $50.	Part of 1935 and into 1936.
(?)	232 M [25]	Unknown			Jan. 1936: $30; Feb. $30.	Part of 1935 and into 1936.

[23] Number probably reassigned.
[24] Daughter of Frank Timlin, #59.
[25] Uncle of W. T. Tucker, #640.
[25] May be James Howe, who is operating on behalf of the Midland Steel Products Co., Detroit, Mich.

NATIONAL CORPORATION SERVICE, INC, OFFICERS, EMPLOYEES, AND OPERATIVES—Continued

Identified by E. E. Mac-Guffin	Identified by A. E. Lawson	Operative Number	Name	Address	Position and Assignments	Compensation	Time of Service
		OFFICERS, SOLICITORS, ETC.—con.					
	(*)	A2	E. C. Vermillion.	Cleveland, Ohio.	(Now secretary Cleveland Manufacturers Assn.).	$300	June to November 1935.
(?)		B2				Advanced by T. H. B. 15.	Aug. 15, 1935.
		20					October to December 1935.
		507	E. C. Vermillion.	Cleveland, Ohio.	Solicitor. See No. A2.		Mar. 1933 to Nov. 1933.
(?)		551	Wagner.		Operative on behalf of the Hazel-Atlas Glass Co, Washington, Pa., in 1934.	$30 per mo. and $5 exp.	Apr. to June, 1934.
(?)		102	Wall			$50 usual monthly rate. Jan. 1936, $30, Feb. 1936, $25.	March 1935 to February 1936.
		44	Al B. Wallace.	Youngstown, Ohio.	Undercover street operative, Indianapolis Novelty Co, 1 job in September 1935 at Coshocton, Ohio, and Columbian Enameling and Stamping Co, Terre Haute, Ind., in October and November 1935.		September to November 1935.
(?)		45	Unknown				July 1934 to November 1935.
	(*)	633	Alfred Wolnik."	128 Berita Avenue, Youngstown, Ohio.	Street undercover, and stool pigeon operative. Operated during the strike in 1933 at the Commercial Shearing Co., Youngstown, Ohio; was employed to break the strike at the plant of the Marion Steel Barrel Co., Oil City, Pa.; operated on behalf of the Hazel-Atlas Glass Co., Washington, Pa., in 1934, to prevent a strike and break up the Union; operated prior to the strike at the Portsmouth, Ohio, plant of the Wheeling Steel Co., where he was exposed. Also operated during the Columbian Stamping & Enameling Co. strike, Terre Haute, Ind.		Oct. 1933 to Dec. 1935.
		634	Unknown				Oct. 1933 to Jan. 1937.
(?)	(*)	81 W	H. Walsh.	609 Fairfield Ave., Warren, Ohio.	Undercover operative in the union and in the Youngstown Pressed Steel Co. plant at Warren, Ohio, on behalf of the Sharon Steel Hoop Co. during 1934 and 1935.	$50 per mo. & $5 exp. plus special remuneration.	Apr. 1934 to Nov. 1935.
		86	Weaver.	Warren, Ohio.	Special operative.		1932.
	(*)	87	Unknown				May and December, 1931.

(²)	323	Ferdinand F. Wierz, C. Welk.	420 Holden Avenue, Clarksburg, W. Va. Lives on the Sharon Line near Youngstown, Ohio.	Undercover operative on behalf of the Fostoria Glass Co., Clarksburg, W. Va.	$35 per mo. and $5 exp.	June and July, 1934, and possibly longer. Jan. to Apr. 1933.
(²)	90					
(²)	78	Charles Welker.				Oct. 1932 and Feb. 1934.
(²)	341	A. E. Wheat.	451 Catalina Avenue, Youngstown, Ohio.			Sept. 1934 to Feb. 1936.
(²)	355	Unknown.	Springfield, Ohio.	Operated on behalf of the Robertson Steel Co., Springfield, Ohio.	$40 per mo. & $10 exp. $35 per mo. to Oct. 1934. $40 per mo. & $5 exp. through 1935. 1936: Jan. through Apr. $45, May $28.75, June $22.50.	Dec. 1934 to Jan. 1935. Aug. to Oct. 1934. March, 1935 to 1936.
(²)	356	Unknown.				
(²)	703	Paul Williamson.				
(²)	705	Unknown.	Detroit, Mich.	Sales manager, Youngstown, 1933-1934. In charge of Detroit office November 1935 to June 1936.	$35 per mo. & $5 exp. $50 per mo. $50 per mo.	April & May 1935. Apr. & May 1935. Apr. to Dec. 1935. Fall 1933 to late 1934 or early 1935. November 1935 to June 1936.
(²)	707	Unknown.				
(²)	709	Arthur Young Wilson.				
(²)	88	B. C. Wood.	Youngstown, Ohio	Sales manager and solicitor.		April to July 1936. Nov. 1932 to Apr. 1933. Apr. 1934.
(²)	651	C. R. W. or L. E. V.				
(²)	204	Young.			$50 per mo. $40 per mo. Feb. 13, 1935 $35. Oct. 1, 1935 $40.	Jan. and Feb. 1935. Feb. 1935. Feb. to Dec. 1935. Feb. to Apr. 1934.
(²)	211	Unknown.				
(²)	210	Unknown.				
(²)	637	Herbert Young	123 Church St., Newton Falls, Ohio.	Stool pigeon in the Newton Falls, Ohio plant of the Newton Steel Co.		
		Wallace Metcalf.	Civil Service Commission, Mahoning County, Ohio.	Assigned to prepare a weekly report bulletin to be rewritten from labor newspapers and operatives reports. This bulletin was used as a promotional sheet among clients and prospective clients.	$2 per report.	Various months in 1934.

² Number probably reassigned.
⁷ Alias Alfred R. Kinlow.

American labor relations that we get any true feeling of their ubiquitous vitality: the sight of holes they leave behind them; their curious methods of self-multiplication; their unexpected liveliness; their powers to contract or elongate themselves into what they hope is invisibility when they are turned over in a spadeful of earth; their quick and noiseless disappearance. Such an intimation of crawling life comes to the reader of any random list of spies. What is unknown about them, the blanks, the anonymities contribute to the reader's restlessness equally with the unpleasant emergence into sunlight of their shape and form. Such a feeling of uneasiness attends the reading of the preceding list which is but a fraction of the pages devoted to the names, identities, and activities of a single agency, the National Corporation Service.

I have said, but who is anyone to know, that spies are born, not made. The metamorphosis of certain hooked men in service would not bear out that contention. Some observers report psychological changes in them during the course of their informing from self-castigation to despair, cynicism, and finally hardened intention. Those who know Red Kuhl say that, after twenty successful years in the business, his repudiation of it was complete and bitter; that he works tirelessly in ferreting out other spies and nullifying their efforts. John Davidson, No. 880, in August of 1936 wrote in his report made for U. S. Steel, "I may as well state right here that George Ferguson who is a movie operator and an officeholder in his local union, and Darrell Kepler, a movie operator who is secretary of the local union are personal friends of mine. I have known Ferguson for twenty years and Kepler for ten years, and now I am selling them out as they tell me most anything."

This might seem to be the ultimate statement of moral

loss. But Ralph Winstead, a labor investigator who has known hooked men in all phases of their operations, says, "Not at all. Those are the words of a man still squirming on the hook. Give him more time and the thought of his treachery would never cross his mind."

The final predicament for the man as individual would seem to be that situation in which he can scarcely remember for whom he is spying. He attaches himself for the moment to the man he was sent to spy against. In his role of good fellow, he becomes all things to all men, and loses his identity, not by retreating into an armor of aliases but by a sort of eviction of his spirit from its tenement. He lives in a moral stupor, needing to make no choices of any kind. This is reported of a famous Russian military spy who died in service of two sides, not knowing, it is believed, to whom he finally adhered, or why.

VI. The Small Fry of Violence

LABOR espionage being not an act in itself, but a preparation for an act, we can take it for granted that the employer who wrote the order for it had some future course in mind. The spy tells him where and when, if not how to act. Since the employer's object is to make collective action ineffectual if not impossible, he has a number of courses to follow even before open hostility breaks. The union leader can be intimidated into leaving, discredited with his followers by framed charges of scandalous behavior. He can perhaps be provoked into violence for which, if the local political forces are well handled, he can be indicted, tried, and imprisoned. Or he may be removed forcibly, perhaps beaten or murdered. All of these things occur, and have occurred with astonishing frequency. The rank and file of union members can be dispersed by the less drastic method of a gentle warning or they can be put in fear of the blacklist if they join the union, although the blacklist, far from being a gentle method, is the most permanently brutal of all, its effects so far-reaching, devious, and final that they are hard to summarize. By these and subtler means the union can be kept futile or inactive.

Though technically but an accomplice before the fact, the spy himself is frequently successful in obviating the need for later action. Sowing mistrust and suspicion he weakens the cohesive agent which binds men together in a common cause. If he remains outside the union he can derogate the idea that there is any practical virtue in a union as such, or as union member he can counsel inaction. If he rises to a position of trust within the union, he can negotiate agreements disadvantageous to its members, and by force of persuasiveness make them believe that this was the best that could be done. If he comes into an unorganized shop he can introduce the company union, his vaunted success at doing this elsewhere being perhaps the greatest talking point he has in favor of his being employed.

How he will proceed in these matters is largely determined by his agency's financial interest in violence. If it purveys the double service of espionage and strikebreaking, which is the relatively more profitable end of its business?

Several interesting practical questions arise here. How soon, for instance, would a double-service agency like Railway Audit, which shows good examples of how a spy can build up a business for his successors, the strong-arm men, find it expedient to milk the protracted job of espionage? Would Pinkerton, whose long suit is spying and whose guard work is limited, operate in the same manner as Burns who do more guard work? Would Corporations Auxiliary, who claim that they do no strikebreaking whatsoever, use the same methods in their undercover work as if they were to reap the harvest of self-provoked violence? Do they feel defeated if a strike occurs in a customer's plant? We have Ross's word for it that they do. We also have President Smith's word for it that his ideal was to harmonize, and that he felt his company had been singularly successful among its Detroit clients. Would he feel his ineptitude at the denouement of the dramatic Frankensteen episode more keenly than would Burns, who had been battening splendidly upon violence in Remington Rand for so many months and who had profitably introduced many guards to 160 bewildered New York clients whose elevator shafts were idle in March of 1936?

These are questions in part and obliquely answered by the record, but let us first study the anatomy of strikebreaking, remembering the while that a great volume of it is conducted by agencies more or less exclusively engaged in the furnishing of strong-arm men. Since these companies were not under subpoena, the Committee intruded only incidentally upon their affairs.

A well-defined caste system exists within the ranks of strikebreakers, better known to employers as guards. The foreman is called a noble. Privates are known as finks, a word taken over, as is, of course, the word "hooker" from the vocabulary of prostitution. The fink should not be confused with the scab who, as free lance, is instrumental in breaking strikes by taking the job of the striking worker. The fink, who scorns work, also scorns the scab. Michael Casey, ex-turbine operator, who allowed he had worked as guard for almost all the agencies, was explicit about this: "A scab and a strikebreaker is different. A strikebreaker doesn't want anybody's job." It was from Mr. Casey's account of his part as soldier in the Middletown sector of the Remington Rand strike (he was engaged in various parts of the field at different times) that we extract among other equally interesting facts, the story of how a fink can pretend to be a scab in order to fill the striker's heart with that alarm which he feels when he sees another worker standing in readiness to take his job away. How without basis in fact is this fear as far as guards are concerned can be known only as we look into the well-nigh universal character of finks. One illustrious instance of their fraudulent claim upon the job is that of the ex-hosiery salesman who turned up in the role of electrical high tension lineman.

Mr. Casey's contribution to our knowledge of how the

worker's fear is exploited is found in this dialogue, concerning the Remington Rand strike:

SENATOR LA FOLLETTE: Whom did you meet at the station?
MR. CASEY: Mr. Bergoff.
SENATOR LA FOLLETTE: Did he furnish your transportation?
MR. CASEY: Yes, sir.
SENATOR LA FOLLETTE: How many men went up in that shipment with you?
MR. CASEY: There was only one shipment made of that 58 men.
SENATOR LA FOLLETTE: The whole 58 went up at one time?
MR. CASEY: Yes, sir.
SENATOR LA FOLLETTE: And Bergoff had transportation for all of them, did he?
MR. CASEY: Yes, sir.
SENATOR LA FOLLETTE: Did you see Mr. Rand on the train?
MR. CASEY: We picked Mr. Rand up about Stamford, Conn., about 7 o'clock in the morning.
SENATOR LA FOLLETTE: Did you see Mr. Bergoff and Mr. Rand in conference on the train?
MR. CASEY: Yes, sir.
SENATOR LA FOLLETTE: Were you in the conference?
MR. CASEY: No, sir; we all sat in the same car.
SENATOR LA FOLLETTE: Did you hear what was said in that conference?
MR. CASEY: Mr. Rand himself made a speech to us.
SENATOR LA FOLLETTE: What did he say?
MR. CASEY: That we was going up to this job and that he wanted us to go into this plant regardless of what happened, we had to get into the plant no matter how many pickets or strikers there was. We was supposed

to get in there as a showing. We hired as millwrights—
I hired as a millwright.

SENATOR LA FOLLETTE: Are you a millwright?

MR. CASEY: I have done a little of that work.

SENATOR LA FOLLETTE: How did he tell you to get in there if there was resistance?

MR. CASEY: Some of them didn't get in.

SENATOR LA FOLLETTE: What did Mr. Rand say about the situation, about how to get in there?

MR. CASEY: He told us to go in there and hire out as so and so, and some hired as watchmen, some as millwrights, and I happened to be a millwright. When we got to New Haven some of them went together, some two together and some three together to this Middletown, about 20 miles. Some went by taxi, and some went by bus.

SENATOR LA FOLLETTE: What did they do when they got to the plant?

MR. CASEY: Some couldn't get into the plant; the picket line was so strong they were stopped. It took me about an hour and a half before I got in, but I finally got in.

SENATOR LA FOLLETTE: How were they stopping you?

MR. CASEY: There were ads in all of the nearby town papers for millwrights, at New Haven, Hartford, and all of the nearby towns, and they figured we were the original fellows answering the ads.

SENATOR LA FOLLETTE: They thought you were legitimate?

MR. CASEY: Yes; they thought we were coming to take their jobs from them as millwrights. We were only sent up as millwrights to get into the plant, and when we got in there we didn't do nothing.

SENATOR LA FOLLETTE: The plant was not running?

MR. CASEY: No, sir.

SENATOR LA FOLLETTE: Was there any violence on the picket line when these fellows were trying to get in?

MR. CASEY: No, sir; not going in.

SENATOR LA FOLLETTE: When you got into the plant, what were your duties?

MR. CASEY: When we got in there, we just hung around and sat around on benches and chairs, didn't do anything at all.

SENATOR LA FOLLETTE: What was Mr. Rand's idea of getting you in the plant?

MR. CASEY: Just to make a showing that the plant was being opened up by millwrights.

SENATOR LA FOLLETTE: You understood from Mr. Rand's speech in the car going up, his idea was that you were to palm yourself off as regular employees, scabs looking for work?

MR. CASEY: Yes. A scab and a strikebreaker is different. A strikebreaker doesn't want anybody's job.

SENATOR LA FOLLETTE: I understand, but you were to give the impression to the men on the picket line you were going to work in the mill?

MR. CASEY: Yes, sir; that we were new men being hired by the company.

SENATOR LA FOLLETTE: And to create the impression they were going back to work?

MR. CASEY: Yes; the idea was they were rehiring men, and if they didn't come back regardless, they were going to open the plant.

SENATOR LA FOLLETTE: And, therefore, the strikers' jobs would be taken by somebody else?

MR. CASEY: Yes, sir; refilled. . . . We were told that when we were leaving that it was a one-day job with a bonus for going up and getting into the plant. Mr.

Rand offered us a bonus himself if we would get into the plant, when he made that speech.

SENATOR LA FOLLETTE: How much was the bonus?

MR. CASEY: We got a $5 bonus if we got in the plant.

Guards, finks, and nobles do not complete the category of strikebreakers. Roundsmen, sluggers, ropers, missionaries, and street operators are names encountered. The term "slugger" defines itself. The word "roper" is not so clear. A man who primarily belongs in the preliminary business of espionage, the roper nevertheless turns up inconspicuously in the open business of a strike, where he operates secretly as shadower, informant, and hooker. The roundsman is a kind of beadle, who in night-watching makes the circle of a given number of guards to prod them into wakefulness. The street operator or "missionary" performs his duties secretly. Mr. Jack Fisher, who has worked for six or seven agencies, said the word "missionary" as used in the strikebreaking business was a new one to him. "A missionary worker? Well, my conception of that would be somebody who is working in a religious outfit." Mr. Casey was familiar with the term. Although he spurned the work of missionaries, he described it:

> "They go around; they have a book or pad with a list of names on and they know the names of everybody in the town; the company gives that to you. You go around these houses—you are supposed to be a salesman—and you get to talking to somebody, the wife or somebody in the family, and try to ask them about the strike. Then somebody else follows you in a couple of days and tries to get them to go back to work."

SENATOR LA FOLLETTE: Trying to break down the morale of the workers?

MR. CASEY: Yes, sir.

THE SMALL FRY OF VIOLENCE

Red Kuhl was more detailed:

"Well, there is different kinds of street work. For instance, if we are going to talk about this New Orleans job, the street operators, they are supposed to get out and make connections with different union men, or preferably a union official, and find out his sentiment and write it in; talk to the businessmen and talk to the wives and the mothers and daughters of these striking workmen that are out of work, and propaganda them, tell them that this strike is silly, 'You are losing a lot of money, and why not call it off and get back to work?' And tell the businessman, 'You are losing a lot of money. You don't have any income, and why not see how you could work it with the city council or the mayor to call this strike off?'"

The missionary will be recognized by the reader as being not so much an integral member of the agency's strikebreaking crew, as an instrument of the employer's expensively laid campaign to create public opinion. In order to draw popular sympathy away from the strikers, he often uses highly paid publicity experts or public relations men who help him to create citizens' vigilante committees by radio and newspaper propaganda.

The use of the missionary worker for other purposes than to break strikes is shown in William Gray's and Dorothy Timlin's employment (women missionaries appear frequently) for the Ohio Power, Gas, and Light Company in Oberlin, Ohio, to work against a municipally owned plant. In the words of Lawson, formerly of National Corporation Service, "they circulated around the town and talked to the people against the plant and tried to show them what a mistake it was to put in a municipal plant." Kuhl was also able to recall similar missionary work done for the Lake Erie Power and Light Company at Bellevue, Ohio.

MR. KUHL: That was again a municipal power plant that the Mayor and probably two or three councilmen were in favor of putting in this power plant. This would be financed by one of the Government agencies, I don't know what it was, the FRA or one of them that finances, and naturally this Lake Erie Power Co. was opposed to it. A fellow named Fiske and myself went up there and opened this job. Our cover was that we told about the bad water, and that in fact they needed a new water plant more than they needed a light plant, but we convinced them, that is, this management of the power company that two of us wasn't enough, and we built the job up to about six.

SENATOR LA FOLLETTE: Was the water really bad there?

MR. KUHL: Yes; the water was bad, it was a good talking point.

This kind of work, however useful to the client, is to the agency mere embellishment. The big money for the strikebreaking agency does not lie in the labors of a missionary, nor is the agency particularly interested, except for gradations of pay, in the fine lines between noble and fink. Money is in violence, the longer and harder the violence the better; for the more guards called to quell it, the more money is spent.

Where is this private constabulary recruited? Who is in it? How is it transported, what are its instructions, what are its methods of warfare? How is it paid off, what is its provision against casualty?

The significance of the answers can be better understood if management's true purpose in calling in the strikebreaker is known. If the agency's interest in violence, and by the same token that of the strikebreaker's, is to prolong and embitter the fight so that a stronger guard will be called out and more money expended through the agency, the employer likewise has a vested interest in strife. His advantage in violence seems to be that it shall, by being attributed to the workers, bring discredit to them, thus alienating public sympathy from their cause. In those states where anti-picketing injunctions are still freely served, violence is provoked in order to obtain an injunction against the strikers. If blame for violence can be pinned on any individual, he may be prosecuted and convicted on criminal charges. The local leader of a textile union in Burlington, N. C., together with several textile strikers, in January, 1936, entered prison to serve terms up to ten years, after conviction as dynamiters. These convictions were obtained primarily on evidence given by or obtained through four police officers from Uniontown, Pennsylvania, later found by the Labor Board to be known undercover agents: two were "looked upon as dangerous characters and considered as experts with the use of dynamite; one had been arrested for bigamy; another had been indicted for felonious shooting with intent to kill; a third served a year for assault." All four had served as deputies in Pennsylvania under the direction of the H. C. Frick Coal & Coke Company.

This objective, if it were known, is obviously not one that would endear to the public the employer or his cause. A very different color must be given to the call for recruits. For this reason he gives his orders, not for strikebreakers, but for guards; guards to protect his plant, and to protect those workers who have not gone out on strike, and for whose lives and right to work he therefore at the moment feels a heavy responsibility. To cloak his true objective, he outwardly assumes that the strikers intend damage to property and violence to human beings. That for many years strike technique, as counseled by labor movement leaders, has been to avoid violence at every cost, is ignored. A state of war is presupposed.

Thus the strike call echoes in the taverns of the finks as a call for the defenders. Red Kuhl is interesting on the subject of recruiting. There is, he says, "a kind of underground grapevine system that puts out this call, and everyone hears it. They have certain places they congregate. For instance, in New York they have a certain place at Forty-second and Broadway. In Chicago it would be down in the Loop around Randolph Street. In Philadelphia, for instance, it is down around the Reading Depot. For instance, these agencies will put out the word to one fellow, and he will go down and spread the word, and they are all around there looking for the job." Jack Fisher further elucidated, "You see this business, you know, is just like a club of boys that hang around certain spots and one tells the other what is doing." He added that there were no officers. "I tell you in this business nobody trusts each other so they can't have any officers."

Before we watch these lowly mercenaries scuttle to new places on the military field map, let us lift the plane of moral choice to where it can better be afforded in a world of economic determinism and resolutely refuse to avert our gaze.

Almost exclusively drawn from the underworld, a good number of them are men of criminal record. The press, quick to draw upon the spectacular as typical, chose Samuel Goldberg, alias Chowderhead Cohen, alias Charles Harris, as fink standard-bearer. His repulsive picture, that of a man whose head was set into a series of chins rather than upon a neck, looks to be the picture of a man of arrested intelligence rather than that of a vil-

THE SMALL FRY OF VIOLENCE

lain. His description as given under a wanted notice by the Chief Inspector of Baltimore, made from information received from the New York City Police Department on a print numbered 39494, reduces his elephantine bulk to the following specific terms: "Color, white; sex, male; age, 40 years; height, 5 feet 8¾ inches; weight, 266 pounds; build, stocky [a euphemism]; hair, black [bald on top]; eyes, black; complexion, dark; birthplace, U. S.; occupation, tailor; residence, —— New York City." Additional description, as it appears on print No. 76566, gives notice of identifying scars and fractures. His criminal record includes imprisonment in Atlanta for conspiracy, four years in state's prison, and four years in Sing Sing for burglaries.

Out of thirteen strikebreakers furnished by Railway Audit for the General Materials strike in St. Louis in 1932, seven were wanted by the police of other cities on charges including burglary, forgery, larceny, pointing firearms, inciting to riot and assault. A large proportion of the strikebreakers furnished to the Pioneer Paper Stock Company of Philadelphia by Mickey Martel, a character known to the police, turned out to have police records. One Dominick Perfetti had been found guilty among other things of stealing an automobile, robbery by holdup, receiving stolen goods, assault and battery, aggravated assault and battery to kill. Another was arrested for being in possession of narcotics. One held, at the time of his arrest for attempted larceny, a six-inch iron pipe wrapped in paper for use in breaking open doors on automobiles. Ralph Golden who, while in service of the American Bridge Company, shot Edward Bergin of Jersey City, a non-picketing bystander, in the back, had been tried for murder and felonious assault.

Mr. James Bambrick, president of the Greater New

York Council of Building Service Employees International Union of Ozone Park, Long Island, testified in the preliminary hearing of the Committee, concerning the character of men entrusted with the safety of thousands of New York apartment house dwellers in the two weeks' elevator strike of the preceding March.

Mr. Bambrick's opening remarks can be given to uphold the contention that strife is fostered for profit rather than kept in check for public interest. "First of all, Senator, I am of the opinion, as president of these various service locals, that for many, many months prior to the strike of March 1, that these various strikebreaking agencies not only were in favor of the strike but they did everything possible to bring on a strike. We have hundreds and hundreds of communications in our files that I would be willing to mail to your Committee to supplement my information here today, showing that as long back as July, 1935, they predicted the strike and they laid out plans which, in their opinion, would break the strike and also break the union."

With this end in view, carelessness in recruiting method becomes a virtue. Mr. Bambrick read clippings from the *New York Herald Tribune* of March 3, 1936, interpolating comments:

" 'Thousands of strikebreakers to replace building service employees who had walked off their jobs were recruited yesterday by the Realty Advisory Board of Labor Relations, 12 East 41st Street, and by a variety of "industrial service agencies" which opened up overnight—'

"These are strikebreakers—

" 'Six men, three of them from New Jersey, were arrested on disorderly conduct charges in a brawl in the office of the American Confidential Bureau at 150 West 52nd Street, in which 100 men took part. Police said that the row was caused by the fact that the applicants were strikers who had gone off the job, but Leo Groom, manager of the agency, said that it was due to an argument among the men as to whether they should be fingerprinted—'

"And I go down further. This is Mr. Groom, the head of the agency there—

" 'Groom said that the Confidential Bureau had been preparing for the strike for 2 months, in which time 8,000 men had registered. In the early part of the day he said strikebreakers were being pushed through the agency at the rate of 180 an hour. About 2,000 men had been sent to work from the bureau, according to police.'

"The next heading goes on to refer to Bergoff, who is supposed to be the most notorious of them all. It says:

" 'Bergoff office hires 2,000.

" 'At 113 West Forty-seventh Street more than 1,500 men were packed into a second-floor hallway, the floor of which creaked under their weight. It was a newly opened branch of the Bergoff Industrial Service, Inc., which has its main office at 551 Fifth Avenue. A man and a girl took applications. They said they had sent about 2,000 men to jobs in office and apartment buildings.'

"Then going on to another agency, part of the same article:

" 'The Standard Industrial Service, of 7 East Forty-second Street, took over a vacant office at 106 West

Forty-sixth Street. All the applicants had to do was put their name and address on a green card and they were assigned to apartment houses, many of them on the East Side and on Fifth Avenue.'"

The results of this procedure were discussed in an article in the *New York World-Telegram* of March 19:

"Leo G. Groom charged today in suing for part of the gains. He demanded $8,300 on his own account, $12,450 on an assignment by John B. Barron, and $1,400 on an assignment by Alexander Cohen.

"During the strike the police seized 18 men with police records in a loft run by the bureau and Charles W. Hansen, the president, said his business had been virtually taken over by gangsters. The men named in today's suit were not involved in those moves."

Thus with two separate interests working harmoniously for the provocation of violence, we see what force is on hand to create it. It is handsomely summarized in a letter from Railway Audit to one of its canvassers out after business:

"A former police commissioner of the city of New York . . . came south during the last textile strike with about 300 guards . . . recruited from the gutter and dregs of New York, Chicago, and Detroit. They were gunmen of the first water and, believe you me, they used every kind of roughneck method known to them to quell the disturbances. The old police commissioner was run out of the State of Georgia by the Governor and given thirty-six hours to leave after he landed, but during those thirty-six hours he did plenty of havoc with his men. We served a number of individuals through this part of the country with guards, not strikebreakers and

THE SMALL FRY OF VIOLENCE

in no instance can they point to us and say that we were mixed up in a fight or that we ever beat up anyone, or that we have employed strong-arm methods. It is true that we did recruit some pretty big men, but all of them were either wrestlers or boxers and every one of them tried to be gentlemen in the handling of the crowds."

Their soldiers once signed up, the immediate job of the agency is to transport them to the employer. We have seen that curious band of fifty-eight finks en route from New York to Remington Rand in Middletown, shepherded by Mr. Bergoff and Mr. Rand. It is a big task, made none the easier by the Byrnes law of June, 1936, which makes it a felony to transport men across state lines with the intent to employ them for interfering with peaceful picketing, a law whose usefulness can be questioned since intent cannot be proved, and since the creation of violence once they have arrived upon the scene is a corollary of their employment. Besides instances of the open infraction of this law, there are indications that its terms are being evaded by the fiction of hiring guards on the spot of the strike, although they are recruited and given their traveling expenses in another state.

Since the famous episode when Pinkerton, rather than send armed men across the border, put guards in one car and their Winchesters in another, agencies have found ways, if not of avoiding obstacles to the flow of business, at least of surrounding them. By bus and by day coach, one can see the unkempt army raced to a likely scene for battle, their untidy habits not improving the condition of the common carrier.

Some of these rides, usually spoken of as shipments, are long. The 1,050 strikebreakers working for the New Orleans Public Service were recruited from Chicago, New

York, and Philadelphia. The Wisconsin Light & Power Company obtained 700 strikebreakers through the Bergoff Service Bureau. Mr. McDade, in charge of several bus loads of men picked up in Chicago, testified:

"Well, the first recruiting originated in Chicago, and they did not have enough men down there, they thought they would have trouble with the generating plant outside of Milwaukee—there were 300 down there then—and they ordered 400 more and we could not get the men in Chicago, and the president of the company advised them to place an order to New York City to bring them in by plane if necessary."

SENATOR LA FOLLETTE: The president of what company?
MR. MCDADE: Wisconsin Light & Power.

After they have arrived in the war zone, as we have learned from the importunate Mr. Rand, the first task is to get them into the plant. Sometimes this is done by ruse; men are brought in before daylight when there is no picket line, or run on the plant tracks through the yard in a loaded freight car. When no ruse is used, the arrivals perhaps club their way to the interior where they find the garrison prepared by the expectant host. A commissary has been set up and cots have been brought in. This unique military task of taking the home fortress with imported defenders has been disconcertingly frustrated by the modern tactics of the sit-down whose object is better understood as we learn the workers' past experience of tactics employed upon outside picket lines.

Inside the walls the men set up such a brand of housekeeping as can be imagined. After two nights, finks were evacuated for unsanitary conditions from a plant in Philadelphia by the Board of Health. Levinson in his important book, *I Break Strikes*, describes finks' barrack life more exhaustively than it was brought out by the Senate. However, the record is not wanting. Describing life in the New Orleans Public Service strike, where a thousand men slept and were fed in five car-barns, Red Kuhl incidentally brought out a fact elsewhere elaborated: that the fink emerges from the strike with no money to show for it, his earnings having been taken away from him through various kickbacks to superiors, fixed gambling games, and by inter-fink thieving. But let us read Red Kuhl whose tale of finance is revelatory of so much else:

SENATOR LA FOLLETTE: Are there different rates of pay between finks and nobles and lieutenants?
MR. KUHL: Yes. Well, I can go down the line, start from the top and tell you the pay. MacGuffin received $50 in salary—
SENATOR LA FOLLETTE: A day?
MR. KUHL: And $50 expenses a day and a bonus.
SENATOR LA FOLLETTE: What is the bonus for?
MR. KUHL: Well, probably if it is a good job, a very good paying job, why, there would be a bonus connected with it.

Williams received $25 a day and a bonus. That bonus was a verbal bonus, and went something like this. For all of the time he laid off the drink or the booze, why, he would receive a bonus. Myself and the rest of these fellows I mentioned, we received $20 a day. Naturally, we make more money on these jobs, you know, when these men are housed up in these barns, and take particularly a streetcar job where there is a lot of money transacted, why, these finks, they keep all the money, you know, that they take in on the cars. And they do a lot of gambling. These lieutenants of the barn take care of the games, and that is their cut. And they cut pretty heavy.

SENATOR LA FOLLETTE: What do you think some of them made on that job?

MR. KUHL: Well, I don't know. The word come out that Williams had himself $15,000 or $18,000.

And then there is another cut. These fellows that operate these streetcars, the money is divided three ways. The motorman gets a third, the conductor gets a third, and the fellow in charge of the barn gets a third.

SENATOR LA FOLLETTE: What does the company get?

MR. KUHL: The company doesn't get anything. But this money goes to the higher-ups.

SENATOR LA FOLLETTE: Oh, I see.

MR. KUHL: For instance, like Mr. MacGuffin, he gets his cut out of that.

SENATOR LA FOLLETTE: What would that be?

MR. KUHL: Well, it would be considerable, because this Whitey Williams wanted to stand in the good graces, and he would cut fairly heavy on that.

SENATOR LA FOLLETTE: How about the finks? Is there any kickback system working?

MR. KUHL: No; only these fellows in charge of the barns. But, for instance, like you take this New Orleans job, what you call a noble or a guard—

SENATOR LA FOLLETTE (*interposing*): I do not call them that. That is what I understand you call them.

MR. KUHL: That is what they call themselves. That is the name. They would get a better rate. For instance, they got 80 cents an hour, and figuring an 8-hour day, why, it was the policy to work 8 hours a day, but it would generally be 12, 14, or 16 hours a day, because these jobs are taken mostly on a cost plus 25 percent, and the bigger this pay roll will run the more the RAI or the Central Industrial would receive from them.

SENATOR LA FOLLETTE: As I understand you, they usually with their clients arrange to do these jobs for cost plus 25 percent?

MR. KUHL: That is it.

SENATOR LA FOLLETTE: And therefore the more the job costs the more they make?

MR. KUHL: Sure.

Kuhl's figures on guard pay are considered high, although they are supported by other veterans in the business. Chowderhead Cohen after twenty years in service was getting nine dollars a day and two dollars daily for expenses. Casey's pay in the 1935 Frigidaire strike on his own word ran as high as nine, twelve, fifteen, and eighteen dollars over a period of six or seven weeks. It is among the lower order of finks that pay seems to run less than Kuhl believed. Allied Corporation Service paid forty-five cents an hour, and Burns between forty and fifty cents. Other variations from what Kuhl considered to be average appear; Burns, as we have seen, doubled their money. Also the kickback system seems to be prevalent elsewhere than in Kuhl's experience. This arises out of a hiring custom similar to that employed in stevedoring where a flock of men like a flock of gulls wait upon the shore for the appearance of a ship. They buy their job from whichever foreman is lucky enough to land the contract of unloading it. The same strikebreakers turn up at every job under leadership of different foremen from whom they purchased it.

The strikebreaker's pay is chiefly interesting as a lens through which we see other measurements of value. It should be compared to the charge for his service made by the agency upon the employer, to the striker's wage demands, and thus ultimately to the relative cost of breaking the strike to the cost of conceding to it. As intrinsic wage it should be compared to the peril in which the strikebreaker is placed.

The inquiry has yielded little data on the first of these comparisons. For such facts to emerge the Bureau of Labor Statistics would have had to be called into collaboration on a study of the wages in question. Red Kuhl's testimony that the workers of the Johnson Bronze Company of New Castle, Pennsylvania, were making only ten cents an hour at the time he was paid lieutenant guard's wages to break their strike for a raise cannot be relied upon, not because his veracity is to be doubted, but because his was hearsay knowledge. Data were indisputable, however, in two relevant instances. The workers for the American Bridge Company on the construction of the overhead Pulaski Highway wanted a twenty-five cents an hour raise. This would have increased the labor cost on a contract running over two million dollars by some one hundred thousand. The company's strike cost, captioned labor trouble on the ledger sheets, totaled to nearly $290,000. The workers of Radio Corporation of America were making a demand at first for specific wage rise, but chiefly for union recognition. In answer to it RCA put on hostilities which cost them around one million dollars.

On the comparison of the fink wage to the danger involved the record is voluminous. For his low wage, the fink—the noble, better paid, is likewise by his tasks better able to avoid the hazards of the fray—risks his life and maybe loses it, protected if at all usually by the compensation laws of the state into which he may be shipped and upon whose mercies he has a minimum of claim. Kuhl's assertion that "they sign them up on a contract where the fink or strikebreaker practically signs away his life" is supported by the following employment contract offered to guards by Industrial Service, strikebreaking affiliate of the Railway Audit and Inspection. Under its terms the strikebreaker all but pays for the privilege of entering the war zone.

"I understand that I am the Employee of the Company to which I am assigned to work by the Industrial Service Company and that the Industrial Service Company is the acting representative of such Company.

"That I will accept workmen's compensation in the state and through the Company to which I am assigned to work. I understand that I am to take the place of former employees now on strike or to guard the property of a Corporation or Company where the employees are on strike.

"I claim and represent myself to be a sober and reliable workman at the trade or duties for which I have been employed. I promise to conduct myself in a sober, reliable manner, both on and off duty during the life of this contract, and in the event of my discharge for any of the following reasons—incompetency, drinking liquor, or agitation, I will reimburse my employer or his agent for all transportation advanced me and subsistence en route.

"Transportation is free after thirty days' work and a ten days' notice of my intention to quit, or at the termination of the contract. If I remain until the termination of this contract or until a settlement has been made between the employer and the striking employees and my services are no longer required, I am to receive transportation back to my point of shipment via the shortest route (No Pullman allowed.).

"I understand that I am to be furnished board and

lodging by my employer during the continuation of the strike or until I receive notice from any representative of the Company that board has been discontinued.

"I fully understand that if I am discharged for any of the above-mentioned reasons or for any reason on the part of the officers of the Company or their representatives, I forfeit all claim to free transportation to or from the work and will reimburse my employer (by deduction from my wages) for any transportation advanced me.

"I certify that I am free from all contagious or infectious diseases, also venereal diseases, to the best of my knowledge and belief and that if it is found upon physical examination that I have any said disease, I am to forfeit transportation advanced me by the Company.

"I certify that I am a citizen of the United States and a voter and that I have never been convicted of any crime and that there is no charge now pending in any court, which, if prosecuted, would result in a conviction of any kind.

"I certify that I have read the above and understand the contents fully before signing."

The violence which the fink is hired to provoke is frequently the violence of mortal combat. That it could occur sporadically or spontaneously as civil disturbance arising out of feud between hostile factions of the American community would tax belief. Yet that it has been a systematized part of American labor relations, occurring with a certain periodicity, prepared for by arsenals and cost-accounted by American management as an expected charge of overhead, has become such a commonplace that it has lost its powers to astonish. The very casualness with which it is accepted is often the result of carefully arranged publicity, itself charged to the strike cost column. Perhaps the volume of the altercation eclipses its specific attack upon human life itself, one broken neck being more interesting news than a surgical ward that is full of them. It is the old story of the large phenomenon, avoidable though it may be, taking on the character of natural law.

Knowing what we do about the fink, it seems idle to speculate as to whether, once debouched from train or bus with new places to see and new faces to knock in, his enthusiasm for his work compels him to exceed his instructions to brawl, or whether instead he brawls in obedience to a straightaway line of authority, upward through noble, lieutenant, agency and finally the employer. It was for his character that he was hired. The fight is on, and all that ensues was expected. Michael Casey's mild description of this eventuation reached a classical height for understatement as he told about the New Orleans streetcar strike. "The only violence," said Mr. Casey, "was blowing up streetcars and stuff like that. The first day there were three of them, I think, got killed—or two."

Management's attitude toward the deputizing procedure points to the expectability of violence. In an effort to relieve employer, agency, and the perpetrator for damage done to person or property, these dangerous and questionable characters are as often as possible made into officers of the law for the duration of the strike. In the same smug letter written by Ivey of Railway Audit to canvasser William Gray concerning the wrestlers and boxers whom he could recommend to handle a mob like gentlemen, he says: "We would not take over the job unless we secured for our men deputization by the local police or the sheriff. If you run into a strike job, tell the president or the owner of the mill that we will not handle the matter unless we secure the help and assistance of the local sheriff as well as his co-operation. It is dangerous to do otherwise."

This is common practice. Although its extent is unknown, much evidence points to the fact that few employers will allow guards to come into their plants, use their munitions, handle their rifles and sub-machine guns and riot sticks without their first being deputized to act as officers of the law. This occurs whether the guards are brought in for the occasion or whether they are so-called company guards. In Harlan County, Kentucky, in a population of 64,000 persons, where there operate between 45 to 50 large coal-producing companies, during one subpoenaed sheriff's term of office 379 deputy sheriffs were appointed. Sixty-five of these had criminal records. In 1936, 163 were in full force, only 9 of whom received their pay from public funds. Their salaries and bonuses for work against union organizers and sympathizers are paid for directly by the coal operators or by Harlan County Coal Operators' Association on assessments on members' coal tonnage. McDade, of Chicago, who took twenty-one armed men from New Orleans to Lake Charles to operate against a longshoremen's strike, testified that "me and these men were all sworn in by the harbor and terminal police of the State." Though sworn in as state officers they continue to work and take orders from the agency, or from the client.

In the complicated issue, later to be described, of the case of Joseph Gelders, various interesting facts were adduced concerning the arrogation of police powers by private property owners. Counsel Borden Burr of the Tennessee Coal and Iron Company which was being questioned about Gelders' criminal treatment, after describing the pitiful conditions in Alabama whereby its biggest tax-

THE SMALL FRY OF VIOLENCE

payers could not obtain adequate protection from the government, explained the plight of his retaining company to Senator Thomas:

SENATOR THOMAS: And your company, realizing the situation, comes in with a certain paternalistic spirit to help the county out?

MR. BURR: No; we come in because it is necessary to protect our property and the lives of the employees. It is not paternalistic at all. It is absolutely proper and necessary, and one that we dislike to have to use because we would much prefer if they were regular officers, but we feel when they are not furnished us that we cannot sit down and allow our property to be destroyed and the lives of employees to be taken.

SENATOR THOMAS: These men that you bring into the system of law enforcement are under whose jurisdiction?

MR. BURR: They are under the sheriff's jurisdiction and under our chief deputy's jurisdiction. The sheriff keeps in close and intimate contact with him.

SENATOR THOMAS: Who selects them?

MR. BURR: As I stated in that return, our chief deputy selects them by sending out to every sheriff in the State practically.

SENATOR THOMAS: The sheriff himself selects them?

MR. BURR: No, sir; you do not understand me, Senator. Our company begins the selection, our company, through its chief deputy, writes letters—you will see them in the files—to the various sheriffs of the State and asks them for recommendations as to men of sobriety and character, and we have a regular application form that they can use to recommend men to act as deputy sheriffs. Then, in addition to that, that information is checked. Then all of that information is turned over to the sheriff and he checks it and uses his own source of information and issues commissions to the ones that he approves.

SENATOR THOMAS: The point I was to bring out, who pays for the services of these men?

MR. BURR: The company pays for them, otherwise we would not have them, otherwise our property and the lives of our employees would be in danger. I am sure the Senator would not want that result to take place. . . .

SENATOR THOMAS: Now, then, if one of these persons does something wrong, assuming that he does, where in the wide world could there be any enforcement or justice obtained by the person who is wronged?

MR. BURR: I would say there would be much more opportunity, because it has been my experience as an attorney that whenever any wrong is committed by one of our regular deputies, or special deputies, for that matter, the courts are open and the company is responsible to the nth degree, both civilly and otherwise. The State would not be.

SENATOR THOMAS: Has the State, through the sheriff or deputy sheriff, ever arrested any of your men at any time for wrongdoing?

MR. BURR: Oh, yes; quite often.

SENATOR THOMAS: Who acts as referee then?

MR. BURR: You mean one of the deputies, for wrongdoing?

SENATOR THOMAS: Yes; one of the men that you pay to enforce the law.

MR. BURR: I would not say that any deputies have been arrested, Senator. I would say this—that correspondence shows it—that 38, as I recall the number, were discharged after employment because their actions did

THE SMALL FRY OF VIOLENCE

not show that they came up to the standards or up to the references that they gave.

SENATOR THOMAS: Discharged by whom?

MR. BURR: Discharged by us, with the approval of the sheriff.

SENATOR THOMAS: At the suggestion of the sheriff?

MR. BURR: Those were discharged by us at the approval of the sheriff. We did it on our own initiative.

At one time even these various aids to company protection looked to be insufficient. A difficulty had arisen involving the importation of scab steam-shovel operators. Mr. Burr read from his prepared statement:

"In the meantime, the Governor of Alabama, upon the matter being presented to him, arranged to give military protection by sending a squad from the National Guard and upon this protection being given, the company was able to operate these steam shovels with its regular employees. The nine steam-shovel operators who were brought in for this purpose, were held in reserve, never used, and returned to their homes during the latter part of June without ever having appeared on the premises of the company."

And later elucidated orally:

"The company, by agreement with the Governor, undertook to furnish barracks, and to equip the barracks, to give the service of water, light, and so forth to the soldiers while on duty."

This custom of supplementing the public police is not unique to the deep South as the chosen examples might lead one to believe. The Radio Corporation of America rejected after a brief stay the services of a rough contingent from an agency recommended by Governor Hoffman after the failure of the New Jersey authorities to allow them to be deputized. The letter itself, signed by Governor Hoffman and addressed to E. T. Cunningham, vice-president of RCA Manufacturing Company, is an interesting historical document:

"This letter will be presented by Mr. Max Sherwood, chief of Sherwood's Detective Bureau, 1457 Broadway, New York City.

"I have been acquainted with Mr. Sherwood for some time, and have been most favorably impressed by his work. He feels that there may be some opportunity for service to your company, and I would more than appreciate it if you can grant him a short interview, or refer him to the proper official of your company.

"With kindest regards, I am—Sincerely,"

It was while ascertainment was being made as to their potential police capacity, that these men were over in the hotel causing an embarrassment to the management by their unpleasant habits for which RCA paid without question. The record shows nowhere any effort on the part of RCA to look into their past or present suitability as protectors of New Jersey citizens. Their sole lack of desirability, it would appear, was that they could obtain from the proper authorities no cloak of impunity for what should transpire in the order of the day's work.

Violence can be precipitated in various ways. Someone throws chairs in an open meeting. Street operatives pose as strikers and start slugging. Strikers are provoked into defensive measures which look like attack. Union officials are called from their homes on fraudulent missions at odd hours, their cars are crowded over to the curb, and they are attacked. Charges of injury by strikers are faked, as in the mysterious assault of a guard in a hosiery strike in Reading. Early in the morning he appeared with a bandaged eye, on the strength of which all guards were deputized. In the same town, during the course of a peaceful strike, an organizer was attacked when walking to his hotel. He was stabbed three times, beaten up, run over by a car, his ankle crushed, one vertebra broken, his sacroiliac dislocated. In the seven-hour battle of the Lake Charles strike in which guards were equipped by the company with machine and riot guns, three men were killed and eight wounded. In the strike of the workers of the Wisconsin Light and Power Company, in which seven hundred men were armed with pickax handles distributed by the management and in which steam hoses were connected with the boilers so that live steam could be turned upon the pickets, two young men were hurt and one killed. The young man was electrocuted by a concealed wire placed by someone whose name was never recorded. That violence can get out of hand and create the opposite kind of sympathy in the public mind from that which it was intended to create emerges from the testimony of McDade who had helped bring the Bergoff guards from Chicago to Milwaukee:

SENATOR LA FOLLETTE: Was he electrocuted by this concealed wire?
MR. MCDADE: Yes, sir.
SENATOR LA FOLLETTE: Do you know who placed that wire?
MR. MCDADE: No, sir; I do not.
SENATOR LA FOLLETTE: Do you know whether it was done by the company or the agency?
MR. MCDADE: I did not even know that it was done until after it happened.

SENATOR LA FOLLETTE: But if it was done by either one it must have been done with the consent of the company, or otherwise they could not have gotten the wire hooked up to the juice, could they?

MR. MCDADE: I do not know anything about that.

SENATOR LA FOLLETTE: Did you have any conversations with the president of the company?

MR. MCDADE: There was a conversation one morning at 4 o'clock.

SENATOR LA FOLLETTE: What was his name?

MR. MCDADE: Way.

SENATOR LA FOLLETTE: Are his initials S. B.?

MR. MCDADE: Yes, sir.

SENATOR LA FOLLETTE: How did he feel about the work that these strikebreakers were doing with their pickax handles and concealed wires?

MR. MCDADE: Well, after the man was electrocuted, he worried about a general march in from Milwaukee of sympathizers to wreck the plant.

SENATOR LA FOLLETTE: Not employees, but just general sympathizers?

MR. MCDADE: Yes, sir.

SENATOR LA FOLLETTE: Well, was he satisfied with the work you were doing, aside from the fact that there had been this aroused public opinion against the company?

MR. MCDADE: No, sir; he wanted more men.

SENATOR LA FOLLETTE: What comments did he make?

MR. MCDADE: Well, he was under the impression there would be a riot the night following the murder.

SENATOR LA FOLLETTE: Did he give you any encouragement?

MR. MCDADE: No, sir.

SENATOR LA FOLLETTE: Did he give you any instructions?
MR. MCDADE: No, sir; there were no instructions given.
SENATOR LA FOLLETTE: Did he make any criticism of the work of the strikebreakers?
MR. MCDADE: Well, he realized he did not have enough men to stand off the crowd. He knew we were unarmed.
SENATOR LA FOLLETTE: Did you talk with anybody else who was connected with the company?
MR. MCDADE: Just the superintendent of the plant, the generating station.
SENATOR LA FOLLETTE: What was his name?
MR. MCDADE: I do not recall his name.
SENATOR LA FOLLETTE: Was his name Vandersee?
MR. MCDADE: I really do not know.
SENATOR LA FOLLETTE: What did the superintendent of the generating station say to you?
MR. MCDADE: Well, he wanted all the men up in front that night and have the lights turned out.
SENATOR LA FOLLETTE: Why did he want the lights turned out; did he say?
MR. MCDADE: He did not want the public to be looking in the plant.
SENATOR LA FOLLETTE: He did not want what?
MR. MCDADE: The sympathizers and the crowd to be looking into the plant.
SENATOR LA FOLLETTE: Did you get the impression he thought maybe the strikebreakers could do better work with their pickax handles if the lights were out?
MR. MCDADE: I suppose so.
SENATOR LA FOLLETTE: You got that impression?
MR. MCDADE: Yes.
SENATOR LA FOLLETTE: Did you talk with any of the other officials of the company?

MR. MCDADE: No, sir.

SENATOR LA FOLLETTE: Were any of the strikebreakers hurt?

MR. MCDADE: I guess there were a few hit, struck by rocks.

SENATOR LA FOLLETTE: To refresh your memory—I only want you to testify what you remember, but to refresh your memory—were any of the strikebreakers or special deputies hurt while they were handling tear-gas bombs?

But here we get into another question, not violence *per se*, but the use of arms. It is the nature of the strikebreaker, the nature of the work he is hired to do, and the authority upon which he does it that must concern us in this chapter. On the subject of authority, Mr. Jack Fisher has this to say: "Of course, you use your own discretion at times. If somebody tells you to do a thing you don't think is right, you don't do it." He adds that if you don't do it, "you are paid off and let go." The orders are explicit and the purpose is implied, both for agency and employer. McDade, on a National Dairy strike in Pittsburgh, "knew of where three cars were ordered out to slug up an automobile, or given instructions to look for a certain automobile and put them in the hospital."

SENATOR THOMAS: What is the purpose of this slugging?

MR. MCDADE: I believe they are active in slugging some of the loyal workers that stay in, to put them out of commission.

SENATOR THOMAS: What is the real purpose behind slugging, Mr. McDade?

MR. MCDADE: Well, I suppose it is to cause trouble, that is all.

SENATOR THOMAS: How?

THE SMALL FRY OF VIOLENCE 163

MR. MCDADE: It is to cause trouble.
SENATOR THOMAS: Why should you want to cause trouble to an employee?
MR. MCDADE: I did not want to cause trouble. I did not do any slugging.
SENATOR THOMAS: Why should your men cause trouble?
MR. MCDADE: I guess they were ordered to do it.
SENATOR THOMAS: Why?
MR. MCDADE: Well, in this here case this car was out turning over milk trucks and we were told to put a stop to it.
SENATOR THOMAS: Is slugging sometimes indulged in for the purpose of selling your services a little bit better?
MR. MCDADE. Well, that might be true.
SENATOR THOMAS: Do you know of any cases where that has been true?
MR. MCDADE: Well, I could not really tell how true it is, but I just heard rumors that some of that work was done.
SENATOR THOMAS: The more rioting or the more disorder there is the more men you would put on, wouldn't you?
MR. MCDADE: Yes; get another order for extra guards.
SENATOR THOMAS: And then the bigger the organization's bill would be, would it not?
MR. MCDADE: Yes, sir.
SENATOR THOMAS: Do you know of any case where that has been been brought about purposely?
MR. MCDADE: I do know in Cleveland, Ohio, in 1921, during the milk strike down there, there was lots of that going on. . . .
SENATOR THOMAS: What happened while you were on this job?
MR. MCDADE: Well, there was considerable violence on

both sides. There were 50 or 60 men put in hospitals. The job lasted a month and was called off.

SENATOR THOMAS: Why was it called off?

MR. MCDADE: There was too much violence; the company could not operate.

SENATOR THOMAS: What tactics could be used by the guards to promote more business for the agency?

MR. MCDADE: Well, some would get out in cars and turn over union machines.

SENATOR THOMAS: Did you use any dynamite?

MR. MCDADE: Well, there was a plant that was dynamited outside of Cleveland.

SENATOR THOMAS: Did you ever fire at other guards?

MR. MCDADE: I never did; no, sir.

SENATOR THOMAS: Was that ever done?

MR. MCDADE: It has been done down there.

SENATOR THOMAS: It was done there. For what purpose?

MR. MCDADE: I presume to increase the guards, possibly.

SENATOR THOMAS: Was anyone hurt in those firings?

MR. MCDADE: No, sir.

SENATOR THOMAS: It was just simply to create more rowdiness for the purpose of selling more guards?

MR. MCDADE: Yes, sir.

SENATOR THOMAS: What other tactics were employed in this strike?

MR. MCDADE: That is about all I know.

SENATOR THOMAS: Do you remember anything about the posting of stickers offering rewards for persons involved in poisoning milk?

MR. MCDADE: Well, I really do not know anything about that.

SENATOR THOMAS: How?

MR. MCDADE: I really do not know anything about that.

SENATOR THOMAS: Did you see any stickers?

MR. MCDADE: I have seen some of them; yes.
SENATOR THOMAS: Did they tell a true story?
MR. MCDADE: I do not know.
SENATOR THOMAS: Was any milk actually poisoned?
MR. MCDADE: Not that I know of.
SENATOR THOMAS: And do you know who put the stickers out and the purpose for it?
MR. MCDADE: No, sir; I do not know that.
SENATOR THOMAS: What other tactics were used, if you remember?
MR. MCDADE: That is all I know. That is all I recall.
SENATOR THOMAS: Do you remember the incident of the daubing of red paint on the house of Frank Taber, the manager of the Taber Ice Cream Co.?
MR. MCDADE: Yes, sir.
SENATOR THOMAS: How did that occur and why did it occur?
MR. MCDADE: Well, the unions were given the blame for it. That is all I know about it.
SENATOR THOMAS: Who was given the blame?
MR. MCDADE: The union.
SENATOR THOMAS: The union organization was given the blame. Were they responsible?
MR. MCDADE. I do not know that; I could not prove that.
SENATOR THOMAS: Do you know who put the paint on the house?
MR. MCDADE: No, sir.
SENATOR THOMAS: You do not know what group put the paint there?
MR. MCDADE: No, sir.
SENATOR THOMAS: Is there any likelihood that it was anyone else besides the union sympathizers?
MR. MCDADE: It might be.
SENATOR THOMAS: Might be?

MR. MCDADE: Yes.
SENATOR THOMAS: For what purpose?
MR. MCDADE: Well, I imagine just to gain public sentiment; that is all.
SENATOR THOMAS: As part of the strikebreaking activity?
MR. MCDADE: Yes, sir.
SENATOR THOMAS: And to create sentiment against the strikers?
MR. MCDADE: That is right.

The most desirable eventuation of violence from the employer's point of view appears to be the manifested necessity of calling out the national guard under cover of whose indubitable protection the shop can be opened for work. We have seen how Tennessee Coal and Iron did not even need to use their scabs after the soldiers turned out. An even more ironical exception to this ironical fact occurred in Harlan County when the troops were ordered out by the Governor to protect the lives of Kentucky citizens against the murderous violence—the average was said to be five killings a month—by company sheriffs. The judge, however, enjoined this proceeding, and the guard did not come in.

It is pleasanter to end with the words of Jack Fisher whose words arouse a feeling of something comforting, mutual, and two-sided about the end result.

SENATOR THOMAS: Have you ever been sworn in as a deputy yourself?
MR. FISHER: I have; yes, sir.
SENATOR THOMAS: How does that change your status of a noble, for instance?
MR. FISHER: Well, instead of being called a noble then you are looked upon as a deputy sheriff. You are given a badge.

THE SMALL FRY OF VIOLENCE

SENATOR THOMAS: From whom do you take orders then?
MR. FISHER: Then take orders from the sheriff of the county that swears you in.
SENATOR THOMAS: Then you forget about your employer, do you?
MR. FISHER: I beg your pardon?
SENATOR THOMAS: You forget about your employer?
MR. FISHER: Well, you take orders from them.
SENATOR THOMAS: From two of them, then?
MR. FISHER: Yes, sir.
SENATOR THOMAS: Did you ever have any fights with strikers and pickets?
MR. FISHER: Yes; I have had plenty of fist fights, protecting myself, of course, after I was attacked.
SENATOR THOMAS: You have never had to strike one of them to protect the property you were protecting?
MR. FISHER: Well, in the flurries of blows I presume there was blows struck on both sides.
SENATOR THOMAS: A general free-for-all?
MR. FISHER: Yes, sir.

VII. Is Gas Politer Than Guns?

I SEE by the morning papers that Mr. Ignatius McCarty is on a roof in Stockton, California, throwing tear-gas bombs at the striking cannery workers. This is no shock to me. Indeed, I should be shocked if it were otherwise. Men like Ignatius McCarty who run so true to form do not occur often in life or literature. Just as there is only one Micawber, one Uriah Heep, one Becky Sharp, one Topsy, one Eva, so is there only one Ignatius McCarty. The mold is broken, but there the caricature stands, deathless in the memory of all who have ever known it.

Mr. McCarty, let me explain, is the San Francisco salesman for the Lake Erie Chemical Company of Cleveland, Ohio, manufacturers of tear gas and tear gas equipment. He has to be constantly on his toes because Erie's chief rival, Federal Laboratories, the company which really dominates the domestic munitions market (the newer Manville Manufacturing Company is not a formidable competitor), has the West Coast too well sewed up to suit our hero. Mr. McCarty at heart seems to believe that, for all the chicanery he alleges of them, Federal really has the edge on Erie because it deals in submachine guns, whereas Erie's main domestic line is nothing but gas. It has become a personal matter with him. He broods about it. He talks about his dictaphone. He fears hopefully that his rival salesman can be found out in some discreditable scandal—a hot party, perhaps a rape.

But let us read selections from Mr. McCarty's perennially fresh prose before we go into a consideration of his mission this morning in Stockton where he is holding a garrison on the roof, and composing, one imagines, between the throwing of Jumper Repeaters and Baby Giants into the workers below, his next epistle to his chief, Mr. Ailes, vice-president of Erie: "Dear Mr. Ailes. You should have seen me in Stockton. I was not only up front but on top. I guess the Federal outfit will be sore when they see my picture in the paper."

If we read him carefully, we shall have to look elsewhere for very little data basic to an understanding of the business of furnishing arms to industry. I draw upon his 1934 correspondence from San Francisco:

"July 19, 1934.

"DEAR MR. AILES: With no stenographic help and only the services of a man from a neighboring concern occasionally to help unpack or pack boxes, with the phone ringing constantly, telegrams, etc., coming in, and calls to be in 4 or 5 directions at once I am just like the story of the 'woman in the shoe.' Fortunately I have the services of a plane due to the patriotic action of a well to do friend who not only loans me the plane but acts as pilot. He is a transport pilot, which means I have one of the best. He supplies me with a parachute (they cost about $300 each) and even kicked because I insisted on at least paying for the gas and oil. I have arranged to have a good radio installed in his plane for convenience in getting weather reports as I think that continuous riding in the plane would be an imposition without some small token of appreciation regardless of his ability to afford donating such services. When this strike is over (if ever) I will either have him pilot me to Cleveland and visit you or come by United Plane. I want to thoroughly go into various matters and I am prepared to go to Washington if necessary to learn why Federal is able to pull the things they do with the Dept. of Justice. My latest information from a purchasing agent of a neighboring county is that this representative is passing as 'official instructor' from the Dept. of Justice and giving the impression (which this man also had until he asked for his card) that he is from the 'Federal Government' instead of the Federal Laboratories. His great angle is to assemble a group for alleged instruction in handling machine guns, and then to display his gas. I must have a machine gun to meet this unfair tactics on his part and if you cannot get a permit to sell I am sure I have enough friends politically and otherwise in Washington to swing the deal. I could sell at least 50 guns and have a raft of sheriffs and police waiting for our gun. I tell them that they would be foolish to buy a Thompson when the latest improved gun is due here shortly. This has stopped Federal in quite a few instances when he was about to sign them up as he is unable to meet this as he doesn't know anything about our gun. I am, as you know, licensed by this State to possess, transport, and sell any and all types of machine guns so that you need no permit to ship me one. Will you advise me if I may be of service in the Dept. of Justice angle as this is the angle which must be met. Only yesterday the Bank of America (subject of a separate letter) told me that this representative told them that he could supply the same type candles we could, and furthermore, that the Dept. of Justice used their stuff and in the minds of the bank 'Dept. of Justice' meant the last word. I, of course, met this with our exclusive manufacture of the candle and by referring them to the local chemical warfare service of the National Guard. I also referred them to our captain of detectives, as if he calls the chief's office (which he did) the 'Boy Scout Cops' will tell him they use both kinds of gas. I also offered to pay for wires to any of the large police departments such as New York, etc., where our stuff is in use. He finally gave me the sketch of what he wanted and I think I have Federal stopped. This man I spoke to is the same one I contacted a year or so ago in an effort to put over daylight holdup protection.

"Herewith a pile of orders which should receive rush attention wherever notation below calls for items being supplied by you. They should have gone to you days ago but with 3 hours sleep a night I simply have reached the end of what I can accomplish and stay awake. This is why I favor plane riding as then I can catch up on sleep as the air at from 6,000 to 10,000 feet is very restful. I have been flying for 12 or 13 years so I have no worries as to accidents, etc."

"A. S. AILES"   "August 25, 1934.

"DEAR MR. AILES: This is to advise you on certain matters which are now in progress.

"(1) You will recall I told you Federal was playing around with a sgt. and cop in the chief's office and that they had been reported as having some $15,000 of gas cached in the hall of justice on the understanding that if used it could be paid for. I have worked night and day running down various clues and rumors and when you realize that getting information out of the chief's office is rather difficult you can appreciate that my success at last in getting to the bottom of matters meant a tremendous amount of digging. Briefly here are the developments of the past week:

"Believing that my investigation had quieted down and

that they could catch me napping the chief and his boys quietly went to the purchasing agent at the city hall and presented a requisition for $13,849.00 of Federal gas explaining that under the emergency that existed they had been unable to comply with the charter provisions requiring bids be advertised because the amount was over $1,000. Through my many connections the bid was only in the purchasing office 10 minutes before I received a tip. I at once went to the purchasing agent and while he was evasive at first I at last convinced him that if he did not want a grand jury investigation he had better play ball legally citing the charter section which (even in an emergency) requires at least 3 bids in open market on purchases of $2,000.00 or more. He stated that the bid was on his desk for approval of the requisition stating that as it was an emergency he would have to approve it. I told him that no emergency had existed as the following conditions completely nullified any claim for emergency such as would justify any purchase being made without 'advertised bids' and allowing 3 bids in open market neither of which method was employed. The conditions being as follows:

"(a) The chief being in possession of an unlimited order from 'public-spirited citizens' directing me to deliver up to $50,000 worth of gas on his order and without cost to the taxpayers.

"(b) Ample gas supplies of all kinds being located in my office 8 blocks from his office and subject to delivery in 10 minutes day or night.

"(c) That I was delivering continuously to the police department at all times under this blank order and at no time failed to deliver material wanted.

"(d) That I was on duty with the police gas squad at all times and reporting to the hall of justice daily.

"(e) That our munitions were superior and that our candles were the U. S. Army type.

"(f) That the material sought to be requisitioned was not delivered to the police dept. until the police had been superseded by the National Guard and had ceased their gas operations or need for gas.

"(g) That the amount of gas supplied by me and originally purchased by the department was ample for all needs and that the additional material called for on the requisition ($13,849,000) was more than 3 times the entire stock of the entire National Guard of this State.

"(h) That the life of Federal gas was only 2 years and that, even if it lasted as long as ours (3 years), it would depreciate at the rate of $4,616.00 per year, or $385.00 per month, and that if what was on hand of our gas was added to this the depreciation would amount to a staggering total of $6,665.00 per year, or over $555.00 per month.

"I next consulted my attorneys to see what could be done on a suit as a taxpayer to stop this bill being paid. I was advised to first call on the mayor. I contacted the mayor's executive secretary and after outlining what would happen if any attempt was made to pay this bill I received his assurance that the requisition would be stopped at once until the matter could be investigated. At his request I placed before him the next morning a written memorandum. The receipt of the memorandum was the cause of things happening rapidly. My friend (Capt. Dullea, captain of detectives and an enemy of the chief) was sent for by the mayor to check on matters. Finding that my statement as to the existence of the blank order was correct the bill was held up. I received a further tip that an attempt would be made to put the matter through by having the supervisors transfer the money to the chief's emergency secret fund (which ordinarily is $10,000 a year) and that then he could pay it secretly out of this fund. I immediately contacted the leader of the opposition supervisors, a bitter enemy of the present mayor, and received his assurance that any attempt in this direction would be stopped. This man incidentally only was defeated for mayor by the present mayor by the slim margin of 6,000 votes. Yesterday I received a call from the representative of the people who purchased the gas, he having been sent to me by the mayor in an effort to save embarrassment over my opposition to the bill. This man explained that if the unions or other people found out that they donated this equipment it would raise hell. I told him that at no time had their names been mentioned and that any information on this must have come from the chief. I explained that he should bring pressure on the mayor and force the return of the Federal gas, otherwise I would file suit as a taxpayer and the whole rotten graft be brought into court. I forgot to mention that, as a consideration for putting over the illegal order, the sgt. and his assistant were to receive trips all over the country and to Havana, Cuba, as well as Federal factory and that they were to tell police departments how Federal gas saved San Francisco.

"The representative who called on me was shown my dictagraph recording equipment and shown certain conversations which had been recorded, and told that these would be used in court. When he left after a 2-hour conference in my office (covered by one of my operatives in the next room) he was convinced that his duty was the forcing the return of this material to Federal and the canceling of the requisition.

"Now you realize that outside of the mere loss of about $3,500.00 commission which this order represents the suc-

IS GAS POLITER THAN GUNS? 175

cessful culmination of this deal would mean my quitting the sale of gas in this State. You realize that if other chiefs and sheriffs in the State found that my own city apparently found Lake Erie so rotten that they had to throw it out and substitute Federal they would no longer purchase our gas, and sales efforts would be hopeless. Realize that I have tried repeatedly to impress you how desperately Federal was fighting me and that they were apparently willing to back their representative to the limit. I have tried to get action on the various items which have given Federal the entry over me in departments, i.e., machine guns, etc.—and have lost a total of $10,000 in commissions so far this year. When to this is added the fact that I have expended continuously more money in education and demonstration and other travel and office expense than I have made in the gas business (with the exception of the period of May and July), you can see that I am fighting for more than mere S. F. Although I have repeatedly asked for more territory, I have not as yet received this, so that with only California, and that saturated with gas, my future in the gas business is not bright. When the expenditure of $350.00 in covering the recent Utah and Idaho conventions is considered and then when an order results for me from same I am unable to fill it, you can realize that something is all wet.

"I have lost sales for 37 machine guns alone in the past 4 months, the news item enclosed being an example of what I have tried to convey to you as to why guns are necessary. This sheriff had no money to even buy $100.00 worth of gas, although I have contacted him for over a year. Federal sells him machine guns and then gets an order for gas as an auxiliary to the machine guns. I have orders on my desk right now for sheriffs' and chiefs' friends who have held up their purchases for 30 days in an effort to give me the business, but gradually have had to give Federal the business on account of pressure of bankers and others that they get machine guns for protection. Every village here has gone gun crazy, and the only way gas can be sold now in the future will be with machine guns. Federal is able to show that the Dept. of Justice purchases machine guns from them as well as gas, that they are instructing the Dept. of Justice men, and as everyone has gone kidnap crazy and have placed the Dept. of Justice on a sort of superman basis, they have the argument that wins the un-informed."

I have deleted here at length. The man has no end.

"With the big State convention of the Peace Officers Association scheduled for October 4th and with no prospect for meeting Federal on any reasonable basis I hesitate to expend any further money on advertising as requested by the committee having the convention in charge. They want me to stage a mammoth demonstration in the Rose Bowl at Pasadena for the officers and the general public; the demonstration they have in mind would cost at least 250 to 500 in demonstration material alone. Their plan is to erect scenery in the middle of the stadium and to have a regular fake gang raid by peace officers with gas attack and mask use, etc. They have arranged for gigantic movie wind machines to blow the gas out of the stadium so that the audience of 90,000 will not be gassed. The convention plans to show the public all modern police methods and the Dept. of Justice is cooperating. Realizing that Federal with its machine guns will naturally take the spot-light (unless we have the gun which for 8 months or more we have been telling about) any expenditure of such money by me is out of the question. Now I have friends on the committee and the whole show was reserved for me both machine guns and gas with Federal shut out of the picture but now that we have no machine gun and Federal will back their man with plenty of money I am not going to attempt to put my money up against theirs. I mention all this to give you a fair picture of things out West.

"I believe that any requests of Dinius for material should be filled from here so as to reduce my stock. I have my office crowded with 3 giant safes so that I have hardly room for my other equipment. One office contains one safe and all empty boxes and is devoted exclusively to gas. The other office has 2 large safes filled with gas as well as closet filled with dummies and catalogs. As long as I have this large stock I must keep all these safes as I will not risk the gas outside of a safe. Only one safe, however, is properly protected with Anakin gas, this safe being my original regular safe, the largest of the three. The other 2 safes, which are 5 foot by 3, were loaned me temporarily by the building during the strike conditions. This letter is being written at 2:30 in the morning and is a hurried effort to get the facts to you without delay. I would have written sooner but I wanted to be able to give facts on Federal positively which I am now able to do. I have just checked by phone with a clerk at the chief's office (without revealing my identity) and learned that the sergeant and assistant and Federal's man have left on their trip."

"September 23, 1934.

"DEAR MR. AILES: Have just returned from a last emergency trip to the riot at Salinas, a news item on which appears herein. I received 3 orders which were not half what I expected, but this was due to the fact that the burning of the Filipinos houses while I was enroute the 108 miles (made it in 2 hours including slow driving in city limits enroute) stopped for the moment the riot. It is expected to break out again tomorrow and if so I will return there again.

"Herewith special information on the orders:
No. 316—This was a present to the highway patrol from the growers' secret fund. They want the check cashed personally by someone and not cashed by the Lake Erie Chemical Co. They suggested that I cash same and then forward you the money but I told them you could have Mr. Pay cash it and then put the money through company account. It is important that this procedure be carried out if we want any further business with them. They took the price list and went off secretly to the committee meeting and gave the inspector of the patrol the check but forgot to include f.o.b. Cleveland charges. I called this to their attention but they told me the money was already issued and the committee disbanded and nothing could be done about it. If I didn't deliver I would not get the order."

"Last Wednesday I drove to Tracy, about 90 miles distant, and addressed the Lions Club; my subject being Modern Police Equipment. I showed our full line including the bank and safe stuff and, of course, included one of my dictagraph outfits. I spoke for 50 minutes which is 20 minutes more than usually allowed. From the way they stuck around afterwards, and the remarks made by the chief, they like the talk. This talk was merely a matter of good will toward the chief who had been a good booster for our products.

"I have about eight or ten invitations a month to speak at various clubs, lodges, and even high schools but I only take those engagements I can't very well get out of taking. Near the end of next month I must talk before a large gathering of Odd Fellows at Stockton. You have to do a lot of things out here to sell gas.

"I am enclosing a clipping from the *Contra Costa Gazette*, Martinez, which you will notice contains a statement that we are the largest tear gas company in the country.

"P.S.—I am advised by the State bureau of criminal investigation and others close to matters here that the longshoreman strike will again go into effect in about two weeks. Better make sure that sufficient long range shells, guns, masks, and clubs are reserved for me here so that in the event of a strike and a bid being called for in accordance with the law of the city charter here that I do not lose out to Federal on acount of inability to deliver. He has a stock here and in Los Angeles of around $50,000.00 ready for the contemplated strike."

Our next brief hurried letter (what could Mr. McCarty do if he had the time for correspondence) is to his president who has apparently shown displeasure at Erie's showing.

"October 1, 1934.
"B. C. Goss,
President, the Lake Erie Chemical Co., Cleveland, Ohio.
"Dear Colonel Goss: This is just a brief hurried answer to yours of the 27th to cover a few questions given therein.

"Regarding your paragraph No. 2 I have not personally seen the pictures as yet but from reports they comprise parts of the many Fox Movietone pictures taken on various days and covering a multitude of minor skirmishes. In one picture or scene as reported to me the following is illustrated: The Federal representative is shown in the middle of the street firing a long range gun at the mob about 350 feet distant and directly at them. Apparently if you saw this part you would think that Federal had driven back this mob variously estimated at from 1,500 to 2,000 men. Now, here is a rough sketch of what happened and from it you can see that Federal's man and the two Boy Scout cops from the chief's office, dashed up at the last minute and after we had driven the mob back at least 250 feet and had ceased firing and the Movietone wagon hearing the shooting had driven up in time to get only the last part of the skirmish and of course Federal's man ran out in the middle of the street and posed firing at the mob. As a matter of information he fired at the two cops who were located up there keeping the mob back and driving them back still further after we had ceased real firing and the captain had ordered them to go up there. One other scene shows the two cops and a third cop with masks hanging on their necks but not in use, running toward the camera with grim expressions as if in actual combat. This scene was taken on the docks while all the newspaper men were around chatting and eating and these two cops from the chief's office and Federal's man were posing around with black paper hard hats on to protect them from rocks. The Movietone man not having anything to do took their picture and asked them to run toward the camera, etc. As I understand, the picture, with a few of these actual scenes in which Federal is posing, is combined with a lot of distance shots of our munitions in action and all credited to Federal. I have a positive statement verbally from the purchasing agent (Mr. Brooks) that not one cent has been paid Federal nor any munitions purchased as yet. A requisition was, however, received from the chief but on my objection to the mayor this was held up and is still held up. I am advised that there is no legal way it can be paid. The Federal man appeared on the front with a machine load of ammunition and guns and passed a lot out one day to various cops but that was, as far as reliable informants have furnished the information, only loaned. Federal's man shot dozens of long range shells aimlessly and without effect and I personally saw them picked up and thrown back. One in particular was picked up by a member of the mob who ran back about 75 feet with it smoking in his hand and threw it directly at Inspector Millikan, Inspector Findlay, and myself; the affair being witnessed by reporters. I then fired a shell in the same direction asking the reporters and Federal's assistants (the two cops) to watch a real shell in action. Our shell having a longer range went over the head of the man who picked up Federal's shell and landed about 100 feet behind him but directly in front of the mob. Another member, thinking it was the same type, stooped to pick it up when it exploded in his face scattering the mob in consternation. I checked at the hospital with a doctor friend and was told that a man was treated for cut ankles caused by the explosion of a shell and no doubt it was this man. Another phase of the picture and the one I think comprises the real meat is that I believe a picture of 60 police officers was taken in the demonstration given by Federal about 6 miles from the front out in the hills and which was supposed to be an alleged training course. To aid Federal the two chiseling cops had the chief order 60 men sent out in uniform to take this alleged training. This is without doubt used and made to appear as San Francisco police using Federal gas. The thing to be borne in mind is that as far as can be determined Federal has no proof of 5¢ of gas sold to the San Francisco police dept. I have served notice on the administration of this city that any attempt to put over this order will result in the finest expose and suit heard in this section of the country. This demonstration of 60 cops was after the real riots were over and had no connection in any way with the waterfront trouble, but was merely a gesture by Federal to help him get an order. I was informed that at least $1,000 worth of gas was used, some of which failed to go off. I reported this in detail to Mr. Ailes. I also cited a recent case where Federal's man gave a demonstration and set a house on fire and also a large field with his burning type of long range shells. I think this fire danger of their shells should be stressed as well as the fact that they can be picked up. I have one of Federal's latest long range shells given me by one of the captains at a police station here. This could be used to get a picture of it being picked up. I have been trying to find time to take a few shots myself using a San Francisco police officer in uniform with a Federal gun and having him fire a shell at me and then pick it up and throw it back. My intention being to get the pictures if necessary without his knowledge as I feel any means within reason is fair in dealing with Federal."

If you are bored, bear with me. The man is a better expositor than I.

"You are familiar with police departments and realize that while I have my information furnished me from unquestioned sources (some from the members of the chief's own office who are friendly) this information is furnished me confidentially and I can't get it in affidavit form. The thing to be done is to beat Federal on this order as then they are out in the cold. We can challenge them to show where they have sold San Francisco police department any gas and they cannot produce a bona fide order. The mayor states that as soon as the chief comes back here, which will be on Monday next, October 8th, he will settle the matter definitely. If we let Federal get away with this attempt here they will give us the laugh throughout the State and we will be discredited, as the chief, who is one of these fake flag wavers who is always spouting about the dangers of Communism and what he is doing to combat it, will be asked why he chose Federal instead of our gas. To justify his purchase he will have to state it is better than our munitions. If we beat Federal we can then show the police department with around $5,000 of our gas and equipment for the past 2 years with our munitions and guns, etc. We can then expose their attempt to put over the order and how they failed.

"In my recent telegram to the Senate Munitions Committee, I had written in same a statement of the fact that Federal had furnished the joy ride trip to the two cops and the wife of one, but my attorney thought that until we can definitely know whether the trip was paid for by the salesman individually or by Federal as a company I should not put this in a telegram to the Senate. I have it from a lieutenant and an inspector from the chief's office that Federal's man furnished the trip, but they of course do not know whether this was out of his expected commissions on the $13,849.00 or whether Federal advanced him the money. I do not know that my stopping the requisition did cancel the trip for several days but that a few days later the trip was again on so that it looks like the representative passed the news on to Federal and was authorized to furnish the trip anyway as a matter of satisfaction and on the feeling that they would eventually be able to put it over. The funny thing about the whole fight I am having with the chief and these two cops is that I hold a regulation police star (7 point) with an inscription on same that I am a member of the chief's office and my own initials are in the center as my identifying number. The chief would like this back but so far has been afraid to ask for same believing that such a move would be unwise as serving notice of an open break. After all these boys have a healthy respect for my dictagraph equipment and know that I can put them in right under their noses. My reputation on this is so well known that I am credited with a sort of uncanny magic in my work, all of which amuses me greatly. I have always contended that the honest man, the one who has nothing to hide, need not worry about dictagraph equipment. This star was not given me through any genuine affection on the part of the chief, but merely as a bluff that he was doing me a favor for having given him $7,500.00 worth of free dictagraph work in the Egan murder case lasting over 13 months. I am known as a bureau of inspectors man, my friend being the captain of inspectors and an enemy of the chief. The chief thought that when he issued me this star and I technically became a member of his office I would then play with him instead of the captain of inspectors. It would take more than a piece of tin to break a friendship of 14 years' standing.

"This letter is being written somewhat hurriedly in an attempt to catch the air mail and at the same time get ready for my trip to the convention at Pasadena tomorrow. The convention does not start until Thursday morning but there will be some doings on Wednesday night and I want to be there for that as well. It is a 475 mile drive to Pasadena over a nice smooth highway and can be made in one day without trouble. I usually drive about 300 miles the first day and then after a good night's rest I then drive the next day, arriving fresh after a short 175 mile drive. My weekly driving is around 600 to 750 miles all the year round as we have no snow or extreme heat and can use our highways 365 days of the year.

IS GAS POLITER THAN GUNS? 185

"The green hand grenades, clubs, and literature arrived O.K. this morning. I will inquire at general delivery, Pasadena for balance. I have my State machine gun license, which is number 9, and authorizes me to possess, sell, transport, and demonstrate any and all makes of machine guns. I carry this with me at all times. Should you send the machine gun, it will be locked in either a safe deposit vault or kept in a vault at the Pasadena police department when not in use. Should it arrive, it will secure publicity as the papers are looking for something new. You can communicate with me either care of the State peace officers convention at the Huntington Hotel or general delivery, Pasadena. I will not leave Pasadena until Saturday night.

"Herewith sketch referred to in forepart of my letter."

They say the fine art of letter writing is lost. I sometimes wonder, what will McCarty do when the thirty-hour week overtakes him. And all those aids to brevity are most peculiarly his; the telephone, the telegraph, the dictaphone. Words come out on him like rash.

"I had hoped business would be good by now so I could take a trip back there for a week or so for additional study and personal contact with you and Col. Goss but so far I cannot see my way clear. I would like to serve a few days looking over various phases of the work and discuss actual field conditions I have found in riots with you and the colonel so that when the great general strike which is expected here not later than September, and which many think is due within a month or so, arrives, I would have the benefit of this additional knowledge. Should any of the large corporations there be open to pay for someone to direct actual gas operations or any opportunity develop whereby I might spend a few weeks there without expense

I would be interested in learning of same. Last year the California Hawaiian Sugar Refinery offered to place me on the pay roll for a month to direct gas training for their men but I told them our business would not allow of such engagement. In the event of the next strike here Sgt. McInerny will attempt to supplant me by claiming to have had alleged training back at the Federal Laboratories in latest methods used in various strikes in that part of the country. I am still of the opinion that were we to produce a good picture of slow burning, fast burning, and jumper candles, etc., we could save tremendous demonstration expense and at the same time give a better opportunity for observation of the action of the various munitions. We could pick an ideal day, ideal conditions and typical places to demonstrate various uses of gas. It is now possible to obtain sound motion pictures in the small-size film. In many demonstrations the wind is blowing 35 miles an hour, the weather is cold, the ground damp and uncomfortable to stand on, and the demonstration is hurried and unsatisfactory. Then seldom is a suitable building for demonstration available and the mere shooting off of candles and shells is more of a fireworks display than a demonstration. If the film were merely shown at conventions or peace officers meetings in various parts of the country and shown to other groups such as Lions, Rotary, and other service organizations having plant executives as members it would more than repay the small cost and produce a lasting impression. You would be surprised at the effect I produce using only a 38 cal. blank cartridge either in a pen or in the riot pistol with the dummy shell you made for me some time ago. Anything in the way of a demonstration proves interesting and the picture would enable officers and others to sit in comfort and carefully observe the effects of each shell. Suitable explanation

IS GAS POLITER THAN GUNS?

could be incorporated either by the sound on film method or if only ordinary motion picture was used I could use one of my recording machines to render a prepared explanation of the film as it was shown. Machines for showing the film would not have to be owned but can be rented for $2.50 per day. . . .

"This letter has become a book so will discuss other matters later."

"San Francisco, Calif., Aug. 6, 1936.

"DEAR MR. AILES: Today I had a visit from Atherton, chief graft investigator, who is handling the investigation of the police department here. He brought with him an assistant and a feature writer from the *Examiner* (my friend).

"I showed him the correspondence with Quinn and other officials and the details of the various deliveries omitting the fact that the Waterfront people paid for same. Eventually it will come out if the matter reaches the grand jury, but no use giving it out at present. He asked me to prepare a statement in sequence with all dates and facts and copies of my letters to Quinn and his replies. He asked if you had any information from our representatives in the cities visited by McErerny, Gurnea, and Rausch as to their boosting Federal products, etc., while there. He stated he had not enough funds or men to investigate each city and that in view of the fact the exposé now would not only benefit us but put an end to future deals by Federal, we should give such assistance. Now, can you secure the following from representatives in the cities in the itinerary I furnished you at the time:

"1. Did McEnerney and Gurnea give any talks or demonstration of Federal products or give out any interviews or statements, etc.

"2. Were any pictures taken or published. (I understand some are in existence.)

"The main idea is that they were S. F. police officers and we want to show they were acting as Federal boosters on a trip financed by Federal.

"Their stop in Pittsburg must have been interesting. Perhaps the agent there can give information showing they went around in the interest of Federal or acted as agents.

"Can each city furnish data on hotels stopped at, amount of entertaining, etc. By each city doing a little we should be able to amass plenty of data to show up this dirty deal as well as prevent same in other cities.

"I received information confidentially tonight that Gurnea was arrested for attempted rape at a city near here and that in spite of this secured a position with the Department of Justice. We are checking this and will advise further. If confirmed, this will remove him from his present post. It happens that the chief at the city mentioned is a very special friend of mine.

"In view of the fact that San Francisco will shortly have another general strike and that plenty of gas will be purchased, the killing of this Federal deal now will certainly put us in the right position.

"A check at the city hall shows the money was not paid to Federal by the usual channels. I called on the city treasurer and he told me to check the secret fund of the chief out of which it was evidently paid. This is a big job but is now being done.

"Can you advise me at once if you can give any assistance on this matter and if representatives in other cities will co-operate. The benefit will be for them as well as it will also kill the story Federal circulated that they were the ones who handled the S. F. situation. I will challenge

IS GAS POLITER THAN GUNS?

the chief to demonstrate the junk and then show it is absolutely worthless by throwing it back at him. I will then ask him to try and pick up a green band or a fast candle. I would, of course, see that waivers of damage were secured to prevent suit, as my intention would be to gas him right."

and

"Aug. 20, 1936

"I am enclosing small order from San Leandro where riot at Caterpillar tractor plant caused the use of quite a lot of gas in the past week. San Leandro is broke, but the gas used came from the sheriff of the county as well as the Oakland department which adjoins. These departments were glad to use up their old stuff so that they can replace with our new jumpers, etc.

"I trust the trouble will be speedily located or the shells which will be returned found to be O.K. as we will be left in a bad position here with no long-range shells. There is always a danger of some chief or sheriff getting peeved about being without long-range shells and telling Federal about it. Tonight Sheriff Odell told me he took his long-range gun out yesterday to take a crazy man out of a house but fortunately succeeded in getting the man without gas. Were this situation to arise and he be without long-range shells we would be in a bad light.

"Would it not be possible to start shipment here of, say, 25 or 50 long-range shells as soon as possible so that in an emergency I would be able to handle matters.

"I am presuming that in calling for all long-range shells you do not mean the new Tru Flite shells just received. I will hold these out until further advised.

"I selected my 5 inspectors today and Dullea is detailing them to me for the demonstration. I have asked Dullea to place Inspector Millikan in charge of the squad and while I will make the talk and explain all maneuvers and answer all questions, etc., Millikan will apparently issue orders for the various attacks, etc. My reason for this is to prevent Quinn criticizing the fact that the representative of a commercial company was ordering police officers around. I have a few remarks to make at the beginning to the effect that our whole desire is to co-operate with any department by furnishing instruction or information at all times but that the only way I can take active part in any riots is as a special officer or deputy sheriff and, not as a representative of the company. This is a crack at Quinn who allowed Rausch to shoot at will without any control. Rausch shot a fellow in the face with a long-range shell and then asked the officers witnessing the same to not say that he did it. I was on the water front as a special police officer.

"While you have never given me any specific instructions on the matter, you have always indicated you wanted me to conduct my operations so as to minimize any chance of a lawsuit against you. I was advised by my attorney to insist on being appointed or deputized by a chief or sheriff before taking part in any riot or other use of gas on criminals. This he stated would then render my actions those of an officer rather than a representative of Lake Erie. You might well insist on this policy in other parts of the country. With the advent of Tru-Flite shells it certainly would be bad if a representative of Lake Erie shot some citizen at close range in trying to co-operate with some sheriff who might then disclaim all responsibility.

"I have been asked to demonstrate the Tru-Flite gun and as there is no suitable place to safely do this I will if compelled to demonstrate its long range, shoot a shell out over the water at about an elevation of 45 degrees knowing that when it lands it will sink in at least 200 feet of water and be safe from recovery. I am bringing a small steamer trunk and all munitions will be locked in this until time for the demonstration as a large crowd is expected. The wardens of the two State penitentiaries will be there, General Mittelstaedt and Chief Hallinan are coming from Sacramento, Sheriff Odell is coming from Stockton and at least 100 other chiefs and sheriffs besides men from all Government departments including Army, Navy, Marine, National Guard, Secret Service, Dept. of Justice, Immigration, Intelligence, etc. Many banks will be represented so that a lot of good prospects will be on hand.

"I am enclosing tonight's *News* showing Federal's latest long-range gun, shells, and jumbo candles were found in the possession of a mob. I looked for our stuff to show up in that line from Burnsides' former method of selling to anyone. I note that one of the mob although a Jew has taken the name of McCarthy. Glad it isn't McCarty.

"Last night I received a wire from Dinius asking how many Baby Giants I could spare, as he had prospects for 30. I told him that these were no good for riot conditions existing where he was at the time of sending the wire. He also wanted .410 pens evidently not knowing they had been discontinued.

"I note that Major Spring will send some suggestions for the demonstration I am giving. I was informed that Captain Rideout in charge of the National Guard gas squad would be at the meeting and so I will invite him to take part. He is a very fine fellow and a good booster for Lake Erie. Both he and General Mittelstaedt are very enthusiastic about the Jumper repeater and their presence and remarks will aid a lot. I will call on both for a short talk. Mittelstaedt will make various chiefs take a sample of the gas, going himself right into same to show that it is non-toxic.

"Other matters will be treated separately. In haste."

The denouement of the farce which we might call Gas Bought Without Bidding, we find in the testimony of Federal Laboratories. Mr. B. H. Barker, vice-president of Federal Laboratories, is on the stand. Senator La Follette gives a question: "Mr. Barker, did you ship any gas and gas equipment to the city of San Francisco during the longshoremen's strike in 1934?"

MR. BARKER: We did.

SENATOR LA FOLLETTE: Approximately how much gas and gas equipment did you ship to that city at that time?

MR. BARKER: I presume between $12,000 and $14,000.

SENATOR LA FOLLETTE: Would it refresh your recollection if I mentioned the sum of $13,809.12?

MR. BARKER: I think that is probably correct.

SENATOR LA FOLLETTE: This invoice was not supplied to the Committee; is it contained in the invoices that are here today?

MR. BARKER: I would say it is.

SENATOR LA FOLLETTE: Were you paid in full for this gas?

MR. BARKER: Yes, sir.

SENATOR LA FOLLETTE: By the city of San Francisco?

MR. BARKER: No, sir.

SENATOR LA FOLLETTE: Why were you not paid by the city of San Francisco?

MR. BARKER: On account of the work of a competitive individual and the refusal on the part of certain officers of the city to honor the chief's request that he have the shipment made.

IS GAS POLITER THAN GUNS?

SENATOR LA FOLLETTE: Did you go out to San Francisco and attempt to collect the bill?

MR. BARKER: I did.

SENATOR LA FOLLETTE: Did you talk to the chief of police and the city officials about the bill?

MR. BARKER: I did.

SENATOR LA FOLLETTE: And what was said in those conversations; what position did they take?

MR. BARKER: The position of the chief was it was a bonafide bill. The purchasing agent said he would not pay it even though it was ordered at 3 o'clock in the morning, and certain members of the council would not agree to the payment.

SENATOR LA FOLLETTE: Why did they say they would not pay it?

MR. BARKER: They would not even discuss the subject with me. I never even saw them, but the inference was they were not interested in having gas used.

SENATOR LA FOLLETTE: Did it have anything to do with the way in which it was purchased?

MR. BARKER: That is pretty hard for me to answer, Senator.

SENATOR LA FOLLETTE: I do not want you to answer if you do not know.

MR. BARKER: To give you a frank answer, I cannot answer that intelligently.

SENATOR LA FOLLETTE: I was under the impression it had something to do with the fact the bid was not advertised.

MR. BARKER: I mentioned at the start there was a taxpayer case brought up by a competitive salesman, and it was badly tied up.

SENATOR LA FOLLETTE: Do you know Mr. Ashfield Stow?

MR. BARKER: I think I do.
SENATOR LA FOLLETTE: Who is he?
MR. BARKER: I cannot tell you. I know he is a San Francisco man and one of the gentlemen I think I called on, with one of the corporations there.
SENATOR LA FOLLETTE: Would it refresh your recollection if I said he was agent for the American-Hawaiian Steamship Co.?
MR. BARKER: I believe it would.
SENATOR LA FOLLETTE: Did you talk to him in San Francisco?
MR. BARKER: Yes.
SENATOR LA FOLLETTE: About the payment of the bill?
MR. BARKER: Yes.
SENATOR LA FOLLETTE: Was anyone else present?
MR. BARKER: Mr. Roush.
SENATOR LA FOLLETTE: What occurred at that conversation?
MR. BARKER: We simply explained to him the situation as it had developed, as we did to other people of similar character; what we were up against, and we asked if there was any possibility of any of the people protected by this material to show interest in the matter so long as the city itself had refused to handle it.
SENATOR LA FOLLETTE: Was any arrangement made as to how the bill might be paid?
MR. BARKER: Not at the moment. There was interest expressed by this gentleman whose name I could not remember and whom you have just mentioned; it was some 2 or 3 years ago; other men expressed interest, and we were told to leave the matter in hand to see if there could be anything done about it.
SENATOR LA FOLLETTE: What other men expressed interest besides Mr. Stow?

IS GAS POLITER THAN GUNS? 195

MR. BARKER: I cannot remember their names, but there were three or four people interested in the dock set-up.

SENATOR LA FOLLETTE: Were most of them connected with the steamship companies?

MR. BARKER: I would say yes; with the dock situation.

SENATOR LA FOLLETTE: Was something worked out with these gentlemen who were interested, or others, so you could get the bill paid?

MR. BARKER: Eventually.

SENATOR LA FOLLETTE: How was it worked out?

MR. BARKER: The actual invoice was deposited at one of the banks before I left, and shortly thereafter the money was sent in.

SENATOR LA FOLLETTE: Which bank?

MR. BARKER: A bank right close to the hotel, to the Palace Hotel.

SENATOR LA FOLLETTE: Was it a branch of the Bank of America?

MR. BARKER: One of the large chain banks; yes.

SENATOR LA FOLLETTE: Who suggested this arrangement?

MR. BARKER: The suggestion was made that if we would leave the bills there—I think probably Mr. Stow, although there were two or three other men mixed up in the negotiations.

SENATOR LA FOLLETTE: I offer for the record a letter from Mr. Barker to the Bank of America under date of November 3, 1934, and will read it.

"San Francisco, California
"November 3, 1934.
"Bank of America N. T. & S. A.,
Market New Montgomery Office
San Francisco, California
"GENTLEMEN: We are handing you herewith a

sealed envelope which we are asking you to deliver on payment to you of $13,809.12.

"When these funds are received by you then remit them to my parent organization, the Federal Laboratories, Inc., 185-41st Street, Pittsburgh, Penn.

"This letter will authorize you to deduct the necessary charges for handling this remittance for us.

"When payment has been received and remittance forwarded, kindly wire E. H. Barker, care of the Biltmore Hotel, Los Angeles, California, so stating and charge cost against the remittance.

"Yours very truly,
"FEDERAL LABORATORIES, INC.
"By B. H. BARKER, *Vice Pres.*"

Did this envelope that you enclosed, Mr. Barker, contain the Federal Laboratory Co.'s invoice for $13,809.12?

MR. BARKER: That is correct.

SENATOR LA FOLLETTE: In that case the invoice there had been delivered to the city of San Francisco?

MR. BARKER: Yes.

SENATOR LA FOLLETTE: Did the company subsequently receive a check from the bank for the amount of the invoice?

MR. BARKER: They did.

SENATOR LA FOLLETTE: I offer for the record a canceled cashier's check on the Bank of America, dated November 5, 1934, payable to the Federal Laboratories, Inc., in the amount of $13,799.47. This check was received from the bank pursuant to a committee subpoena. That is the check which you received, is it not?

MR. BARKER: I never saw the check. That is undoubtedly

it, however. I was not in Pittsburgh at the time it came in.

SENATOR LA FOLLETTE: Do you know who provided the $13,000 to cover the amount of the invoice?

MR. BARKER: No; I do not. I have a very definite idea, but I could not say positively that I know.

SENATOR LA FOLLETTE: You don't think the bank just made a mistake in sending a check?

MR. BARKER: Oh, no, no. I could not tell you the corporation or the people that actually put it up. I don't know.

SENATOR LA FOLLETTE: I offer for the record a copy of a letter from Mr. Barker to Mr. Stow, dated November 20, 1934.

SENATOR LA FOLLETTE (*reading*):

"DEAR MR. STOW: I have been extremely busy since I returned to Pittsburgh, which will account for what I would term a fairly lengthy delay in dropping you a note of thanks and appreciation for the part you played in our recent negotiation in your city.

"We will not soon forget, I assure you, the peculiar tangle that we found ourselves in, and to find you not only willing to advise, but ready to protect the activities of the people who, in good faith, had been dealing with us, will remain in our memory long after other things have been forgotten.

[Laughter.]

The "things" sort of slipped your mind, didn't they?

"It is unlikely that there will be any reason to be back in your city soon. I certainly will want to call upon you again, if that privilege is accorded me again, and in closing I hope I am entirely honest when I trust that the rumorings of more trouble on the coast will not be harmful to your interests, or that of your own firm.

"Again thank you, I am,
"Yours very truly,
"Federal Laboratories, Inc.
"B. H. Barker, *Vice President.*"

Now, Mr. Barker, does that refresh your recollection any as to who agreed to put up the money for this purchase?

MR. BARKER: You have already refreshed my memory, and the minute you did I knew who it was. I could not have told you previously. I have not been back there since.

SENATOR LA FOLLETTE: Did Mr. Stow put up the money?

MR. BARKER: I don't know that he did. I don't think so.

SENATOR LA FOLLETTE: Who do you think did?

MR. BARKER: Probably he was the man that negotiated it, but I could not say positively, and he never told me. He said, "Leave the bill there and it probably will be covered." That is why I asked the bank to wire me to see if it was before I left the west coast.

Thus in the small commotion of Ignatius, so diligently put down in the few hours left at his personal disposal after the wear and tear of the patriot's day, we find a syllabus of study by whose guidance we can pursue each subject to its lair. Scarcely a pertinent point eludes his imploring pen. Even the implorations, most of which, believe it or not, I have deleted, are of significance. "Give me more violent means that I may outwit mine enemy by force. Be it my course to busy giddy minds with foreign quarrels."

To the munitions salesman the enemy is not the worker, striker, communist, radical, or malcontent whose menacing existence he, in collaboration with his indispensable agent, the detective, is forever stressing. The striker is but the proving ground for his wares. He falls in the line of battle. He has the bad luck to cross the field. To Mr. McCarty, as to the industrial collector of private arsenals, the true enemy is the competitor. The head that pops above the trenches is nothing but a rising cost.

Perhaps it was reading too much McCarty, who is always on the wire, that sent me to the telephone this morning to check into the true state of affairs in Stockton where McCarty thinks it worth his while to be. A department of federal government informs me that the women in Stockton are making twenty and twenty-two cents an hour on piece work and the men nearer thirty. They want more, and they want union recognition. The employer's dreaded apparition materializes: a market lost to a rival more successful in keeping down his labor costs. Throw faster, Ignatius! Ignatius, with Federal for the moment quelled, feels his bosom swelling. He can afford to be magnanimous. According to the breakfast paper he halts hostilities for a moment and allows a bus load of school children to escape down the street.

The industrial munitions business is very similar to the business of espionage—the same generalities hold for each. It watches the bush for signs of conflict like a cat with its eye on a nest full of fledglings; or rather, a nest full of eggs. (Tempted, one seeks the precise figure of speech in vain.) Intent upon hatching out trouble, it warms each hopeful situation like a hen. Or like a cowbird, even, leaves an egg of its own in every nest.

The literature in this field is excellent. Mr. Roush, writing to a lawyer in Los Angeles in November of 1934, when he was a San Francisco salesman for Federal Laboratories, says in facetious despondency: "Just a line to let you know that I am still alive and still waiting for a nice juicy strike up here. The darn things don't happen often enough to suit me. I honestly believe I can join the Ancient Order of the Ghouls pretty soon. However, all joking aside, I have been in close contact with the powers that be and it all looks as though we will have further business up here in a short time."

Earlier in the year he wrote Vice-president Barker: "Good news, I hope. The milk strike is supposed to break today. The strikers presented their demands this morning, and we are standing by to await results. I was in touch with Captain Hastings, of the sheriff's Communist squad this morning and he is up in the air as to what will take place. . . . If we are going into the strike areas and lend a hand to the Department of Justice, we feel that two DM Gas Masks for ourselves are a necessity. We would also like to stock about 6 No. 204 Long Range DM-CN Gas Projectiles in case of emergency. I will let you know as soon as possible the outcome of the milk strike. Here's hoping it is a good one. Best regards."

A certain air of gaiety marks much of the Federal correspondence on this subject. Another salesman, writing from Los Angeles to Barker, says: "I think someone should get out a restraining order on the President of the U. S. to prevent him from stopping all these strikes. It seems to me that his actions are absolutely in restraint of trade—that is, as far as we are concerned."

The Pacifists unwittingly contribute their amount to the munitions business by setting aside National Students Anti-War Day. Mr. Roush writes to the home office: "Next month should be a good one. Another strike is expected in the Imperial Valley for the cantaloupes. The national demonstration on April 6 of the Pacifists and the crops that will come in that month in the north. Harvest season starts about the middle of June and continues throughout the summer, and if everything works out the way the labor side of the question is concerned, things will be popping."

The wish, of course, is father to promotion. Herrick Foote, salesman for Erie, succinctly puts his case in a letter from New Haven in April of 1935. "I am doing a lot of missionary work in anticipation of a strike this spring and I am in a position to send in some good orders if it will only mature. Wish a hell of a strike would get underway. Fraternally yours." Two months later he is sending in hopeful reports that the textile workers are demanding an increase.

Meanwhile another salesman is watching the steel industry. Writing on July 1, 1936, he can give considerable encouragement to Ailes, his chief:

"The proposed drive for the unionization of this trade will certainly stir up a lot of trouble sooner or later. I am keeping in close touch with the United States Steel Corporation Headquarters in Chicago, which, as you are aware, includes the many subsidiary companies. I shall contact the other companies at the earliest opportunity and shall endeavor to have them prepare for the trouble before it breaks upon them. Bendix Corporation, at South Bend, Ind., were threatened with a strike day before yesterday, but yesterday it was settled by a compromise between the company and the employees. If you have any line on any strikes or threats of strikes in my territory or vicinity, I hope you will post me as soon as you learn of it."

It takes the smallest company, the Manville Manufacturing Company, to put it in a nutshell. "I had figured," wrote its Secretary-Treasurer to a salesman, "that once you had been in the field you would, no doubt, realize that the best places in this line are in large industrial centers or, at least, centers where labor is employed in large volume." And elsewhere, in a letter from a sore salesman who had just learned that his customer, Hazel Atlas Glass of Charleston, was really interested in prevention of the looting of its employees' automobiles parked for the night shift, "My dear Charlie: Well this thing is not so hot, as there is no labor trouble here, and what they want is just a couple of revolvers and a box of shells."

The munition trade's second similarity to the detective business is the secrecy of its every transaction, a chief reason for the difficulty in estimating the size of arsenals set up by private industry. Blind shipment is the rule. Goods destined for plant use are delivered to homes, to railroad offices, or even to the public police. They are fraudulently identified on the package, marked as hardware or other merchandise. Bills are submitted to the home addresses of company officers, to manufacturers' associations, or to the personal attention of the highest officials to avoid scrutiny of clerical employees who would spread the news.

The whole object of this, naturally, is to keep secret the names of the customers, who might stand to lose, besides the efficacy of their weapon which is partly that of surprise, the esteem of the public if their purchase should become known. Employers are loath to admit that their gas, gun, or shell purchases have anything to do with expectation of labor trouble; their excuse for laying in arsenals has usually to do with expectation of burglary, pay roll holdup, or some other sort of attack. Mr. Paul Litchfield, president of Goodyear, was amusing on this

IS GAS POLITER THAN GUNS? 203

point. La Follette asked him, "Are you familiar with the fact, Mr. Litchfield, that the Goodyear Tire & Rubber Co. made purchases of gas and gas equipment?"

MR. LITCHFIELD: We have from time to time, yes; under different circumstances.

SENATOR LA FOLLETTE: I offer for the record a statement of expenditures by the company for munitions for the years 1933 to 1936, inclusive. It shows total expenditures for these years in the sum of $22,491.32. It appears that the purchases of the company for the year 1936 aggregated $15,703.49. Were these gas and munitions purchases made with your approval, Mr. Litchfield?

MR. LITCHFIELD: They were.

SENATOR LA FOLLETTE: And made with your knowledge?

MR. LITCHFIELD: Yes.

SENATOR LA FOLLETTE: Is it or is it not a fact that members of the flying squadron in Akron were given an intensive training course in the use of tear gas and other munitions during 1935 and 1936?

MR. LITCHFIELD: I was away in 1935. I do not know of anything of that sort being done in 1936.

I would like to explain the purchase of this tear gas, and so forth, as to why we did it.

SENATOR LA FOLLETTE: Yes.

MR. LITCHFIELD: The first purchase was in 1933. As you know, the banking situation was such at that time that all the banks in Akron practically failed; there were no banking corporations in Akron, and we had to get the money down from Cleveland; we were paying cash, and we were carrying between $2,000,000 and $3,000,000 in currency in our vault, because of the very uncertain conditions on account of the banking situation;

and that is why these purchases were made, under my instructions, to afford a better defense of the pay-roll money in case of attack.

SENATOR LA FOLLETTE: In that year you spent $418.50.

The invoice gives pertinent information on the remainder of the purchase. When they were expecting a strike, Goodyear Rubber paid $7,551.40 to Federal Laboratories on March 16, 1936, and made an additional purchase of $15,000 within several days.

The obstacles put in the way of Senate examination by Federal Laboratories in both the Nye munitions and the La Follette investigations illustrate the munition industry's reluctance to identify its customers. During the Nye hearings, Federal Laboratories was twice subpoenaed. When early in 1936 the Munitions Committee's agent arrived with the second subpoena in his hand, the company officers sent him off to see their lawyer. As soon as his back was turned, they themselves disappeared for a week beyond his recall. During this subpoena-dodging period, the company changed, retroactively for the years 1935 and 1934, its whole system of bookkeeping. Invoice binders they took to a locomotive works, an excellent hiding place, it would seem, for quantities of matter. Correspondence they took to a secret vault under the elevator. Ink eradicator did the rest. When the records were restored to their places and ready for subpoena (although it is not clear whether or no certain correspondence does not still repose underground), the commission paid to R A & I on sales for which that agency acted as their agent appeared as credits to an alias and became obscured almost beyond deciphering.

As in espionage, this secrecy goes all the way down the line. It shrouds the destination of goods, and it shrouds

IS GAS POLITER THAN GUNS?

the participation of the sender. Sometimes the name of the buyer is withheld even from the salesman.

Mr. C. B. Dinius, reporting his sale of gas, chemicals, grenades, and gas masks, amounting to nearly $3,900 worth shipped to the special agent, Mr. L. T. Benson of the Chicago, Milwaukee & St. Paul, said, "We are certain this material was for the Anaconda Copper Company, although Mr. Benson did not disclose that to us, and you will have to handle the matter diplomatically in order to explain how you happen to know about it." Sometimes lawyers act as the intermediaries. In another letter to his chief, Mr. Dinius wrote from Seattle, "I have been working with a prospect here, attorneys for a large corporation that are doing business up and down the coast, and they were to order gas equipment for Washington and Oregon. They would not tell me who their clients were but asked me if I could instruct their man in the use of the gas at the different points where it would go in the territory." A letter to Ailes from salesman Paul Kilian in Detroit in 1933 says, "Ship to James V. Mills, chief of police, city of Flint, Flint, Michigan, the following: Ten no. 16 gun clubs; and ten dozen (1-0) no. 16-A shells for same. These are to be shipped by express today, in accordance with my talk with Major Spring, and I should, in the natural order of things, arrive in Flint on Monday morning. When they arrive I will have to go up there again for instructions purposes.

"Do not bill the City of Flint for this material. Instead send the bill to the Manufacturers Association of Flint, 901 Industrial Bank Building. Mail it for the attention of James Farber, Manager. Mr. Farber is the one who telephoned me this order this morning.

"For your own information only, I have reasons to believe this material is for the Chevrolet Motor Company, but they do not want it advertised or generally known that they are the buyers."

In the fall of 1935, Kilian can report that a solicitor had at last been successful in seeing Alfred Marshall, Director of Personnel for Chevrolet. He encloses the solicitor's report.

"Having made an appointment to see Alfred Marshall, director of personnel relations, Chevrolet Motor Company division of the General Motors Corporation, over the phone yesterday, I called this morning at which time his secretary, a Mr. Nettle, advised that Marshall had been called to one of the plants and would not return until late in the afternoon. I left and returned at 4:15 P.M. After a wait I saw Marshall and we had a nice long talk, during which I showed our Tear Gas items and discussed same at length. Marshall had already seen the Jumper-Repeater and seemed to consider it a very valuable item. He said, however, he did not feel this a propitious time to bring up matter of gas, citing the General Motors management have taken the attitude they do not want to show anticipation of trouble of any sort by the purchase of such materials, which, incidentally, was the reason this company once partly equipped the Flint Police Department."

John Young, President of Federal Laboratories, in a spacious letter on how to make forts out of one's plants, worked up for one of several Pittsburgh Steel Companies with whom he has at times been in conference ("One of the United States Steel plants, or one of the Jones & Laughlin or independents, I could not say which"), reveals to us why he and not a man like Roush reaches the position of chief executive. Salesman Roush evidently did not know how to meet the caste questions brought up when he wrote, "I am still unable to promote the sale of sickening gas as the departments are all fearful of the reaction against them if they gas the wrong parties." Not so Mr. Young who can include such a thoughtful suggestion as, "Further, in case of labor trouble your employees could be brought in the —— Gate which lies in a less desirable neighborhood and in that way eliminate any trouble at your main gate which could be considered objectionable to residents in that vicinity" or, in other words, bring the finks in through the slums. Mr. Young's letter also brings up and turns over that extremely important subject of who is to throw the bomb. For although Erie has such a weapon as a Jumper Repeater grenade, whose chief selling point is that the victim cannot toss it back, since it goes off spasmodically like defective sparklets, leaping hither and yon at the impetus of explosion, the curse of gassing is that someone beside the man in the front office must throw the bomb, or, for that matter, if a gun has been bought, shoot off the tommy. This letter reads in part:

"April 23, 1935.

"DEAR SIR: Following our conference in your office on April 17th, we have made a survey of your several plants in connection with your Mr. —— and our Captain Alden Baum, to determine requirements for protecting your property and employees from sabotage and destruction in time of social unrest.

"Our study has been made with the view of carrying out your wishes that preparations be made without any show or evidence to aggravate the present situation and that any means of protection to be employed should be of humane character. Our recommendations have been restricted to protective measures which would not endanger the lives of any citizens.

"Our experience in the past has taught us that it is both unwise and very expensive to wait until the emergency is upon you before preparing for it. We have, therefore, prepared one recommendation for immediate action and another recommendation to be carried out systematically at the first sign of emergency.

"We recommend that a select list of police officers be trained by us in the protection of property under such conditions, and we have already conducted some classes of instruction for these men. In this manner we are able to give them the benefit of experience of other people who have gone through similar trouble. This training will enable these men to perform the work that a much larger force would otherwise be required to do.

"We have shown on Exhibit 1 attached hereto a list of materials which should be procured immediately and held in your possession. We consider this equipment essential as permanent equipment at each plant.

"We have shown on Exhibit 2 attached hereto a list of materials which we have recommended be procured at a time when trouble is more imminent at a particular plant, but not too late to have it on hand when needed. Further training classes would have to be conducted for additional police to use the equipment in our secondary recommendation, and time should be provided to conduct these training classes with the new equipment.

"There are some specific features pertaining to each plant which require individual attention, and we cover them briefly herein:

"——— PLANT

"Owing to the small number of police officers here we recommend that each police officer be equipped and trained as a unit so that in times of emergency your police force can act as a training cadre and will be equipped and expand to a force of sixty men.

"Provisions should be made at this time to take over rooms in buildings strategically located about your property where all sides of the property can be under constant surveillance, such as rehabilitation of your old watch houses equipped with telephones, and the corner office of the new cafeteria building adjacent to —town Gate. . . .

"We recommend that you equip one old touring car to be used as a reserve car to reinforce any position which may be attacked in your plant (your General Superintendent has the details of this recommendation at hand).

"We recommend the removal of such hazards as the dynamite magazine, piles of debris, as well as small size pipe plugs which make admirable ammunition for rioters.

"We recommend the anticipation of laying down of an emergency fire and steam line and the staggering of gondola cars along the open side of your plant.

"We recommend the immediate contacting of the Pennsylvania Railroad, Pittsburgh & Lake Erie Railroad and Baltimore & Ohio Railroad police authorities with the view of arranging a plan of co-ordination.

"We find this plant more open than the average industrial plant due to the small percentage of property that is enclosed by a fence, and consideration should be given to enclosing more of it as promptly as possible.

"——— PLANT

"We believe that your existing police force at this plant is adequate, and it will not be necessary that each man be equipped as a unit. However, we recommend the re-allocation of men at the following stations:

"1. The establishment of a watch house at the Scull

Crusher, same to be equipped with a private one line telephone. Two men should be placed at this station.

"2. Four men to be placed on duty at the —— subway, and the establishment of a watch house with a telephone in the hospital adjacent thereto.

"3. Two men to be placed at the Center Street main gate. (We recommend further that the hauling of slag through the Center St. main gate cease and be kept closed at the first sign of trouble.)

"4. Four men to be placed—two at the 'Y' (Railroad Terminal) and two at the Steel Works Hospital, the latter being assigned to duty of patrolling the river bank.

"5. Two men to be placed at the —— Street subway.

"6. The establishment of a reserve force of six men to be held at the main gate and used in connection with your armored car to reinforce any point which may need additional man-power or equipment.

"7. We recommend the immediate contacting of the Pennsylvania Railroad, Pittsburgh & Lake Erie Railroad and Baltimore & Ohio Railroad police authorities with the view of working out a plan of co-ordination; and that arrangements be made at this time for four men to be detailed from the Pennsylvania Railroad, to be stationed as follows:

> One man at the 'Y.'
> One man at the 'Y' side of the ramp.
> One man at the —— side of the bridge.
> One man at the freight station.

(See Supt. John G. Sersch of Penna. R. R. for co-operation.)

". . . (Each plant is considered separately.)

"GENERAL CONSIDERATION

"We recommend at this time that some provision be made for the adequate protection of the main gas line from —— serving the last three mentioned plants as this is a hazard, and would mean a complete shutdown if this line was cut.

"We believe that you have no fear of approach from the river side of any of your three properties, and no extra men need be considered for this work other than the two men already suggested for at the ——, at the Steel Works Hospital station.

"At the present time the —— Plant survey has not been made and this, together with a report of further training of your police officers, will be submitted at a later date.

"Very sincerely yours,

"FEDERAL LABORATORIES, INC.

"JWY:GO   ———— ———— *President*"

It should not be necessary to describe the results of putting arsenals into the hands of irresponsible and frequently vicious characters, deputized as officers of the law. We shall see the small fry of violence at Black and Decker. We have seen it at New Orleans and Remington Rand. It is necessary only to know the coincident placement of gas or gun reserves and of strong-arm guards, either temporarily put on or kept as regular force, to know where industry does not stick at the idea of endangering the community as well as its own workers by making militia out of thugs.

There is some federal pretence at protection of citizens from promiscuous ownership of arms in the requirement that machine guns should be taxed and registered. Some states exact that tear bombs should bear registration numbers and be licensed. This small protection is broken down where the employer or the detective agency is in collusion with the police or with other branches of local government. McCarty amply described this danger.

Federal Laboratories went the whole way by making their commissioned agent a California state official, chief of the Division of Investigations, who had the last word in issuing tear gas and machine gun permits. It can be imagined that few amenities stand between the local government of Harlan County and the coal operators in the stoppage of whatever sales the munitions companies are successful in promoting.

A more typical instance of collusion than bloody Harlan offers would be that of West Point, Georgia, where the Bureau of Internal Revenue had an occasion to investigate purchases through the local police officer of three machine guns which had, as a result, escaped taxation. These guns were shown to be for the use of and loaned among three employers and were paid for by the West Point Manufacturing Company. They were used promiscuously by, among others, guards from the Pennsylvania Industrial Service, deputized by the county. In extenuation of this transaction Mr. Eugene Ivey, head of the branch office of the R A & I of which, the reader will remember, Pennsylvania Industrial Service is a subsidiary, wrote a letter saying that:

"The West Point Manufacturing Company mill officials asked the writer personally about the use of these guns. . . .

"Those people have been so long in a small community without any outside interference whatsoever that they run things to suit the best interest of everyone concerned within the small community. I happen to know that the police department and the mill officials are very close. I happen to know that the mill is always giving assistance to the city and its department not only for maintenance of streets, etc., the laying of pipe lines, and the giving of assistance to the fire department whenever the city might call upon them and whenever the city shows to them that it is for the best interest of the mill employees and the people of the town, who, incidentally, are the mill employees."

That it becomes a three-way collusion against the public is illustrated by the fact that he signed this letter as District Manager of Federal Laboratories, Inc., and testified that for a year and a half he had run the munitions and detective business out of one office. In New Orleans these two firms openly conduct their offices together, having both names upon the door. This collusion between the munitions and the detective agencies is further established in many instances by interlocking directorates, by similar lists of stockholders, by commissions given to detective agencies for sale of gas and arms. E. E. McGuffin, head of the National Corporation Service, was a taker of these commissions from Erie Chemical Company.

As McCarty so ably pointed out, the munitions firms strive to give the impression that they are performing a service for public law and order. They play up the educational nature of demonstrations whose real purpose is dual: to use up old stocks of gas and create the demand for more, and to play upon the love of excitement that makes a good policeman a good policeman. A most effective way to create the impression that an alliance exists between the munitions company and the military or the police is to hire old officers to be salesmen. The case of Colonel J. J. Johnston who obtained his commission in the U. S. Army is one in point. Two short letters about the Colonel describe neatly a situation of many facets. Mr. Ailes is writing to his President, Colonel Goss, in February of 1936:

"We have moved $3,000.00 or $4,000.00 worth of stuff down to the sheriff's office in care of Colonel Johnston in preparation for immediate delivery should serious trouble break out. . . . Colonel Johnston has been appointed chief assistant to the sheriff without pay, and it does seem that if there is any business to be gotten that we will get it. Trouble is not only brewing at the rubber companies but also at the Columbia Chemical Company, where we have sold a considerable amount of material."

In June, Erie recommended his services to Remington Rand in the following letter:

"Colonel J. J. Johnston of Akron, Ohio, who is now acting as our agent, will be very glad to come down to Marietta with a complete line of our products if you desire him to do so. Colonel Johnston was in charge of the defensive measures of the rubber companies at Akron when they were threatened with a strike sometime back. He was also in charge of the guards at the Ohio insulator plant when they had a riot last summer, and was further employed by Columbia Chemical Company at Barberton, Ohio, when they were threatened with violence. Colonel Johnston is a very experienced man and his advice would be quite valuable to you if it is necessary to adopt means to protect your plant or the plant personnel. . . ."

There are other ties that can be tightened. RCA, harangued and canvassed to death by detectives and munitioneers, received in June of 1936 a letter from Federal Laboratories drawing attention to the fact that this company acted as national sales agent for RCA Police Radio and Gun Detectors and offering "a sensible way of controlling strike disorders without bloodshed. We are prepared to furnish you with the necessary equipment

IS GAS POLITER THAN GUNS? 215

and train your guards in its use." A follow-up letter on the next day stressed the impressive information that "Chief Colsey of the Camden Police Department has suggested that I get in touch with you and he joins in recommending that you purchase and have on hand a reasonable amount of tear gas equipment and that you allow us to train your guards in the use of this equipment, in connection with the Camden Police Department. . . . Trusting that you will allow me to do this [go over equipment with them] while the situation is still in a more or less peaceful state. . . ."

In this letter we fall upon the one single most important fact in the modern trend of industrial munitions from guns to gas; the doctrine that gas is more humanitarian than guns, a doctrine predicated on the theory that one or the other is necessary since the striker is put in the category of criminal, barricaded bandit, or escaped lunatic. From one end of the industrial map to the other, employers listen to this seductive sales talk, putting in an occasional order, to be on the safe side, for a machine or sub-machine gun. The result is such sales as that of the Philadelphia & Reading Coal & Iron Company which bought $17,000 worth, or 7,500 tubes, of gas to be used in closing bootleg coal mines; the one day's purchases by the Frick Coal of Pittsburgh of $1,584; the Jones & Laughlin Steel Corporation, $1,920; the Bethlehem Steel, $1,400; the two purchases by the waterfront employers of San Francisco of $1,531 and an additional $2,659. These figures do not seem large, although even in themselves they give no indication of the size of the garrison accumulated over a period of time. The invoices examined by the Committee show a sale to industry of $1,040,621 worth of gas over a period of about two and a half years. This figure is known to cover only part of the sales. Moreover, one must remember in looking at it that the financial measurement is no indication of the effectiveness of gas in intimidating workers, that the workers are rarely armed except with homemade weapons, and that its greatest virtue as disperser is its unexpectedness.

A work order of the Lake Erie Chemical Company, elucidated on the stand by Mr. Ailes, gives something of a picture of the various devices which have been promoted on the market for the suppression of the strikers, who are usually designated in circulars as rioting mobs. Gas fountain pens, Baby Giant gas projectors, Baby Giant gas shells, watchmen's clubs, watchmen's club shells, gas riot pistols, gas riot pistol shells, hand grenades, Universal CN—meaning tear gas, and DM—meaning nauseating gas, long range field guns, long range shells. These are some of the wares which are promoted by a concern dealing primarily in gas. Federal Laboratories does a similar business, plus a business in guns.

A candle is a gas grenade. A grenade apparently has three ways of disbursing its gas. One is ignited in such a manner that the gas is allowed to go off slowly. One shoots the gas instantaneously without bursting the bomb. The third grenade explodes by a charge of powder inside. Erie's grenade, known as the Green Band, has a container of iron or steel. A circular issued by the Erie Chemical Company says of this grenade, one of its most touted products, "The gas from the Green Band grenade is invisible, making it more effective and terrifying because it is not possible for the rioter to determine where the gas cloud begins or where it ends as in the case of the burning type munitions." In other words, the strikers will be unaided by their sense of sight and will not know what has happened until they begin to inhale the gas. It explodes violently, tears into ribbons which are thrown with considerable force in all directions from the point of burst, with possible severe injury to anyone within a radius of approximately fifteen feet thereof. The instructions which are sent out for the use of this grenade caution the user not to throw it into a crowd unless very severe treatment is necessary, "as the pain from the high concentration of this gas in the eyes, nose and throat is almost unbearable." These gases are admittedly in the experimental stage of development. There is no authoritative diagnosis of their powers of permanent injury. The companies who sell them formulate their sales talk to create one of two different impressions. Those customers who wish to be assured that it is harmless, receive comforting statements as to the mildness of its effect. On other occasions, however, where the customer indicates that he means business, he receives such assurances as this sales circular provides: "When rioters have been subdued with nauseating gas they will not invite another dose until the memory of the last experience becomes very dim indeed. What does K.O. gas do to the victim? (The effect of this gas varies considerably with different individuals and with the amount inhaled.)

1. Violent nausea and vomiting.
2. Sense of suffocation as if several men were sitting on chest.
3. Intense pain in chest and head.
4. Above effects last, if subjected to a good dose, from several hours to a whole day, but without producing permanent injury."

The long range Tru-Flite shell, developed within the last year by Lake Erie Chemical Company, has a range of 500 yards and can be shot accurately 150 yards. "All purchasers of Tru-Flite projectiles are warned that serious injury or death may be caused should the projectile strike any person while in flight. This shell is not suitable for use against mobs if serious injury or death are to be avoided." According to Mr. Ailes, this is designed for one purpose only: to be used against barricaded bandits (whose numbers would not seem to warrant going into large production). Yet in June, 1935, Mr. Ailes heard from his salesman Herrick Foote, a letter optimistically reporting upon the textile workers' demands for an increase in wages: "I hope you have something definite as to the new long range gun as we will be in a bad way if this strike gets under way and we have no long range guns."

Much is made in the testimony as to the humanitarian characteristics of gas as over against bullets and guns. It was established on the stand that both gas and its projecting equipment could produce very serious injury; if not death, under certain circumstances. The salesmen urge upon its users that they never attempt to go into action without gas masks. The *San Francisco Herald Examiner* bought two gas masks for the use of its reporters who were going into the strike areas. No such precaution exists for the strikers and no immediate treatment for its effects is made available.

A still further hazard than the intrinsic one of putting these instruments into the hands of irresponsible men emerges from the record. These men, who so frequently steal property from the employers who hire them, may also steal the munitions and sell them for small prices to anyone who wants them. One firm, troubled by the public opinion which was aroused over the incident of a child's being hurt by a repeater candle which had been thrown into an automobile, could give no other explanation for the fact than that the strikebreakers had been selling stolen goods.

The argument over toxicity goes back and forth, salesman and customer both offering ingenious and consoling rationalizations concerning the use of something which is no good at all if it is not very bad. The Anthracite Institute, who wanted to get the bootleggers out of their mines, found themselves in a hole with the miners. If a gassed man tried to get out of a coal opening so fast that he fell and broke his leg and had to stay inside with a heavy concentration of gas, how would the result be diagnosed?

As about other instruments of warfare, how one feels about the use of gas apparently depends upon how close one has been to battle, either in person or imagination. The guerrilla character of the attack, the fact that but one side is armed with it (labor buys neither gas nor guns), the fact that it is no respecter of nostrils but befouls the air for everyone in the area, even the small fact that its users refuse to go into battle without masks, as they also refuse to go in without being made into officers of the law; these are squeamish considerations of military deportment. Its acceptance as a technique of maintaining employment relations is revelatory of an attitude so profoundly undemocratic and so much more important than the means, that the use of gas must be regarded as not an evil in itself but a symptom. We must consider this true, even after we take into account that it is so new, and we are so ignorant of its long-time effects, that the workers who have experienced this allegedly humane treatment may yet, because of it, become charges on the public and burdens to themselves.

The attitudes toward the distribution of the means of life and the stratification of castes implied in the following tale are apt to make all but the immediate victims feel that these social phenomena in a political democracy are more toxic than the gas itself.

The story is told in two affidavits. The first I shall quote only in part to give the background. They both are dated February 23, 1937.

"Less than a month after the election several hundred farmers of Crawford County were cut-off the WPA and thrown onto the Resettlement where they received on an average of about $20 a month and some families receiving as little as $10 a month to live on. Many of the City WPA workers were also cut-off and the conditions of the farmers and workers were made much worse than they had been, many of their incomes cut to half of what they had been and even less. This was clearly a violation of the peoples mandate to the President and to the Administration when they returned them to office in the recent election.

"For this and for other reasons we were determined to get these workers and farmers together in this mass meeting and there let them decide what action they would take to meet these problems which we faced.

"At this mass meeting on January 11th, held in the Chamber of Commerce rooms in Denison, Iowa, which was attended by several hundred farmers and workers, a grievance committee of 7 members was elected to represent these farmers and workers and was instructed by them to take up their grievances with the proper authorities, namely, the Board of Supervisors, Crawford County Relief Administrator, Ora Malone; Crawford County Director of Relief, Miss Selma Kluss.

"It was further decided by this mass meeting of workers and farmers that if their duly elected grievance committee was not recognized by the Board of Supervisors

IS GAS POLITER THAN GUNS? 221

and Relief authorities that they would remain in the courthouse until their committee was recognized.

"The mass meeting further cautioned all farmers and workers that there was to be no violence whatever on our part and that we were to remain perfectly peaceable even though we were subjected to an attack, or even though violence or violent methods were used against us.

"The grievance committee, of which I was a member, upon securing a hearing with the Board of Supervisors and Relief authorities were told by them that they would not recognize this committee.

"Thereupon the Committee informed the farmers and workers in the Lobby of the courthouse of this decision, and since the Committee was not recognized they could not take up their grievances with the proper authorities.

"The farmers and workers then, in carrying out the decision that they had previously agreed upon, declared a 'sit-down' strike to stay in the courthouse until their duly elected Committee was recognized and the Constitution of the United States was once again re-established in Crawford County.

"This action by the Board of Supervisors and Relief officials was clearly a violation of the Constitutional rights of these people, of that section of the Constitution which guarantees the right of the people to peaceably assemble and petition their government for a redress of grievances."

The second tells the story:

"AFFIDAVIT

"State of Iowa,
Crawford County:

"I, Lillie Johansen, being first duly sworn on oath, state that I was present at the Crawford County courthouse in Denison, Iowa, on January 11, 1937, at the time when a gas bomb was exploded by one Percy Cavett [deputy sheriff of Crawford County].

"I was sitting on a bench on the north side of the relief office door which is located on the West side of the Lobby on the second floor of the courthouse.

"My daughter, Geneive, age 10 yrs., was sitting on the floor right in front of me. I seen Cavett coming up the stairs with bombs in his hands. Lehfeldt, City Marshal, also had a bomb in his hand.

"When the bomb exploded the room filled quickly with gas and smoke. My daughter, Geneive, was choking and crying. I done my best to help her outside. When we got outside we had no coats or hats. I was so weak I could not walk and my husband had to help me through the door.

"My baby, age 20 months, was with his father and both of the children were choking and crying and rubbing their eyes. They were taken to the hospital where their eyes were treated by Miss Kraul, the nurse of the hospital. My baby was sick all night and we called the doctor who said the baby had taken cold from exposure and the effects of the gas. He still has a cough and I believe it is caused from the gas. I was at the courthouse because we had no fuel and nothing to eat.

"Frank North gave us 50 cents and with that I bought bread and I borrowed coffee from Mrs. Kilgore, My Neighbor, as we had a little lard, we ate bread, lard and coffee until Friday at which time we received $4.25 from the Relief office to buy groceries."

VIII. Collective Firing

IT IS a truism that no institution likes to see itself die. Founded for a given purpose at a given time, its purpose may malinger long after its time wears away. But the professional staff, once assembled and delegated by the directors of an institution to do their work for them, settles down upon the situation like a hen upon eggs.

The longevity and insistent busyness of the National Metal Trades Association, a collective labor-bargaining union of manufacturers in metal, may be in part accounted for by the zeal of its staff to hang on to a good thing when they see it. It is not a large staff. Each of the twenty-five branch offices has two or three workers; a general officer, secretary, and employment manager. At their head is a commissioner who has been with the association for thirty years and who makes a secure living, as do his subordinates, in the role of professional labor advisor to employers. This commissioner is not sought out in times of stress as is a lawyer in a blackmail case, or a doctor called in for broken ribs. He is permanently retained by manufacturers susceptible to his doctrines who, in conference with him, renew their faith in them. Therefore he and his subordinates throw their hearts and brains into perpetuating an association whose only financial margin goes into salaries and which, without doubt, many of its members hang onto unquestioningly only from force of habit. The constitution which it adopted in 1909 is long outworn. The world, the law, and the Supreme Court have overtaken it. But its adherents cling to their orthodoxy with the faith of a congregation which has been carefully and prudently led clear of the attractions set for the sinful in a godless world.

This faith of the National Metal Trades Association is that of the Open Shop, and it has held unremittingly to it in and out of prosperity, in strike and in lockout, since 1901 when there broke down an agreement with the union entered into two years before by some forty metal trades manufacturers. In the thirty-six years intervening between their taking the vow and Commissioner Homer Sayre's testimony before the Senate Committee early in 1937, the association had achieved a membership of 952 employers within a single industry, and that membership was concentrated in the most heavily industrialized territory of the United States. It has no members west of the Mississippi and none south of the Mason and Dixon line. The infidels in scattered parts it leaves to other open-shop associations or to the voluntary teaching of its members who have plants in those outlying territories.

It is frivolous, of course, to ascribe to the machinations of the hired help, the instigation or resolute continuance of such an engine of labor control as is revealed in the workings of the National Metal Trades. I mean to say merely, as Senator Thomas clearly brought forth in his questioning, that these machinations cannot be overlooked, as they should not be overlooked, in any affair of state. The housemaid sometimes gives a closer twist to history than does a conjunction of imponderable forces. Yet the robustness of the Association cannot be dismissed in such easy terms. Nothing about it can be easily dismissed. That is why I devote a special chapter to this one subpoenaed non-profit agency whose methods of hooking, spying, bribery, employment, and payment of hirelings differs slightly, if at all, from those of professional companies in the business for profit. Its significance lies in its different purpose, management, and means of enforcing its policies. Perhaps the most important triumph of the inquiry, not even excepting the Harlan County hearings, the investigation into the National Metal Trades Association yielded up data on economical and efficient methods of coercion which are bound to appear long after the professional agencies have made their separate exits. Since it is a non-profit organization without dependence upon customer good-will, exposure can do little to extinguish its activities, nor is it likely that any legislation devised to hamper the operations of the professional agencies will stand in the way of its future smooth performance. The National Metal Trades Association has much to teach the groping employer who may feel elderly and helpless as he tries to cross the street without the aid of those who have in the past tenderly given him an arm.

In itself nothing more nor less than an employers' closed shop, it has the sole purpose of presenting to the workers in the metal manufacturing trades an unbroken front and of maintaining an unbeatable means of defending this front against breakage. Its theory is simple; all members pool their pay-roll strength against any man who attempts to combine with others against an employer. Since pooled pay-roll strength is not only pooled money to an amount that would make combined union dues look like sparrows' tears, but a totalitarian grip upon the labor market amounting to control of all jobs in the industry, that worker is brave, foolish, or drunk who would attempt to beat the game thus fixed for the house.

If the theory is elementary, the device employed to tap this latent police power cheaply and quickly is as simple as a spoon. The industry assesses itself for insurance payments on each eligible worker whom it employs, and tosses the assessments into a strikebreaking kitty. Although, according to the Constitution, those eligible to membership shall be "persons, firms, or corporations engaged as principals owning or controlling manufacturing plants, operating principally in the metal trades, or in trades employing metal workers as hereinafter classified," the corporation or owner must join for each of its plants in the jurisdiction of the association. Thus the corporation joins as employer rather than as owning principal, and the number of owners is much smaller than the figure conveyed by the length of the list of members. A given corporation may operate fifteen plants, only seven of which are in the territory serviced by the association and, of these seven, two may be foundries and for this reason ineligible to join. Thus it could take out only five memberships, each in the name of a manufacturing plant. The narrowing control by line of authority within and the fan-wise spread of control by indoctrination without are easy to see.

Each employer-member pays into the kitty twenty cents a month for every operative or eligible worker he employs; that is, providing his assessment never falls lower than ten dollars a quarter. Also he may not be assessed on more than 6,250 operatives quarterly. If he fails to report quarterly on the average of the maximum number of operatives he employed in each month of the quarter preceding, he will be assessed according to his last report plus a ten percent penalty, a penalty which will go up by another ten percent for each omission of the quarterly report. These pooled dues, plus the fifty-dollar initiation fee for every member, are divided into a general and a defense fund, the defense fund pre-empting, in fact, all but current salary and office expenses. In November of 1936 its defense fund, or war chest, amounted to $214,-928. Not an overpowering sum in itself, it induces the same sobering reflection as does a detachment of National Guard, the thought of how much power lies behind it.

It is this help which is rushed to the aid of the boy with his finger in the dike wherever the sea may look angry: Rushed with this proviso; that the boy hold his finger in the prescribed way. The Constitution is very explicit as to this: "In the conduct of labor disputes, members must proceed in the manner which the Constitution and By-laws prescribe, failing in which they shall forfeit all right to the financial or moral support of the Association, except as special relief measures may be authorized by the Administrative council. . . . Should the Commissioner and a member disagree as to the measure or method of relief to be afforded during a strike or lockout, such member may appeal to the administrative council and its decision shall be final."

Elsewhere the association is more lenient with its members. In its Declaration of Principles it announces to employees that "we will not admit of any interference with the management of our business . . . the employees will be paid by the hourly rate, by the premium system, piece work, contract or other system, as the employer may elect; . . . it is the privilege of the employee to leave our employ whenever he sees fit, and it is the privilege of the employer to discharge any workman when he sees fit." But following these announcements, it leaves this eye in the needle for the member to crawl through. "In case of disagreement . . . not affecting the economic integrity of the industry, we advise our members to meet such of their employees who may be affected by such disagreement and endeavor to adjust the difficulty on a fair and equitable basis."

If a man goes soft, and settles a strike independently

of the administrative council working through their commissioner (this administrative council has upon it K. T. Keller, president of the Dodge Corporation, and some eleven others of equal importance), he must take his punishment. There is nothing unfair about the penalty. Presumably he read its constitution before he joined his union: He knew what was coming to him. He has to repay the association all the money they have spent on his strike. He has to forfeit his past dues, and he is apt in the bargain to be suspended or expelled. These are the sanctions which the association can hold over their members in the maintaining of their uniform policy.

If, however, he plays along, using the tactical procedure advised by the Commissioner, his strike expenses are paid and the strike is broken for him by the token of his membership in the convenient and worry-saving organization, in itself a flying squadron of employers, similar in concept to the flying squadron of the Goodyear Rubber Company but superior far in force, since the Rubber Flying Squadron is merely composed of loyal employees skilled in versatility, to be thrown into any trouble-stricken department as scabs. The "affected member" notifies the commissioner, or the secretary of his local branch, of his trouble and keeps them advised of any changes in his situation. This forthcoming aid, that for which he paid his dues, is described by Commissioner Sayre: "According to our constitution, if a member should have a strike and the administrative council approved the combating of the strike, the association would furnish him up to 70 percent of the total number of men that were reported for assessment purposes: for example, if a man reported 100 men, under that plan he would be entitled to be furnished 70 men."

SENATOR LA FOLLETTE: You would furnish him 70 men to replace the services of those who were on strike at the time?
MR. SAYRE: If it was authorized; yes.
SENATOR LA FOLLETTE: Do you furnish guards?
MR. SAYRE: Simply for the protection of the property and the men.

That there is more than automatic lip service behind this arrangement and that the members feel a responsibility toward each other in times of distress was shown when the Lindemann and Hoverson Company of Milwaukee regrettably found itself unable to make use of the association's customary ministrations because of a Wisconsin statute which reads:

"Any person who, for himself or as agent or officer of any firm, joint-stock company, or corporation, shall use or employ or aid or assist in employing any body of armed men to act as militiamen, policemen, or peace officers for the protection of persons or property or for the suppression of strikes, whether such armed men be employees of detective agencies, so-called, or otherwise, they not being authorized by the law of this State to act in such capacity, shall be punished by a fine not exceeding $1,000 or by imprisonment in the State prison not less than 1 year nor more than 3 years, or by both such fine and imprisonment."

The executive committee in regular and special session discussed this quandary, finally resolving it by a simple gesture of condolence. They sent the company three thousand dollars to spend as they thought fit.

True to precedent set by the other agencies, the National Metal Trades Association opened their revelations with a lifting fog of aspiration. Senator Thomas was splendidly responsive to their mood. As former professor, he slipped back in spirit to the class room where he met, as if they were his colleagues, Commissioner Sayre and his singularly unprofessorial assistants, Abbot and Stringham. The association, as Mr. Sayre pointed out, was interested in safety, harmony, and education. But in contradistinction to the claims of other agencies, more particularly to those of Corporation Auxiliary, the National Metal Trades Association had really dabbled rather importantly in educational work. It had, he said, collaborated with the University of Cincinnati in the first cooperative course of engineering ever given in the United States, whereby a boy goes to school a certain number of weeks and works in the member plants a certain number of weeks. "Our primary interest," said Mr. Sayre, "in all of these things is to try and get the employer and employee to believe that their interests are mutual. Now, we have also done a great deal of work in apprenticeship throughout the country. In addition to that, a number of years ago our organization recognized that a bad foreman in a plant could do a great deal of damage, I mean by partiality, and things of that kind. The foreman should understand the problems of the men and management. We developed quite a course on foremanship training, which is being used quite extensively in our member plants. You might be interested in this thought: After this course was developed—and I believe your men have copies of it—the problem, of course, was how to teach it. Naturally, we could not have a man going around to each plant, so we had our department go into a town and ask the plant to send one or two of the most capable foremen, and then we instructed him how to become a leader in his plant, and he goes back and teaches that course in his plant. There you have a man that is familiar with the personnel and the conditions surrounding the doing of that particular job, and we think it is very effective."

SENATOR THOMAS: Effective in what sense, primarily?
MR. SAYRE: Effective in establishing co-operation between employer and employee. That is our primary interest.

Mr. Sayre mentioned, but never fully defined, various departments—that of "industrial relations, sanitation and so forth." Espionage is developed in the employment department. Here again the mutual-benefit association manifests its superiority over the professional detective agency, for according to the commissioner, through the medium of its central employment agency, able at any time to produce a worker of given qualifications, it needed to do no hooking. In his words: "I mean we have the men. We do not go out and buy information. We just have men that go into a plant and are asked to report on conditions as they find them in the plant." The plants, billed through the association, pay for the men. The reports are relayed to the member through the association. Here again its non-profit character is claimed to be an advantage to the member for reports are not built up in order to get more business.

How Mr. Sayre's contentions hold up we shall see from further depositions, for when the prelude is over and the birds have sung and the romance of brotherly love has been set forth in its ancient beauty, we get down to the old story; the old story with a sharper, more final ending. The spies and the strikebreakers are there, marshaled with the finesse which thirty-seven years of practice within one organization can give to its officers. And in addition to these sometimes inconclusive weapons, the workers contest, although proof of their contention is not a matter of record, that the National Metal Trades Association holds over the worker the longest, most complete blacklist probably ever assembled in this country since it is alleged to be composed like a round robin by an overwhelming majority of an entire industry. The unions claim that during periods of prosperity, when employers are putting up a cry as they do now for more skilled workers, some of the most highly skilled men in American industry are wandering jobless and are supported by public relief, having been made into industrial vagrants by the means of the blacklist.

Certainly it is a highly skilled worker against whom strike insurance is taken out. The operative against whose favorable views on collective bargaining the employers have collectively insured themselves is defined in the constitution of the Metal Trades as a "machinist, pipefitter, millwright, blacksmith, boilermaker, patternmaker [patternmakers are craftsmen with years of training behind them; their numbers are said to determine the rate of speed at which production goods can be made, and therefore the rate of expansion in recovery], carpenter, structural ironworker, polisher and buffer, brassworker, ironship builder, sheet-iron worker, electrical worker, coppersmith, machine operator, and helpers and apprentices to any of the above. Workmen in any kindred trades may likewise be so designated, at the discretion of the Administrative Council."

Piecemeal data was the best that could be obtained about blacklisting, much of which seems to be done by telephone in the routine of calling up the last place of employment. There are some letters like this addressed to Mr. Blatchford by the American Metal Ware Co., dated May 21, 1934:

COLLECTIVE FIRING

"DEAR SIR: Per recent conversation, we submit below, list of names of men who were not taken back into our employ:

"Tinners: Joe Anderson, 3060 N. Avers Avenue, Chicago, Ill.; John Birdie, 2970 N. Ridgeway Avenue, Chicago, Ill.; Lester Loeffler, 614 N. Latrobe Avenue, Chicago, Ill.

"In addition to the above, wish to submit also the following name; this person was involved in the difficulty in our factory, but we had cut him off some time previous to the general walk-out, but he was active in agitation and it might be well for you to have his name on your files, which is, John Stec, 953 Winchester Avenue, Chicago, Ill.

"Trusting the above answers your requirements and assuring you that a copy of this communication is being sent on to Mr. Abbott as per your request, remain

"Yours truly,
"AMERICAN METAL WARE COMPANY
(signed) P. J. DAUBLE."

Provocative testimony concerning the blacklist was found in the responses of E. C. Davison, mayor of Alexandria, Virginia, at the time he testified, and general secretary-treasurer of the International Association of Machinists which has 130,000 members. Mr. Davison has been active in the organized labor movement for forty years. Senator La Follette inquired: "Has the International Association of Machinists had any experience of blacklisting by the National Metal Trades Association?"

MR. DAVISON: Yes, sir.
SENATOR LA FOLLETTE: State it.
MR. DAVISON: We have numbers of members of our association who find it necessary, because of this blacklist,

to change their names in order that they may secure employment. Their records are furnished by these employers to such an extent that men have been forced to travel all over the country, have become tramps, as the result of that blacklist.

"Some years ago we found a way by which that has been offset to some extent by permitting these men to change their names and keeping a dummy record of them in our headquarters. Of course, we keep a record of their original names. In addition to that, we at one time operated a shop in the city of Norfolk known as the Hampton Roads Ship Repair Corporation and we furnished the men a reference under the Hampton Roads Ship Repair Corporation. That reference would break the reference that the National Metal Trades Association would be furnishing to their members under another name, and when they would go to seek employment their references were carried through by the Hampton Roads Ship Repair Corporation.

I myself was a victim of that blacklist in 1901. That is how I started in the labor movement.

SENATOR LA FOLLETTE: Relate that experience, briefly.

MR. DAVISON: After a strike had broken out in the city of Richmond in 1901, which was the original Metal Trades strike, no doubt, among other names my name was sent to the National Metal Trades Association and I became blacklisted and could not get employment even in my own home city, or in my State. Every place I would go men whom I had worked with before that, who had later become foremen and master mechanics, told me frankly they would be very glad to give me employment, I was a good mechanic, but they could not do it because my name had appeared on this list. I finally drifted into Newport News, Va., went to the New-

COLLECTIVE FIRING

port News Shipbuilding & Drydock Co., changed my name to Hutchinson and worked under that name. I think the men who employed me knew what my real name was, they had worked with me before, but they shielded me to that extent. The moment my real name was known—there was some kind of system going on that I did not understand—of course, I would become discharged, the foreman was notified to lay me off. I would promptly go the next day to another department of the shop under another name and I would work there 2 or 3 weeks until I was found out. Other men were having the same experiences.

After leaving Newport News, I went to the western part of the State and later became a general foreman in a shop in Danville, Va., and as general foreman I became interested in the general manager and he supplied me with one of the lists that were circulated of men who had been employed and who had taken part in the 1901 strike, and my name was on that list. In other words, I was supposed to blacklist myself although I was general foreman at that time.

I later became foreman of another establishment and a list was shown to me; it was not given to me but it was shown to me, and any men who had that name could not be employed. That is how I learned first what a blacklist was.

Then I found later on, traveling in Cincinnati, which at that time was the headquarters of the National Metal Trades Association, that all men who sought employment in the machinist trade had to be certified by the National Metal Trades employment office. They kept a card record and file, and when that file was turned over to the employer that signified the man was not to be employed. Why, the men just did not get employment until large numbers of machinists throughout this entire country became tramps as the result of that blacklist, up until almost the beginning of the war. When the war started machinists were needed so badly that the blacklist proposition broke down. I understand, of course, that it has been reopened since. I have not received copies of it since then, but we have instances that have come into our office where we have a number of men who are members of the grand lodge, who are foremen and who are other executives—the companies at times will tell us about these things; their membership is kept confidential in our files—we have numbers of men whose names are kept in our files that the local lodges know nothing whatever of, in the communities in which they are working, in order to preserve and save these men from being discharged because of their affiliation with the union. We have quite a file of them.

SENATOR LA FOLLETTE: Is it your experience that this blacklist is maintained through information furnished by undercover operatives of the association or detective agency?

MR. DAVISON: To a large extent, but I think through the employers as well. The employers who have a strike in their plant pass on information furnished by these spies and designate the men as agitators and as interested in unions, and in order to keep that class of men out of employment in any of these establishments I think that list is partially furnished by the employer, based on information furnished by these spies."

Since spying methods of the association so closely resemble those of the professional agencies, it may be superfluous to describe them. In contradiction of Mr. Sayre's statement that it needs to do no hooking, one of the grossest examples brought forth in the course of the inquiry occurs in the record on National Metal Trades, although it may be said in its extenuation that the applicant was naïve as to what was meant by the phrase "investigating experience" in the advertisement he answered. After hearing the deposition read aloud, the commissioner said, "This is the first time I knew that there is any misrepresentation, and as far as the National Metal Trades Association is concerned, it will not tolerate any employee making any misrepresentation with respect to the work of this association."

Carl Eckhardt, being duly sworn, deposes and says in part:

"In and about the second week of January, 1936, I noticed an advertisement in the *New York American*, a paper published daily in the city of New York, asking for an experienced machinist with investigating experience. I answered this advertisement with a letter addressed to post office box 248, 110 East Forty-fifth Street, New York City.

"On or about August 6, 1936, I received a letter signed by Joseph Holman, asking me to call at room 2609, 70 East Fifth Street, New York, N. Y.

"I went down to the office and saw the signer of the letter, a Mr. Holman. He represented himself as Captain Holman, an officer of the United States Government. The name on the door of the office was National Metal Trades Association and the name of L. A. Stringham also appeared on the door. Captain Holman stated to me that their office was a branch of the United States Government investigating sabotage in industrial plants where Government contracts were being fulfilled. He offered me a job in one of the plants in which I was to watch out for the sabotage and make daily reports on any suspects. Holman stated I would get $250 a month. To prove that he represented the Government, Captain Holman pulled out what appeared to be an official credential from the United States Government. Captain Holman stated I was to quit my present job. I was then working as an assistant superintendent for the Esemco Co. at the Bush Terminal, Brooklyn, N. Y., making $48 a week."

Mr. Eckhardt continued at some length as to the usual agency concealments from the tyro, and as to the true nature of his task.

"I then went over to the Boston office of the National Metal Trades Association and saw the manager, by the name of G. H. Wilson. Mr. Wilson gave me instructions as to what my duties would be. He evidently did not consult with the New York office because he told me that I was to join the local union of the International Association of Machinists and try to become an officer of the union. He told me I was to get to know about the union's activities and report back to him. He stated frankly that the Association wanted to keep the union out of the Boston Gear Co.

"It was then that I learned for the first time that the National Metal Trades Association was nothing but a spy agency used for the purpose of interfering and breaking up unions. I said nothing to Mr. Wilson but I immediately returned to my home in New York City.

"I subsequently went up to the New York office of the National Metal Trades Association to ask them to reimburse me for the time I had spent in Hartford and in Boston. They refused to give me any compensation and have continued to refuse to do so. I received several communications from Mr. Holman asking me to come down to the office. When I did not come down he started visiting my home. I told him that I would not do any spying and refused to have anything to do with any association which did spy work in unions. He then became very unpleasant and warned me not to say anything about what had transpired between the association and myself. He threatened me and told me that if I did not keep secret what had happened I had better watch out.

"He called several times when I was not at home and spoke to my wife and also warned her. Attached hereunto and marked 'Exhibit 9' is an original note which Mr. Holman left at my home asking me to get in touch with him.

"Because of these constant threats and intimidations, I wrote to Senator La Follette in Washington, D. C., on or about October 6, 1936. As a result of an interview with the agents of Senator La Follette's Committee, I am making this affidavit.

"(signed) CARL ECKHARDT."

Four days later, Joseph Holman, known to the New York office of the Metal Trades Association where he was employed as Holub, appeared at the witness stand to deny the story and to write his signature, which he did with visible fright, for comparison with the handwritten note accompanying the submitted affidavit. The compared signatures were photostated and appear in the printed hearings for handwriting experts to ponder over. To a layman they are strikingly similar.

The association employs spies in two different capacities. Special contract operatives do undercover work within a member plant. General operatives go into a community for a member and investigate local public attitude toward labor organization. One hundred and four known special contract operatives were rotated among seventy-nine firms by the association from March, 1933, to July, 1936. The majority of them received $200 and $175 a month, less shop wages. The member was billed anywhere from $25 to $50 a month more than the spy received, the margin being more often $50 than $25. One of these operatives still, so far as the record shows, at work in the same place, has been employed in the Delco Remy Company, a subsidiary of General Motors in Anderson, Indiana, since March 3, 1933, at a cost to the association of $200 a month, less shop earnings, and a cost to Delco Remy of $250, less shop earnings. At one time during his service this spy became a member of the Communist party, in line with the well-nigh universal practice of confusing, intentionally or otherwise, the worker, the firm, and the public as to the identity of the organizing problem involved.

The run of the mine report from a spy for Metal Trades has no more and no less dirt for the check weighman than that of the spy working for any other agency. Canvassing proceeds along the same lines. The operative is up to the same old tricks. Here is spy Frank Shults signing himself as D. G., doing the double motion of scratching his head to sharpen his wits and rubbing his belly in self-satisfaction. We first find him in Erie, Pennsylvania, writing his friend and boss, Bert Stringham. He has not yet settled down to work and there is something footloose and adventurous about his mood that betokens the knight of the road.

"DEAR BERT: This is not a report but more in the nature of a personal letter. Want to thank you for the cooperation in re the car. Car came through to Erie fine, Buick 29, master six, some job, and you ought to be in it when it takes the hills. Its a coupe, and with all that power it sure rambles. Now just a few words about Erie; your friends here are very quiet, not a thing at the union labor hall last night. Not even the janitor. Night before carpenters met. Met Mr. D. E. J. and learned his wants. Business here very bad and laying off a lot of men. Standard Stoker is about the only ones who are doing anything. Trouble in Girard. All settled up about 0.06-cent raise.

"Nothing else of importance, so will close. In case I receive no instructions from you will send weekly statement to you tonight.

"Respectfully,
"FRANK SHULTS
1134 West Ninth Street
Erie, Pa."

By November he has himself in hand. His membership in Local 101 of the International Association of Machinists has been accepted and signed by national secretary-treasurer Davison. Let us read his letter in part only; true to its genus, it is long. He reports a meeting of Local 101:

"Suggested that a committee of three out of work members be appointed to act as an organizing committee and look up several men who had paid in sums of 25 cents to $2.00 on application and had not been heard from since this committee was to go out and look these men up and also try to see other machinists and get them to join the union and to pay their own expenses and serve without pay.

"This was called absurd by Shults, who said that if those who were working were not interested enough in trying to better their conditions to do this work it was absurd to think that out of work members were going to spend time and money trying to organize, this and the fact that the Grand Lodge was thinking the matter over of giving Erie some help on organizing work, some of the other members then spoke along the same lines and criticized the Grand Lodge for not getting on the job and the matter was allowed to drop, no action taken."

By December he is really in his stride, opposing union plans on a practically circular front.

"Erie, Dec. 1st, 1933.
"Machinist meeting at C. L. U. Hall, Friday evening, December 1st, 1933.

"Federal local organizer, Winter, had requested some of the members to let him come in and explain his pet scheme of taking all machinist into the Federal local then telling them that they must join the machinist union, the member who proposed his coming in stated that Winters advised that his organizing of the Glacker Mfg. Co. was being held up because the machinist at this plant refused to pay in $5 to join the machinists' union while it only cost the rest $2 to join the Federal local, and unless he could take the machinist in at $2 he (Winters) couldn't organize the plant. Several members seemed to think it was all right, but after some discussion a member (Shults) took the floor and objected to allowing the man to enter, told them his scheme was unconstitutional and that he knew it, that the member of this machinist local ought to know it if they read the constitution and that any man who wanted to join a trade and didn't think it was worth $5 to belong probably wouldn't amount to much as a member, and would probably expect the local to help him get a raise the first week he belonged, that the thing to do was to settle it once and for all, tell Mr. Winters that machinist must join the machinist local or else they couldn't join anything in Erie, this action was taken and Winters was denied the floor."

James Matles, Grand Lodge Representative for the International Machinists for New York, New Jersey, Philadelphia, and Connecticut—in whose territory twelve large and other small manufacturers, among them Otis Elevator, Worthington Pump, and Yale and Towne, employed undercover men supplied them by Metal Trades—described the spying activities of one John Cole. Cole appeared in Hartford, Connecticut, on a picket line of employees locked out from the Pratt and Whitney Aircraft.

SENATOR LA FOLLETTE: What was the occasion of the lock-out?

MR. MATLES: The vice president of the Aircraft Lodge of the union and four union members were discharged. A committee recommended their reinstatement. Unable to secure their reinstatement they ordered the union membership, the employees of the plant, to stop and remain at their machines as a protest. They were making an effort to reinstate the officers and members of the association. When they appeared at the office of the company the company declared the entire plant fired, all the employees fired, and instructed the foremen to tell them to leave the plant. The employees obeyed that order to leave the plant, considering themselves fired. Considering that situation a lock-out, naturally, they put up a picket line to prevent strikebreakers from going in, in an effort to settle this dispute.

SENATOR LA FOLLETTE: About what time did this occur?

MR. MATLES: This occurred sometime in September of 1935.

SENATOR LA FOLLETTE: Proceed.

MR. MATLES: John Cole applied for membership in the organization while on the picket line. He stated that he was hired in that plant one day before that lock-out, and since he was one of the boys he walked out together with the boys, that he intended to be a good union member and join the association. No one in the department where he claimed he worked for 1 day recollected or saw him in that department. It is our conviction that he appeared after the lock-out took place, when he appeared on that picket line, and did not see the plant before the lock-out. He became very active on the picket line during that lock-out.

SENATOR LA FOLLETTE: Was he taken in as a member of the union?

MR. MATLES: He filled out an application and was taken in as a member of the union, because there was quite a bit of confusion, there was nothing on hand that could be pinned on him, and there do occur instances where a man is hired the day before a lock-out and wants to join the labor organization. It is nothing unusual, and for this reason he was admitted to membership.

SENATOR LA FOLLETTE: Did he hold then a union card at the time he was active on the picket line?

MR. MATLES: Several days after that he was issued a union card.

SENATOR LA FOLLETTE: Did his activity on the picket line have anything to do with his getting the membership?

MR. MATLES: That convinced a large number of strikers that he was an active union man and might be of help to them.

SENATOR LA FOLLETTE: What did he do on the picket line?

COLLECTIVE FIRING

MR. MATLES: He was involved in the picket line himself, carrying signs on the picket line, participating from early in the morning until late in the evening, attended all meetings, made himself active on all committees, relief committees and order committees that are attached to any lock-out or strike.

SENATOR LA FOLLETTE: Did you attend any of the meetings of the local of which he was then a member?

MR. MATLES: I attended the meetings after that lock-out. I was not in Hartford during the lock-out itself since it lasted only a few days. I attended meetings at which John Cole was present. At all meetings he took an active part in the discussions of the meetings.

SENATOR LA FOLLETTE: Did you observe anything about his activities as a member of the union in these meetings?

MR. MATLES: We became very suspicious because of the fact that he pushed himself too much to the front, trying to get himself elected as an officer of the organization. The employees began suspecting him and began staying away from the meetings. It was common talk that there was something wrong with John Cole, and that resulted in a drop of attendance in meetings from 300 to 400 down to a dozen, which meetings I have attended personally, and when it dwindled down to a dozen, John Cole was still one of the loyal union members attending all the meetings.

SENATOR LA FOLLETTE: In your judgment what effect did the activity of Mr. Cole have upon the union?

MR. MATLES: None of the officers of our union were recalled to work, 18 of the officers were all fired, blacklisted in Hartford. Some of the rank and file members were called back to work. As soon as they would return after a meeting, a foreman by the name of Rice in that department would go over to our members and tell them everything that happened at the meeting, and they should keep their mouths shut and stay away from meetings, or they would be fired. This resulted in intimidation, and that was the reason the employees stayed away from meetings.

It reached the point that when I came to attend the meeting of the lodge I saw no important business taken up at the meeting of the lodge, and then the meeting was officially closed. I saw groups of members remaining in the hall and they asked me to remain and stay for a while, and after John Cole would leave they would convene another meeting. That was the official meeting, without John Cole, in order to take up the business of that meeting. Everything would go blank while John Cole was around there. That was in the later months of his membership in the organization.

SENATOR LA FOLLETTE: Was anything ever done about Cole's membership in the union, in view of all this discussion?

MR. MATLES: I might say, Senator, regarding these operatives that you have supplied here on that list that the National Metal Trades Association has supplied, most of these men have been under suspicion, but we have found it difficult to expel a member before we had conclusive proof. It happens that the men are influential people that the Metal Trades Association sends into our association. They have good personalities, they happen to get in good with the boys, they secure the confidence of a portion of the membership, and you are running the risk, when you haven't got conclusive evidence that they are spies and rats, that if you throw them out a portion of your membership will support them and create dissension in the organization, and it is for this reason that we have to be extremely cautious before we are in the position to eliminate or expel anyone on the suspicion of being a stoolpigeon.

SENATOR LA FOLLETTE: Anything else about John Cole that you have would be of assistance in this investigation.

MR. MATLES: John Cole was getting a small salary and was keeping an apartment there for $40 a month in Hartford, and generally lived well. He took time off from work many times and did not put in a full week's work. He intended to run for office in the lodge elections, where I was present to install the officers, and since he was suspected already at that time, and there happened to be a vacancy in the office of sergeant at arms, the president thought it advisable to appoint him temporarily as sergeant at arms in order to keep him from being nominated for an important office, such as secretary or president. It worked out well. He accepted the sergeant at arms job, although he was not satisfied, and that permitted us to elect a slate of officers without John Cole in an important post.

Two days after that the president, Raymond Dunn, was fired by the company. That was the second president of that lodge was fired. The man who was president during the lock-out was also blacklisted. He is one of the best grinder hands that I ever came across. This man is now driving a bakery wagon because he is blacklisted and cannot get a job as a machinist. His name is Axel Benson.

There is a cry of shortage of skilled mechanics in Hartford. I think if the Metal Trade Association would let us put in every man that they have blacklisted, every skilled machinist that they have blacklisted, that they would have 10 machinists for every opening in their plants.

About the life and works of other association spies, Mr. Matles is equally specific. He then generalizes:

"I might say on the whole that from my observation of these stoolpigeons, the Metal Trades Association is having difficulty in finding real mechanics to do stoolpigeon work for them. In most cases these men do not know their job and cannot put in a day's work, while good men and good machinists are being kept out and blacklisted in these communities. Today you will find these machinists that are blacklisted have taken jobs as janitors, half-shot salesmen, and other occupations that they were driven to, without being able to work at this trade because of the fact they are blacklisted."

In the matter of strike-prevention, Commissioner Sayre, like President Smith of Corporation Auxiliary, has met professional disappointment. Sayre says: "We believe that the greatest amount of good that we can do for our members is the prevention of labor difficulties rather than the combating of them after they occur."

SENATOR THOMAS: Then you would be a bit out of harmony with a certain witness that we had here who, when he heard of a strike, prayed that it was going to be a very bad strike, the bigger the better.

MR. SAYRE: Well, there is no doubt about that in my mind.

SENATOR THOMAS: You like peace?

MR. SAYRE: I think there is nothing worse than a strike. I think it is a terrible thing. I think it is a terrible thing both from the point of view of employer and employee. I have seen thousands of men that have been called out on strike for no reason at all, and their families have suffered, they have lost wages, and any concession that they might get, regardless of that, it might take them years to make it up. I think that the worst thing that can possibly happen is labor difficulties.

SENATOR THOMAS: Have you made any statistical study at all of the result of strikes in general, whether they have actually been economically paying propositions?

MR. SAYRE: Paying propositions?

SENATOR THOMAS: Yes.

MR. SAYRE: I cannot conceive of any strike being a paying proposition.

SENATOR THOMAS: Well, if it brings about an increase in pay for the employee he may look at it as being a paying proposition in that way.

MR. SAYRE: Well, probably, but as a rule a man goes out on strike and he loses more, in the amount of time that he is out on strike, than he gets back in increased pay.

Feeling as strongly as he does about strikes, it is but logical that he should aid employers to break them as quickly as possible, both for their own and their employees' good. It seems as gratuitous to examine the strikebreaking service furnished by the commissioner as part of his professional duties as it did to examine his variety of espionage. Down to the last detail of recruiting, deputizing, getting into the plant, and inciting violence, it exactly duplicates the guard service offered by professional agencies. The manner of financing operatives is the only difference, transportation, subsistence and wages of finks and nobles being paid out of the strikebreaking kitty.

Lawrence Pfohman, Metal Trades' contribution to the

Addressograph Multigraph Company of Cleveland during their strike in May, 1935, had, on the occasion of his being sentenced to Joliet Penitentiary for robbery in 1924, attempted to kill his judge. Thenceforward his offenses had been confined to playing con games and passing bogus checks. The president and general manager of the Addressograph sent thanks to the commissioner for aid in behalf of his Board of Directors.

"We feel that our 'investment' in National Metal Trades Association is a real asset, both in normal times and during periods of labor strike. I want to thank you particularly for the force of guards, who protected Company property during the recent trouble. I have never had contact with a more capable, intelligent and efficient group of that kind.

"With kindest regards and best wishes, I am

Yours sincerely,"

Sixteen of the forty-three guards arrested for inciting violence at the Black & Decker strike in Kent, Ohio, had police records, obtained from the Federal Bureau of Investigation. They were charged with offenses ranging from rape and abandonment of a legitimate child, to robbery and shooting with intent to wound. Charles A. Gadd, machinist and union business agent who was on the spot, describes the activities by which the association was laboring the reconcilement of worker and employer in Kent.

SENATOR LA FOLLETTE: When did the picket line form at the Black & Decker plant?

MR. GADD: About May 2.

SENATOR LA FOLLETTE: Was there any violence at the plant prior to that which took place on June 18?

MR. GADD: Some time before that there were four automobiles and a truck came up to the gate. There were 18 or 20 men got out of the truck and tried to open the gate. The gate was locked and they were unsuccessful. Of course, there was some opposition from the pickets on the picket line. They got in the cars and left there. The leader of them said they would be back in about 10 minutes and if they did not let them in then they were going to shoot hell out of them. They had guns drawn at the time they were there.

SENATOR LA FOLLETTE: At the time they made this threat?

MR. GADD: Yes, sir.

SENATOR LA FOLLETTE: What happened next?

MR. GADD: Well, they left there and about a week before June 18 the sheriff of Portage County, Sheriff Burr, came up there and he said he had some deputies he was going to put in the plant for guards, and some of the pickets recognized some of them as the ones that were trying to break in the gate there before, and they told Mr. Burr that he better get them out of there because they were not residents of Portage County, they did not want any thugs in there, that they could watch outside of the plant all right. They asked him why he did not get people from Portage County as deputies. So he left with the ones he had with him.

SENATOR LA FOLLETTE: Please describe what took place on the picket line on the morning of June 18 before the violence took place.

MR. GADD: There were three people on the picket line, and two trucks drove up there, they smashed right through the gate, and a bunch of them jumped out of the back end of the truck.

SENATOR LA FOLLETTE: Were there any other pickets there besides the three you mentioned?

MR. GADD: There were only three on the picket line. Others were away from the plant.

SENATOR LA FOLLETTE: How many?

MR. GADD: I suppose about 12 or 15, but they were far away from the entrance of the plant.

SENATOR LA FOLLETTE: Why were they back away from the plant?

MR. GADD: There was an injunction against the pickets which said they could only have three at each gate. There were two gates.

SENATOR LA FOLLETTE: Did it limit the territory where the other men could approach the plant?

MR. GADD: I believe it called for 1,000 feet from the entrance.

SENATOR LA FOLLETTE: State the circumstances that led to the violence.

MR. GADD: Two trucks drove up there at 6 o'clock in the morning and crashed through the gate, men jumped out of them with sawed-off shotguns and tear-gas guns.

SENATOR LA FOLLETTE: Approximately how many men were in the trucks? Do you remember?

MR. GADD: Well, there were forty-some. I was under the impression there were 49 of them altogether. They started shooting tear gas and shooting with the shotguns. They had some of the pickets that were suffering from gas taken to the hospital. One picket was shot in the right leg, gassed, and some of the other pickets were slightly wounded. One, by the name of Gray, was shot in the face with some buckshot, and then they proceeded to go down into the plant.

SENATOR LA FOLLETTE: Were any women hurt?

MR. GADD: Yes, sir. There was a Mrs. Broffman or Brockman, I do not know how she spells her name, I think it was Broffman; she had a gas shell explode right at her feet. She is still suffering from the effects of it. I was in contact with her last week.

SENATOR LA FOLLETTE: When these trucks drove up to force the gates of the plant, did the pickets who were back away from the gate come to the assistance or try to resist the entrance into the plant of the trucks along with the three men who were there under the permission in accordance with the injunction?

MR. GADD: They got inside before they could get up to the gate, that is the truck got inside before these men who were away could get to the gate.

SENATOR LA FOLLETTE: What was the occasion for the use of gas and shooting into the crowd?

MR. GADD: Well, it was unprovoked, there was no reason for it.

SENATOR LA FOLLETTE: Were the three pickets at the gate resisting the entrance of the truck?

MR. GADD: They could not stop the truck. If they had got out in front of the truck they would have been run down.

SENATOR LA FOLLETTE: Did they indulge in any violence? Did they throw anything?

MR. GADD: There wasn't any violence. The truck was inside the fence.

SENATOR LA FOLLETTE: If I understand you now—I want to be corrected if I do not understand you—if I understand you there were a dozen or 15 men congregated 1,000 feet away from the gate.

MR. GADD: Yes, sir.

SENATOR LA FOLLETTE: There were three men at the gate?

MR. GADD: There were two men and a woman, I believe, at the gate.

SENATOR LA FOLLETTE: And this truck drove up. Now, did anything happen to these men who were standing back of the 1,000-foot line? Did they rush toward the gate before this shooting and use of gas took place?

MR. GADD: No, sir; they did not know anything about it until the shooting started.

SENATOR LA FOLLETTE: Following the attack of the guards, what took place?

MR. GADD: They went down into the plant. The strikers secured guns from some place, or somebody did, and a battle went on, was carried on from about 6 o'clock, the time they got down in the plant, until about 11:30.

SENATOR LA FOLLETTE: How many men were outside the plant at this time?

MR. GADD: Up until 11:30—of course, the crowd kept getting larger as the news spread—up until 11:30 there were probably 300 outside the plant, that is out on the street, running by the plant.

SENATOR LA FOLLETTE: What else took place?

MR. GADD: Well, they kept firing into the plant, and the ones in the plant kept firing out, and there were some of them wounded in the plant. Three of them, I think, were very seriously wounded. One of them got out of the plant some way over the back fence, went to Cleveland, the hospital there. Two of them were taken to the Ravenna Hospital at Ravenna, Ohio.

SENATOR LA FOLLETTE: Were any of the people who were outside of the plant injured?

MR. GADD: I do not think there was any of them injured, only a couple that had medical attention after the first attack was made at the gate when they went in.

SENATOR LA FOLLETTE: Did the guards remain in the plant?

MR. GADD: They remained in there until almost dark, I could not say just what time it was. It was in June, the days were pretty long. They remained in there until the sheriff came to get them out. They told the sheriff he could take them out if they were disarmed and take possession of all the guns, ammunition, and things like that, and he agreed to do that if he could get in.

SENATOR LA FOLLETTE: What was the occasion for the evacuation of the plant by the guards, if you know?

MR. GADD: I did not just get your question.

SENATOR LA FOLLETTE: Did anything occur there which made it necessary for them to take the guards out of the plant?

MR. GADD: Yes, sir.

SENATOR LA FOLLETTE: What was it?

MR. GADD: They were firing into the plant all the time, and the guards were useless in there because they had them scared so bad they were all lying on the floor so they would not get shot. After some of them got wounded they wanted to get out, because the crowd kept getting larger and larger all the time. There were probably 5,000 people around the plant before they got out. There was no firing of any kind from their side after about 1:30. They were afraid that the crowd would rush the plant and do them bodily injury down there, so they wanted to get out. We accompanied the sheriff and deputies down into the plant and gathered up all the guns and stuff we could find there, provisions and stuff that they had there in the plant.

SENATOR LA FOLLETTE: What was done with the guards after they were taken out of the plant?

MR. GADD: They were taken to the Kent jail.

SENATOR LA FOLLETTE: What was done with them there?

MR. GADD: Well, I think they were fingerprinted and booked on a charge of shooting to wound, or something like that, and then were placed under bail, $1,500 each, and then they were released. I do not know where they went then.

senator la follette: Were there munitions found in the plant?

mr. gadd: Yes, sir.

senator la follette: What kind of munitions?

mr. gadd: There were five sawed-off shotguns, five tear-gas guns, long-range guns, one full case and one part of a case of long-range tear-gas shells; there was quite a quantity of small arms ammunition, shotgun shells, and there were about a bushel-basket full of revolvers and automatic pistols.

senator la follette: Did you find any food?

mr. gadd: Yes, sir. There was enough food there to last them for a week or more, I suppose.

senator la follette: After the guards had been removed, were you able to come to any agreement with the company?

mr. gadd: Yes, sir. Two weeks after that we got a signed agreement with the company.

senator la follette: What did it provide? Were any concessions made on the part of the management?

mr. gadd: Well, the management granted a 5-percent increase and adjusted some of the wages of the employees in the lower brackets. I understand that has been taken care of, the adjustment of the wages in the lower brackets, and the relationship between the employees and employer now is very good.

senator la follette: What is the name of the president of the company, if you know?

mr. gadd: Mr. Lamb; W. J. Lamb, I believe.

senator la follette: In the course of your negotiations for the agreement which was entered into subsequent to

COLLECTIVE FIRING 257

the removal of the guards, did you have any discussion with Mr. Lamb about the hiring of the guards?

MR. GADD: After the agreement was signed he said he did not hire any guards—that they turned the settlement of the strike over to the agency. He did not name the agency at that time.

SENATOR LA FOLLETTE: It has been developed in the testimony that it was the National Metal Trades Association.

MR. GADD: That is right.

It was in the association-conducted strikebreaking activities of the Columbian Enamelling and Stamping Company of Terre Haute, Indiana, that the militia maneuver was played again so successfully. On June 18 in 1936, protected by four police cars, a van load of forty guards broke through the picket line with such repercussions of violence that the Company appealed for protection of the National Guard. "On July 22, a one-day general strike was called of all labor in Terre Haute"—I am quoting from a press release of the National Labor Relations Board—"It ended when 750 militia were marched into the plant, martial law was proclaimed and picketing forbidden. Under this protection the plant was reopened, and by September 15, it was in full operation by former strikers, one half of whom had returned individually, and by new workers brought from the outside."

It is supererogatory to describe, in the light of its practice, the group faith or attitude of this employers' association toward social legislation. The commissioner testified that Mr. Clarke of Fyffe and Clarke, the association's counsel in Chicago, had advised them that the National Labor Relations Act did not apply to manufacturers, a decision which was convenient, to say the least.

This attitude is well clarified in the association's attitude toward other employers of the industry who refuse to adopt their tactics or toward those association members who, disillusioned with the method, or failing sympathy with its aims, become recalcitrant.

Mr. Stringham's ire was drawn by such an attitude on the part of George E. Deming, vice-president of the Philadelphia Storage Battery Company and part-owner of the Philco Radio and Television Corporation. Mr. Deming's company employs approximately ten thousand hands, and he signed a union agreement with seven thousand of them in Federal Local 18368, affiliated with the A. F. of L. Stringham's sarcastic letter to his chief Sayre reads:

"No. 18368, Radio and Television Workers Federal Labor Union, affiliated with the A. F. of L. is the largest Federal local in the A. F. of L. and the A. F. of L.'s strongest organizer is Geoge E. Deming, Vice President of the Philco Company.

"Deming is the employer member of the Mayor's labor committee and is the 'yes man' for the labor racketeers on the board. Deming insists that employers sign agreements with the unions.

"26 percent of the tool and die work in the Philadelphia area is Philco work. 70 percent of Philco work is farmed out on contract.

"Frank C. Castelli, who has a fair-sized tool shop and recently spent a hundred thousand dollars on new equipment, has been a successful bidder and done fair business with Philco. Castelli's shop was recently affected by strike, about 50 percent remained loyal and stuck with him, and he continued to operate with the assistance of the Metal Manufacturers' Association. Deming, Vice

President of Philco, pulled his work from Castelli's shop, hailed Castelli before the Mayor's Labor Board and insisted that Castelli settle with the strikers, run a union shop with a union agreement, or he would never receive another dollar's worth of Philco work. Castelli told him to go to ———, he would not sign a union agreement if they took the shop from him.

"Deming severely criticized the S. L. Allen Company for not settling with the union, also the Metal Manufacturers for helping the Allen Company. He says it's wrong, that the Allen Company should recognize the union. Deming is the best thing the A. F. of L. has in Philadelphia, and his constant agitation in favor of the A. F. of L. is adding strength to the organized labor movement.

"This man should be broken down. Can you suggest anything that we can do to off-set his activities."

The S. L. Allen strike procedure toward which Mr. Deming had felt critical was the one in which association finks had been evicted from the plant for insanitary conditions by the Board of Health. Prior to January, 1936, the Allen Company had been negotiating with the union, aided by conciliators from the Pennsylvania and U. S. Labor Departments. At that time they decided instead to turn to the Metal Trades who were soliciting their business but whom they could not join until they repudiated their collective bargaining activities.

Mr. Gerard Swope also comes in for his share of disapprobation as a dangerous man for industry. Of him Mr. Stringham complained in 1935.

"During the difficulties of a few years ago, when the International Brotherhood of Electrical Workers were attempting to 'close shop' the electrical industries and were not only discriminating against manufacturers' products, but were championing local, municipal, and State legislation with a view to licensing electricians in various municipalities, counsel for the manufacturers and associations, during their deliberations, woke to the fact that there was a leak among their own group and through an investigation it is said that Gerard Swope was not only informant for the other side of the fence, but was keeping them thoroughly advised and alive to everything that went on in the manufacturers' meetings."

Legislation is dealt with consistently. When the Common Council of Terre Haute passed an anti-picketing ordinance, the Commissioner wrote of his pleasure, to Mr. Werner Grabbe of the Columbian Enamelling and Stamping Company:

"This simply is an indication of what a determined stand can accomplish if the objective is sound.

"You are one of the best soldiers that I have ever come in contact with. Accept my congratulations.

"I am sending a copy of your letter together with a copy of the ordinances to all of our branch secretaries."

This was affirmative. When legislative dangers arise, one can expect to find Mr. Sayre in a resistant mood. Members are asked to bring to the attention of their Senators and Congressmen their disapproval of the Wagner Disputes Bill and the Walsh-Healey Bill. When the Social Security Bill comes up, we find him writing to a member in Indiana:

"DEAR MR. SMITH. I was very much interested in your letter of the 11th regarding the social security legislation. We are preparing at the present time a bulletin on this subject which we expect to send to our members in the course of the next week or ten days.

"I talked over the long distance telephone to the secretary of the Michigan Manufacturers Association, who had sent out a similar bulletin on August 31st. He told me that when these notices were posted, the employees said that they didn't realize that the money was to be deducted from their pay envelopes, but rather felt that it was the rich who were paying the bill.

"We intend to make this notice as brief as possible and at the same time include all of the facts so that employers can use all or any part of it in their notices to their employees."

And soon enough a bulletin-poster appears, prepared by counsel. Whether or not the same counsel who had advised the association that the Wagner Disputes Act did not apply to manufacturers, is not recorded. Its beginning paragraph read thus:

"THE NEW FEDERAL TAX ON WAGES

"The new federal tax on wages goes into effect January 1, 1937. As of that date the law requires that we subtract one percent from the wages of each employee who is under sixty-five years of age and pay it to the federal treasury as a tax on his wages. This tax was enacted by Congress in 1935 as a part of the 'Social Security Act'—but is to be used for the general purposes of the government. This will be the first direct federal tax on wages. It is in addition to all other taxes. The law provides that it shall gradually increase until it is three percent after 1948. When the plan for registering the twenty-six million wage earners to whom this tax applies is completed, the 'Social Security Board' is expected to commence registration."

The zealot, as over against the profiteer, thus makes his appearance with a vested clergy. As we have said before, the National Metal Trades Association is an institution, and institutions are tough to kill and slow to die. In unsympathetic times they often pass into a sort of self-induced coma, a period of suspended animation. Sustained by a sense of virtue and patience, they await a Second Coming.

IX. The Field of Honor

IN MOST civil wars one side fights to win away and one side fights to save. Since government, the property right, and the taxing power are usually in the hands of the defenders, they have both more money to fight with and less need of money. The rebels are in the situation of a new housewife who has to outfit her establishment with everything from broom to salt before she can sweep or cook. In counter-revolution, where the terms loyalist and rebel are almost reversed from their customary usage, these relationships are not necessarily true, the vested interest having been, it hopes, only temporarily ousted and it being still in possession of an accretion of the subtle power of habit, as expressed in institutions.

Yet in most civil wars we should be surprised to find the defenders fighting with nothing but money. A fight rarely occurs over property interests in the raw. These interests have been translated into terms of social custom or religious observance. A few leaders with their tongues in their cheeks may see through the transparency to the pure economic issue involved. But they pick their officers from among those who, having received its highest privileges, find beauty and meaning in the status quo, and who are willing to fight for it with their lives. The sons of the generals are found far out in the field. The heir-apparent is restrained with difficulty from risking his neck. To be sure they have to swell their lower ranks with mercenaries. Since they have not widely distributed the privileges which they are seeking to maintain, they are not apt to have the young volunteers on their side. These have enlisted with the opposition and are contending for privileges which they have never had. It is customarily in the ranks of the conservers that paid soldiers are found, working at war as they would work on the roads, earning their livelihood at so much a day. But no matter how many mercenaries have been rounded up for the royal colors, their ranks are usually led and infiltrated by men who believe deeply in their cause.

Here, on the contrary, is a civil disturbance on a large scale, call it war or not as you like, in which no true defender risks his neck. And this in spite of the fact that, although he is not the maker of the war, the defender in this instance is the maker of the disturbance since the mutinous army who is moving upon the stronghold is ordered by its officers to employ peaceful means of gaining their objective. From top to bottom, the industrialists' army is made of men who are paid to fight. No one exhorts them, unless one might call Mr. Rand's importunities-with-bonus an exhortation. No one gives them black, brown, or red shirts to wear. They do not even ride away to the wars, they are shipped. No one explains to them—an oversight which cannot be charged to the makers of most wars—that if the battle is lost, all is lost, heaven, home, and mother, all that life holds sweet, most of all honor. To stir the finks to the exaltation of holy battle would take more than the reading of the minutes of a meeting of a Board of Directors. Mothered in vinegar, all that they owe the system which they are hired to defend is that it furnished dregs to spring from.

It is thus that the issue is kept from emerging. If we were allowed to see it more clearly we could elect with righteous passion to stand on one side or the other. If we ever saw Mr. Morgan, Mr. Rockefeller, or Mr. duPont charging at the head of an infantry of embattled stockholders, preferred in the van of the common, the thing would look simpler. Or if we should, alas, find the chairman of the board of U. S. Steel or his aide-de-camp from its subsidiary, the Tennessee Coal and Iron Railway Company, beaten and bleeding in the deep woods eighty miles from Birmingham where lay Joseph Gelders, we could snatch ourselves from out the twilight zone of apathy in which moral outlines are extinguished. Or if we ever found one corporation counsel down in Harlantown with his gun in a window to lay low a lad of nineteen—but we never do.

It is because we so quickly lose the sense of contrast that we do not bestir ourselves against the causes of violence. By the time we are ready for school, injustice and greed have been prettied up by other names. In fear of that most dreadful jibe of all, that we are being unrealistic, we check our pity sharply. This is an old fact known well to the poets. The Jews say it best in a proverb: "May all those things to which you can become accustomed, not occur." Stevenson and Browning said it. Keats said it, for a different context.

"And now
How can I hold myself in jeopardy
Of blank amazements that amaze no more?"

The significance of violence, that is, of attack upon blood and breath, escapes us when we are not there to see the wound bleed and rigor gather or, slower misery, incapacity set in. Our protective obtuseness is the cause of tabloid technique. The reporter has to flay us with words and pictures, for he knows that our own world closes down round us as closely as a shower-bath curtain, and that life has no vivid meaning as it spreads outward in concentric circles into anonymity.

Probably it should not be otherwise. There is no reason to exacerbate our nerves with thoughts of all the people in this world doomed to die elsewhere than in their beds. The immunity we build up against the thought of violence is only a part of the immunity we set up against the thought of death by decay, or the fact of death itself. It has to be unimportant to us so that we may live. Furthermore, who wants to live forever in this earthly frame, with a face like a turkey's neck and toothless gums? How much more beautiful, perhaps, to be brushed off in the bloom of nineteen years, like Bennett Musick of Harlan, now a youth for history, a short while ago pledged to a pedestrian life of wages, marriage, and children, and dark work in the mines, with possible additions of hernia, deafness, or tuberculosis, unemployment and relief, church socials and deaconhood, grandchildren and, finally, unmentioned burial in a soft pine box.

The bequest of life from testator to heir is not the breath in the body but breath immediately outside it; that which is about to be drawn in, or that which has just been exhaled. Whether this air is damaged by its tenancy, or whether it is purified thereby, is for the solitary man, as it is for race and nation, the measurement of spiritual progress. If the signs of history are to be read at all, between the Piltdown man and a man measuring the corona of the sun, there has been a rarefication of air. Not all the difference between these two evolved creatures can be measured in terms of physical self-preservation. The crablike movement backward into brutality, so highly thought of nowadays, is a freakish development as inorganic as the gall on a hazel bush.

In reckoning the cost of espionage and strikebreaking we should therefore take notice of the intangible losses, or rather weights bearing down against the upward effort; the encouragement to betray and to expect betrayal; the destruction of hope for a better life; and those titanic impersonal losses, the pre-emption of the machinery of justice for private gain, and the rape of public opinion. These form a subtle disaster whose victims cannot be listed.

The battle is fought on a less ambitious level. Let us look to see if management gets what it is gunning for. The aim of espionage and strikebreaking is to keep the worker a citizen of a tributary state. The first tactic is to take away his implement of warfare, in other words to get away from him his union, and failing this, to get the man; alive if possible, dead if necessary. The blacklist is the prison in which he can be incarcerated for the duration of the war, which is to say, indefinitely.

The Senate will never have statistics on the economic casualties of this prolonged engagement; how many independent unions have been destroyed; how many company unions have been introduced by spies; how many organizers and officers framed, slain, or sent away. But, thanks to the inquiry, volumes of documented description of these practices now exist. How these ends are accomplished we know, because for hundreds of individual instances we have the last detail of data. For the extent and penetration of the practices we have to take as gauge that industry has spent millions of dollars in its belief in the efficacy of espionage to keep labor impotent in its efforts to organize. How many large unions, like that in Flint which was reduced from 26,000 to 122, have been brought down in membership to literal nothing, or how many unions have been forced to live underground, to meet in cellars in the small hours of morning, and retain their membership by mail is not important to know, in order to gain a workable idea of its effect. If we have down in black and white, as we have, the names of hundreds of men discharged as a result of their being spied upon, we do not have to know the names of all workers who have been thus discharged. The length of the cumulative, or even the current, blacklist need not be computed after we know that, like an anaconda, it can swallow many times its own size in men and then go back to sleep and regain its pristine shapeliness.

If we knew every name that had ever appeared on it, we should not have the beginning of wisdom about the blacklist. Its first effects are drastic, but later, as is true of the deterioration that sets in under compulsory idleness for any cause, there is no measuring the height or depth of its effect. Likewise with the disintegration of unions over a long period of years. If we knew the names of all union failures brought about by spying in the past, and the sum for which their strikes have failed, we should still have no manner of calculating the total loss, because the profit accruing to a country whose workers are achieving new levels of living is too subtle to be measured in figures, the whole of the profit being much larger than the sum of its parts. We now have all of the facts and figures about certain union fatalities. But even of such cost-accounted instances the total computation of loss is impossible to make. I know of no cost accounting system, social or economic, that would convey the volume or importance of a single action taken on either side in the Tubize plant in Hopewell, Virginia. Dates and figures are available for almost every act in that labor trouble from the insertion of the Burns spy at canvasser insistence for the sole purpose allegedly of looking into efficiency, since management claimed there was no labor trouble, through the propaganda and counter-propaganda of incitation and tattletale, down to the violent strike, the permanent lockout, the moving elsewhere of the plant, and the leaving behind of a stranded population. We know the approximate numbers of those spied and reported upon and discharged, the wage, the cost of the spy, even the cost of the three cigars bought for "the boys at regular detective purchase price of twenty-five cents apiece"; we know the dates of almost every action. We know how many revolvers were sent in and how; by collusion with what department of government they were obtained; fifty of them, by automobile. And a box of badges and two packages of night sticks.

But who can measure the economic displacement that comes from reducing skilled, semi-skilled, or even unskilled workers from the position of wanted to that of unwanted; of engineering independent men into the positions of mutineers? It is even difficult to compute the public cost of a man's change of status on the rolls of the United States Treasury from that of an earner to that of a dependent on public funds. Somewhere along the line the collapse has to be socially supported, for with the loss of the courage of his bowels, the worker loses his economic attack, as a pianist loses his attack upon the keyboard with lengthened and uncertain synapses. The economic value of public opinion is easier to measure than the economic value of confidence, or lack of it, in the worker. We have practice in appraising the economic value of public opinion. Advertisers have been setting a price on it for years. Men are paid huge fees for flattening it out here and perking it up there, trimming it into shapes like a Japanese hedge. We have never seen a merchant or a manufacturer in the relief office with a pair of calipers measuring the equally relevant cost in money terms of a low wage policy.

As to the personal casualties on the field of honor, each man will have to see them for himself. For all but the slain and his mourner, there will be a different way of viewing the event, since the event, though social, has to be seen through a single pair of eyes. When a mother straitens the body of her child between her two palms, the whole of life, its beginning and its end, is placed between these two polar fields. When many social forces converge and press downward into a single event, infrequently their pressure shapes a shining incarnation of what we mean by life rather than by society. In the experience of a solitary man we sometimes view life clearly, if only for a moment. Society can be measured in past and future terms. When we talk about society we talk of progress and improvement. The word has comparative forms. A man's life, on the contrary, may not be compared with another man's life, past, present, or future. It is here and now. It never was before, and it is soon gone forever. Like art, it does not improve upon itself. Its value is absolute and irreplaceable.

Further than this, as the affidavits read, the deponent sayeth not. May I, instead, give the single experiences of men for the reader to evaluate in his own terms of loss or gain?

First may I present the bewildered Mr. Jesse V. Souder of Woodbury, New Jersey, some eight miles from Camden, where, prior to June, 1936, he was for six years employed at experimental and tool work for the RCA Victor Company and where he was a member of local number 103 of the United Electrical and Radio Workers. In all fairness to the union movement and to Mr. Souder, it must be said that it is not upon activities of such innocent souls as his that the structure of labor organization is reared. Mr. Souder is what is known as an amateur, with the passion, preoccupation, charm, and remoteness of a man who has a hobby. His love is the camera. Like a grain of sand drawn into a blower, he was pulled into a great event. Let us hear him on the witness stand.

SENATOR LA FOLLETTE: Were you arrested in Camden on July 7, 1936?

MR. SOUDER: Yes, sir.

SENATOR LA FOLLETTE: And were you taking pictures of this melee between the Camden police and—

MR. SOUDER: I made a few snaps; yes, sir.

SENATOR LA FOLLETTE: Where were you at the time?

MR. SOUDER: I was down near the ferry.

SENATOR LA FOLLETTE: Describe briefly just what took place prior to your arrest.

MR. SOUDER: On this evening, another man and I were headed homeward. The crowd had left and we were going to the ferry entrance to go home, and we had rounded the corner, and about 60 feet in front of us I noticed a disturbance. I pointed to it and tapped the man on the shoulder and said, "Oh, oh, look there." I stepped backward about 10 or 12 feet to make a better working condition for the lens I was using, which was a 135 millimeter lens, with a 1 by 1½ negative—

SENATOR LA FOLLETTE: How did you happen to have a camera with you; did you anticipate there would be trouble there?

MR. SOUDER: I had made a few pictures from day to day and at that time I had not anticipated there would be any trouble. We were going home, but this broke right in front of us.

As I raised my camera like this (*indicating*) I heard

some man shout, "Give it to him," and at that, two clubs went up and came down on a fellow. They loaded him in the patrol wagon and then they brought out another man and this same man shouted again, "Give it to him," and up went the arms again and down came the clubs, and they loaded him in the wagon. The fellow who arrested me, Officer Wright, came down the pavement on his horse and said, "Get off, everybody." He was directing the crowd and I turned around and walked backward and had gone 10 or 12 feet when I heard someone say, "I want to go across on the ferry." He said, "You can't go this way; you have to go around." Supposing he meant me, too, I headed into the street and I had gotten back about 15 feet in the street, back past the rear ends of the cars that were parked there, when this officer advanced up opposite me and shouted, "Hey, buddy, you with the camera, you are under arrest for snapping pictures of evidence." I turned and came right in to him. By that time other officers had collected there. They took hold of my wrist and marched me over to the patrol wagon, and about the time we got within 12 or 15 feet of the patrol wagon this officer yelled, "What is that he has got?"—that is, the officer the other witness described. Someone answered, "A camera." Then this officer said, "Smash it." They smashed it and took out the film and tore it in pieces and scraped it up in a pile and set fire to it and burned it. The officer that arrested me claimed that I was causing a disturbance and that I yelled, "Get those cops and kill them," and that I also said, "We ought to tear down the American flag and put up the 'red' flag," all of which was a falsehood. I never said a word from the time I left until I got to the police court except to say, "Please don't break my camera," and I doubt if anyone heard it but myself, because after seeing two men clubbed, I guess you are not so brave and don't talk so loud; if you are, you beat me.

SENATOR LA FOLLETTE: Now, was this a grand-jury proceeding?

MR. SOUDER: Now, then, the trial that he gave me was on the 29th. There was this man Wright who testified against me. There were two officers that corroborated him, and a third also differed. He said, "No; this man didn't say that. The man I arrested said it. But he did say that we ought to tear down the American flag and put up the 'red' flag." And it was also said that the officers were in the employ of RCA. All of the time I never said a word. And so after the judge had listened to the testimony, he didn't give me or my witness a chance to testify. The prosecutor just turned to the judge and he said, "Your Honor, it sounds to me like a case for the grand jury." The judge says, "I find this man guilty and hold him without bail for the grand jury."

SENATOR LA FOLLETTE: And were you held without bail?

MR. SOUDER: Well, then they put me in the prisoners' pen, or anteroom or whatever you call it, while they were making arrangements. And while there this city detective, Vernon Jones, came along and says, "You shouldn't be in here." I said, "You was there, wasn't you, Brother? It seems to me I remember your face." He says, "I was." I says, "Did you hear me say any of the things which they charge me with saying?" He said, "I did not." Then they took me over to the prosecutor's office and changed my bail from no bail to $1,500. And due to some rearrangement or mistake, or something in the wording of the matter, the printed matter, I was in jail 3 days, from Wednesday noon until Saturday at 10:30.

SENATOR LA FOLLETTE: Had you ever been in jail before?

MR. SOUDER: No, sir. That was the first time.

SENATOR LA FOLLETTE: Did you make bail?

MR. SOUDER: Well, the union furnished bail for me from somewhere.

SENATOR LA FOLLETTE: And you subsequently were indicted by the grand jury? Did they return a bill against you?

MR. SOUDER: I was indicted; yes. I am indicted now. I am out on $1,500 bail on a criminal charge.

SENATOR LA FOLLETTE: What was the charge in the indictment; do you know what the bill charged you with?

MR. SOUDER: Inciting to riot, I believe.

SENATOR LA FOLLETTE: How much was this equipment worth that you lost in this situation?

MR. SOUDER: Well, I have a list of it here, and it is practically $533.50. Now, that equipment they still hold. They haven't returned any of it, and I did see some of it the first 2 or 3 days in court. This officer brought it in and was exhibiting it around among the officers and showing them the workings of this camera, the automatic focus, and so on and so forth, but since then I haven't heard the first thing about it.

SENATOR LA FOLLETTE: Have you been back to work at the RCA?

MR. SOUDER: No, sir.

SENATOR LA FOLLETTE: Since the strike?

MR. SOUDER: Because of my arrest I have not been called back. I am a fairly good mechanic and I have samples of work here to show my ability, if you care to see them. And because of my arrest I have sort of been blacklisted from other plants. I have been around, here and there and yonder among the most, that is, small plants and large plants, and, of course, you are required to fill out an application and at least give four names of places where you have worked, have been employed. And when they come to RCA they say, "Uh-huh, how long did you work there?" "Six years." "Why aren't you working there now?" I tried to explain they had a strike and there is a lot of us that haven't been called back. They say, "Well, was you active in the strike in any way?" I says, "No; I took no part in the strike. I am a member of the union, but that is all." I says, "I didn't take any active part in it or anything." "Well, how was it you wasn't called back?" And finally quizzing, they say, "Well, our personnel department can find out. You might as well tell it." So I told them a true story, rather than have them go and get an untrue story. They generally come back and say, "We will investigate and let you know, but we don't want any trouble-makers around here." That has been the story.

SENATOR LA FOLLETTE: Are you employed at present?

MR. SOUDER: I am right now in a sort of a minor job.

SENATOR LA FOLLETTE: When did you secure that job?

MR. SOUDER: The 7th of January.

SENATOR LA FOLLETTE: You are here under the subpoena of this Committee?

MR. SOUDER: Yes, sir.

SENATOR LA FOLLETTE: You are excused.

MR. SOUDER: Now, I will present this as a detailed description.

SENATOR LA FOLLETTE: Let it be given an exhibit number.

MR. SOUDER: Yes. And I also have a chart here showing the street as it laid and the distance I was away from the offices, and their position and everything, and it has exact measurements and the exact position of all.

Let us next view the event through the business-like eyes of Mr. Edward Bergin of Jersey City. When Mr. Bergin drew fire in the back from the American Bridge Company through the gun of its protector, guard Ralph Golden, tried once in the past for murder, and once for felonious assault, he was walking along the building operations of the Pulaski highway, looking for the worker to whom he had loaned some money. It was a raw day in November and Bergin turned his back to the wind to light his pipe. Something hit him. It didn't feel like much, but he fell down, and some policemen rushed up and told him he was shot. They took him to the hospital where he experienced paralysis of both legs and of bladder and rectum. After ten days this paralysis receded, but he developed (I quote the doctor's statement) "a bilateral phlebitis of the legs whose danger is the danger of an embolism's breaking off and landing in the brain or lung, death following this occurrence in about 99 percent of cases."

All this was in the early winter of 1931. Mr. Bergin was a structural iron worker, drawing $160 a week. In the winter of 1937 when he appeared in Washington in answer to subpoena of the Senate, he was again, after years of idleness, employed and drawing eighty-five dollars a week. Both legs were bandaged to his thighs to enable him to stand. His case had dragged for three or four years until it was nearly outlawed before some lawyer encouraged him to sue American Bridge. During that time—but Mr. Bergin is laconic. I shall let him tell the story. "I had to pay the hospital bills and the doctor bills. I had two girls going to college at the time. I had to discontinue that, I could not pay for it. I was dispossessed four times. I had to go on relief. I was in the hospital fourteen months all told."

It was a profitable job for Golden. Any fink could call

it good. He got off without a scratch from court (although the legal fees for their labor troubles paid to Merritt Lane seemed excessive to the American Bridge), and in the bargain he drew $5,600 from American Bridge at the rate of fifty dollars a week. The company settled out of court with Bergin for $4,000, expressing resignation and even some contentment at the eventuation of the nervous business. Bergin himself got $2,500 out of the affair.

In the extravert Mr. Bergin's story the tragedy, whatever it was, was faced with demi-comedy, like a veneer on the front of an abysmal drawer. The American concept of opportunity; the ambitious workman following the exhortation to save and be thrifty; the social rise through the benevolent leaven of red schoolhouse and college: the whole notion shot to hell with a gun. A two-million-dollar contract protected against all comers by a soldier enrolled from the records of the police, a man with an itching trigger finger who could not tell a match in the wind from an assault upon the rights of property, couldn't tell left from right, and, lamentably important to Mr. Bergin, could not tell front from back.

Mr. Bergin being on his feet again, so to speak, let us next view the phenomenon through the eyes of Jack Barton, and very tired eyes they are, affecting his beholders with an overwhelming sense of weariness. Tall and pallid, though young lifting his voice with difficulty, making no uneconomical changes of posture, he sat to be examined upon the extraordinary events of his recent life. His physical depression and the fact that he volunteered nothing, yet attempted to hold nothing back, invested his testimony with a mood of understatement which moved the audience more than did the extravagant detail of crime and bloodshed embellishing so much of the testimony.

Mr. Barton, now of New York, from June until Christmas of 1936, lived in Bessemer, Alabama, a purely industrial town, where the Tennessee Coal and Iron Company has a large rolling mill and where there are ore mines and the U. S. Pipe shop. Before June he had lived in Birmingham whither he had removed from his native Georgia. His early days upon a farm and later as electrician must have given him no premonition of the ordeal which was to put a sculptor's knife to a conventional boyish face, leaving upon it communicable lines of moral grandeur.

In 1917 Barton joined the union, in 1934 became a member of the Communist party, and later its regional secretary at ten dollars a week. Here at last was what Pinkerton was looking for; what the entire machinery of espionage had been allegedly set in motion to find, and what they so rarely turned up. Indeed, out of the innumerable witnesses and deponents, those spied upon and those discharged, from one end of the country to the other, Mr. Barton was one of those very rare people who complied with the detective's qualification of being dangerous; that his youth and apathy lent him the description of bashful could not alter this fact. Mr. Barton said, and said out loud, to a United States Senator who was in no sense badgering him, "I have been a member of the Communist Party for the last three years. After I came to Birmingham I became a paid employee of the Communist Party, that is, their secretary." Senator Thomas, unarmed though he was, did not blench. Stoutly he brought forth the question, "Is the Communist Party a legal party in Alabama?" To which Mr. Barton replied, "Yes, sir. It has been on the ballot since 1932."

THE FIELD OF HONOR

In a year and a half Mr. Barton had been arrested four separate times. Once he was arrested at the home of a friend on the charge of being a Communist suspect. The arrest was made by Milton McDuff, the head of the McDuff Detective Agency of Birmingham, who, according to Barton, holds no authority from the city, merely directing the raids and ordering the city detectives to make the formal arrests. McDuff is the son of a sheriff of Jefferson County, a job which, according to a member of the state patrol, used to net its possessor more than the salary of the President of the United States.

At the beginning of the year 1936, Barton married Belle West, a nineteen-year-old girl of Scotch-Irish descent, born in Atlanta, Georgia, a member and leader of the stenographers' and typists' union. Into their new home they took a friend, Beth McHenry, a correspondent for the Federated Press. A second girl, a Dorothy Malakoff, left a suitcase of clothes with them for safekeeping. Two weeks after their marriage, there broke into this menage, without knocking and without warrant, Milton McDuff and two city detectives. They found the suitcase. They found, by looking at the typewriter where Mrs. Barton was working, the typist union records, and they found a pile of copies of *The Daily Worker*, of liberal magazines, and some publications of the A. F. of L. Snatching up the suitcase, the records, and the magazines, and taking Mr. and Mrs. Barton and their guest in charge, they hustled them off to the jail where they photographed and fingerprinted Mr. Barton and Miss McHenry and kept them for thirty-four hours.

The charge made against them this time was a violation of the Downs ordinance of Birmingham which said it was unlawful to possess more than one copy of literature advocating the overthrow of the government. Their commandeered publications all had second-class permits to go through the mail, and none of them advocated the overthrowing of the government by violence. Senator Thomas was inquisitive about this point. He pursued it. "Were the documents read in court to convince the court, or was there any need of it?" Mr. Barton answered, "It was not necessary, because the police did not present it. When it was called, the prosecutor asked for several postponements which were granted. The prosecutor asked for postponements on the ground that he had not been able to read the evidence, and about the third postponement the judge said if the evidence was not there, he would throw the case out which he did."

Barton's third arrest occurred in a Birmingham restaurant on a charge of vagrancy. In court he was also charged with having given a fictitious name on a previous occasion. For this admitted offense he was fined five dollars and costs, amounting in all to twenty-seven and a half dollars. The judge threw out the charge of vagrancy since Barton could prove he earned ten dollars a week and that, at the time he was picked up, he had had thirty-five dollars on his person. On this occasion he was held incommunicado for seventy-two hours before the charge was placed against him. He was then allowed to get in touch with a lawyer, and made a $300 bond.

About his fourth arrest I shall let Mr. Barton speak in detail, since robbed of its detail it passes over into the realm of irreality.

MR. BARTON: On July 19, in Bessemer, our home was raided and the Bessemer police, at that time—that is, when they came to the door—they knocked on the door and they showed me the search warrant which called for the searching of the house for liquor.

SENATOR THOMAS: Prohibition exists in Alabama yet, does it not?

MR. BARTON: Yes, sir.

SENATOR THOMAS: It was a perfectly legal search warrant, was it not?

MR. BARTON: Apparently; as far as I could see it was perfectly legal. It was signed by the mayor of Bessemer.

SENATOR THOMAS: Were you taken to jail after that searching expedition?

MR. BARTON: Yes. When the police officers came in they just looked around and saw some magazines in an open cabinet and they piled these up without examining them very closely and told me I would have to go to jail with them. I asked what the charge was, and they said it was possessing Communist literature, and I was taken to jail right away.

SENATOR THOMAS: Was that an actual charge, having possession of Communist literature?

MR. BARTON: No; there is no such charge as that. The law states, "Literature advocating the violent overthrow of the government."

SENATOR THOMAS: Who questioned you at that time?

MR. BARTON: The police chief showed me a photograph of me that had been taken by the Birmingham police and asked me if it was my picture. I said "yes," and was taken back to the cell, and a few minutes later I was brought back into the warden's office and questioned by a man that I later found out was A. D. Maddox, who was employment manager of the rolling mill of the Tennessee Coal & Iron Co. in Bessemer. Also a city alderman of Bessemer.

SENATOR THOMAS: What questions did he ask you?

MR. BARTON: Well, the main thing that he wanted to get out of me was as to who the leaders of the Communist

Party were, that is nationally and locally, particularly locally. He had a long list of people. He would read from this list and ask me if they were leaders or members of the Communist Party. He started out with nationally known people. The first few people he asked me about were Heywood Broun and Mrs. Roosevelt and several other nationally known liberals, all well-known people (*laughter*). I cannot think of their names right now.

SENATOR THOMAS: How did you answer it?

MR. BARTON: Well, of course, I denied it. Then he went on to the questions about local people. His list of local people included practically all of the trade-union leaders in Alabama. He began with the President of the State Federation of Labor and went on down.

At that time there was a strike in the ore mines of the Tennessee Coal & Iron Co., and he questioned me very sharply on whether the leaders of the ore strike were Communists or not. A large number of these people I did not know at all; I had never heard of them. He mentioned a trade-union official by the name of Yelverton Cowherd, who is chairman of the Americanization committee of the American Legion (*laughter*). Cowherd he accused of being a Communist. He said Cowherd was very clever, that he covered up his Communist activities by his work in this Americanization committee and violent attacks on the Communists.

He mentioned different individuals. There was one preacher that he mentioned, a Bessemer preacher that I had never heard of, that he tried to get me to say he was a Communist. Some of the questions I answered and others I did not.

He became very abusive and said I was a traitor to the South (*laughter*), that I was working for an outside organization, that I should be sent to Germany, where they knew how to treat Communists, and stuff like that, which lasted altogether about an hour and a half; that is, the questioning. At that time there was no one in the warden's office but Maddox and a uniformed cop.

SENATOR THOMAS: Did you attempt to get an attorney?

MR. BARTON: Well, I did not myself. My wife was with me when I was arrested, and I knew she would try to get one, so I did not make any effort to get one.

SENATOR THOMAS: What was the offense with which you were charged when the formal charges were put?

MR. BARTON: I have a copy of the law here, if you would like for me to read it.

SENATOR THOMAS: We would like to have a copy of it for the record. That is the Downs ordinance, is it?

MR. BARTON: It is not the same as the Downs ordinance. There are slight differences in it. . . .

SENATOR THOMAS: What took place at the trial?

MR. BARTON: Well, I was arrested on Sunday evening, and Monday morning I was brought into the courtroom. My wife was in the courtroom and she told me she had been unable to get a lawyer. That is, the only lawyer that would take the case was in the Circuit Court, in Birmingham, and would not be able to come out that day. We told the judge this, and he said he would give us a half hour to get a lawyer. Well, it was not possible to get a Bessemer lawyer, and it would take about a half hour longer to get one from Birmingham to Bessemer. I did not have a lawyer when the half hour was up. I was brought up for trial, and I again asked for a postponement of the case until the following day, which the judge refused.

The first part of the trial was the testimony of the

police officer. He piled the literature that he found in my house, or what he said he found in my house, on the judge's desk and testified he found it in my house. The judge asked me if this was correct. I said I did not know whether this was the literature I had or not, I would have to examine it, but the judge said this was not necessary and asked me if I wanted to say anything in my defense. I said I would like for somebody to read any passage in this literature advocating the overthrow of the government by force or violence; that is, any passage that violated the law. The judge said, "That is not necessary. It is all Communist stuff and you cannot have it in Bessemer." Most of this literature was not Communist publications. The only Communist publication I had was the magazine *The Communist*, of which I have a copy here. It was the July issue of *The Communist*. If you want it for the record, I have a copy of it.

SENATOR THOMAS: We can get that in the library, can we not? . . . What was the outcome of the trial?

MR. BARTON: Well, the judge sentenced me to 180 days at hard labor and a fine of $100, this fine to be worked at 50 cents a day if the fine was not paid. I asked the judge to permit me to appeal the case to a jury. He said I would have to raise a $300 appeal bond and would have 5 days to raise this bond. Then I was taken back to the cell again.

SENATOR THOMAS: Were you subsequently released on bond?

MR. BARTON: No, sir. My wife visited me practically every day and told me what efforts she was making towards getting a bond. We found it would take $2,000 worth of property to make a $300 bond, which was impossible to make among our friends in Jefferson County, and the city of Bessemer refused a cash bond, and besides we were not able to raise $300 in cash in Birmingham. On the fourth day my wife wired the International Labor Defense for a bond and they wired $300 back. That arrived on Saturday morning. The lawyer that had been retained, Harvey Emerson, of Birmingham, took the $300 to the Indemnity Insurance Co. of North America for the purpose of making out a bond. My wife took the bond back to Bessemer, got me to sign it, and then took it to the mayor, but the mayor was out of town, and the judge who tried me said he would read the bond, that he had the right to approve it or not to approve it. He read the bond over and said he could not accept it because it was not a Bessemer bonding company. My wife was sent from one place to another, to see one official and another official, and then finally she was sent to the Bessemer Bonding Co., the only company in Bessemer, and the official of this company first agreed to make the bond. It was merely a question of transferring it from one company to the other. But he said before he made it he would have to go to the city hall. He went to the city hall and when he came back he told my wife he would not be able to make the bond, that his boss was out of town and he could not reach him.

All this took up most of the day until 6 o'clock. That was the deadline to make the bond. Six o'clock came and the bond had not been made, therefore, the deal could not go through and I was not released on bond.

SENATOR THOMAS: You stayed in jail?

MR. BARTON: Yes, sir; I stayed in jail, in the city jail, in Bessemer, for about a week, until my lawyer applied for a writ of habeas corpus in the circuit court. Then I was transferred to the county jail for 2 or 3 days.

senator thomas: How long were you there?

mr. barton: Three days, as I remember.

senator thomas: What happened as the result of the finding of the writ?

mr. barton: The hearing was before Judge Goodwin in the circuit court. The writ was applied for on the ground I had been denied counsel, had been denied trial by jury, and that this law was unconstitutional. Judge Goodwin denied the writ of habeas corpus and I went back to the Bessemer jail to serve my sentence.

senator thomas: How were the conditions in the jail you were in?

mr. barton: The city jail that I was in practically all the time was a very old building. The warden told me it had been condemned several times by the State prison commission as unfit for human habitation. If you want me to go into details about conditions there, I will do so.

The cell I was in was about 10 feet by 7 feet; it had four bunks in it, and a toilet, with no running water; no way to bathe or to wash. This cell, although it was made for 4 people, usually had 8; in other words, from 8 to 14 prisoners in it.

senator thomas: Did you count as many as 14?

mr. barton: Yes, sir.

senator thomas: While you were there?

mr. barton: Yes, sir; particularly over weekends. They would throw in a lot of drunks and offenders of that kind that stayed in from Saturday until Monday.

It was impossible to get any sleep. I mean this cell was the drunk cell, it was a cell for anybody regardless of his condition. There were violent drunks in there, usually, and it was impossible to sleep. There was no way to wash or to keep clean at all. The bunks were very dirty, the mattresses looked like they had never been changed, or washed, or aired, or anything.

While I was there the mattresses were not aired at all. The food consisted mostly of syrup and biscuits, that is for breakfast. For lunch and supper I had corn bread, syrup, biscuits, and a slice of bologna. This food was impossible to digest.

This was a cell for the white prisoners. The Negro prisoners were separated, of course, and the conditions in their cell were just about like the white prisoners'. There was no privacy at all. The women's and men's cells were right together, with very small partitions. That is, you could see right through.

Do you want me to describe the work that I did while I was a prisoner?

SENATOR THOMAS: I want your description of the other prison first, and then the work.

MR. BARTON: The conditions in the county jail, do you want that?

SENATOR THOMAS: Yes.

MR. BARTON: The conditions there were very good. It was a new jail and, compared to the city jail, it was very good. You got plenty of food. It was not so good, but there was enough of it.

SENATOR THOMAS: Did you do any work while you were in jail?

MR. BARTON: Yes, sir; I worked on the roads, that is, doing repair work in the streets, and I worked in the parks. The work consisted of digging up the streets, making repairs, and work of that kind.

The first day that I was sent out to work I was shackled; that is, heavy chains were put on my legs. That had never been done before to a white prisoner. They do shackle the Negro prisoners, but they are carried to work in trucks, to and from work, they do practically no walking with these shackles on.

On this job that I was on I had to walk about 14 miles a day with the shackles on me, which caused my legs to become infected and for several days I was unable to work. When I got well again I was sent out to do the same kind of work, without the shackles. We worked from 7 o'clock in the morning until 5 o'clock in the evening.

senator thomas: How long were you in?

mr. barton: From July 19 until about October 12. Then I was transferred to the sanatorium.

senator thomas: And where is that?

mr. barton: The sanatorium is in the outskirts of Birmingham, in Jefferson County.

senator thomas: What were the conditions there?

mr. barton: The conditions there were very good; that is, I was treated very well. The conditions generally were good.

senator thomas: What was the occasion for your transfer to the hospital on October 17?

mr. barton: Well, after I had been in this city jail a month I had lost 15 pounds and my health started going to pieces. I finally got so bad that I could not hardly work. In the meantime Joseph Gelders, of the National Committee for the Defense of Political Prisoners, came to Bessemer and started a campaign to have me released or removed to a sanitorium, because of my health.

At the time I went to jail I had bad lungs, that is, they had not bothered me for years, but the conditions in the jail caused this trouble that I had had in the past to come back again.

senator thomas: Had you an arrested case of T.B.?

MR. BARTON: Yes, sir; this had been 4 or 5 years ago. I lost so much weight that I was transferred to the sanatorium at the behest of Mr. Gelders.

SENATOR THOMAS: What was the reason for your transfer? Can you give me some details on that?

MR. BARTON: I would say definitely it was because of the campaign that had been started around my case. This Mr. Gelders had organized a delegation, or delegations, of liberals and trade-union people to take part in the campaign for my release, and several delegations had requested the mayor of Bessemer to give me a medical examination. After a couple of weeks the mayor did agree to give me an examination, and as the result of this examination I was transferred to the sanatorium.

SENATOR THOMAS: When were you released from the sanatorium?

MR. BARTON: On November 11.

SENATOR THOMAS: How did it happen that you were released from there?

MR. BARTON: The lawyer that had been retained had appealed my case to the Court of Appeals of Alabama, that is, had made an application for a writ of habeas corpus to the court of appeals, and at that time, on November 11, the court of appeals ruled that this law was unconstitutional and I was freed from the sanatorium. I was freed as a prisoner. . . . I came north for medical treatment.

On that day of Barton's testimony, which was the middle of January of the year of our Lord, 1937, Mr. Borden Burr, counsel for Tennessee Coal and Iron Company, and Mr. Le May, assistant to its president, came on the stand again a moment, to clear up some points before Mr. Joseph Gelders should be called upon. One of these points had to do with taxes. Mr. Burr said: "May I give you one piece of information that I was not able to give you this morning, Senator? You asked about the amount of taxes. I was able to ascertain that our tax bill approximates, for the State, county and city taxes alone, one million and a half annually."

To this the gentle Thomas replied, with that fine precision of attack seen best when very large men sit down at the piano to play Bach, "Did you make any donations toward the upkeep of prisons?"

MR. BURR: "No, sir."

SENATOR THOMAS: "Just for the guards?"

MR. BURR: "Just for the quarters. The only expense was for the two quarters I referred to this morning, as I explained, for the National Guard during that particular strike. That is the only expense we had."

After this, shortly Mr. Gelders came on, a tall, cadaverous man whose features are drawn in a fine elaboration of outline such as can be found in Schongauer. Although very grave, Gelders gave off none of the emanation of tragedy that made Barton's testimony so painful for the hearer. This was perhaps for several reasons. The physical damage which had been done to him, though it had nearly killed him, was recoverable. Also he had approached the labor movement as a disciplined and intellectual man, behind him a long variety of experiences to teach him lack of surprise. Born in Alabama and schooled for some time in the University of Alabama, he later went to Massachusetts Institute of Technology, then to war. Later he became assistant credit manager in a department store, and worked at various occupations for the next ten years, including that of third helper in the open hearth furnace for a previous witness of the morning, Karl Landgrebe, now vice-president of the Tennessee

Coal, Iron and Railroad Company, but superintendent of one of the works when Gelders had worked for him in the furnaces. In 1930 Gelders went back to college, and in time became assistant professor of physics in the University of Alabama, a position which he left in 1935 to be representative of the National Committee for the Defense of Political Prisoners. In August, 1936, he moved his headquarters to Alabama.

Gelders began his own testimony by describing his unsuccessful efforts to enlist various public citizens in behalf of Barton, who was losing weight rapidly. Most of them refused to see him. A few young ministers joined him. They employed a doctor to examine Barton, and requested of the mayor, Jap Bryant, that Barton be taken out of jail long enough to go to the doctor's office for an x-ray. This Mayor Bryant refused. Gelders and Mrs. Barton finally decided to interview Gelders' old friend Arthur Green, solicitor of the Bessemer Cut-off of the Jefferson County court. His conversation proved to be so startling to them that they sat down as soon as they got out of his office and made notes upon it. Green said, upon being introduced to Mrs. Barton, " 'I know all about this Barton case. I was the one who had him arrested. We meant to get you, too, but you were not there when the arrest was made. . . . Why, all of you people are always covered.' " This is quoted from Gelders' reconstructed conversation. Mrs. Barton asked Green if he knew anything about a committee waiting on Buck Harrison, the bondsman Mr. Barton had gone to after the Insurance Company of North America bond had been turned down, telling him not to make Barton's bond, and that if he did, "it would be the last one he'd ever make."

"Green said, 'I know all about the committee, too.' He added that 'the industrialists' were behind it.

"I told Green that such procedure was unconstitutional and that, in the Barton case, the very law under which he was convicted was unconstitutional. I reminded him that he had taken an oath to uphold the Constitution. Green replied, 'I know it's not constitutional, but some things are law that are not constitutional. That's the way we do in Bessemer. The T.C.I. controls Bessemer, and you won't get very far with your teachings here—why, even I have been called a radical here more than once. Now, Joe, I'm going to tell you something confidential. Milton Fies has been saying that someone has threatened you, and you'd better leave town; and, Joe, I'd advise you to, too. Why don't you let someone down here run these things and you stop?'

"I explained to him that I was here to stay; I told him he was mistaken in believing that Barton's aim was to incite violence; that he evidently had much misinformation on the subject.

" 'Why, I didn't know there were two kinds of Communists. I thought all Communists were "Reds," ' he answered. 'Why, the Communists are the ones who started that ore-mine strike awhile back. All the leaders in that A. F. of L. are Communists. All they do is to start trouble. . . . Why, we've been in the very throes of communism.'

"Mrs. Barton asked, 'Would you do the same way with A. F. of L. leaders as you did with the Barton case?'

"Green answered emphatically, 'I sure would.'

"MRS. BARTON: 'Mr. Green, when they came to our house they had a liquor warrant, and they didn't even look for liquor.'

"GREEN: 'Oh, I know that. I was the one who had that done. That's the way we always do. If we want to search and don't have anything sure on the person, then we send a liquor warrant and search the house anyway. Somebody called up and said you had literature there, so we sent the men with a liquor warrant and searched. We use that a lot.' "

From here on I insert Gelders' testimony without comment.

"I went to a meeting with Mrs. Barton, who was at that time acting in some capacity within the organization of the International Labor Defense. . . . When we came out of the meeting we somewhat suspected that we were being watched, but we mounted the streetcar and came into the downtown part of Birmingham and thought no more of it after that. Then Mrs. Barton went one way and I went another. I got on the bus and went out to the part of town where I resided, got off the bus, and walked in the direction of my dwelling.

"I had walked only a few steps when I heard footsteps behind me, and I walked a little faster and heard that the footsteps behind me were going faster, and I turned slightly to see who was in back. As I did the person following me took two long running steps and hit me on the head with a club of some kind. I turned to defend myself from him and saw him quite clearly. This person has later been identified, as I will tell you directly as Walter J. Hanna. From now on I will use that name in describing him."

SENATOR LA FOLLETTE: How do you spell that?

MR. GILDERS: H-a-n-n-a. I stood facing him and holding him off at arm's length for possibly no more than 10 seconds, when I suddenly realized this was not an attack by one man. I do not know precisely why it came upon me. It may have been for several reasons. Of course, I had heard much about this kind of attack, and I may have heard a car stop beside us there, but I immediately turned and ran; and I had run but a few steps when I ran directly into another person, whom I have since identified as Dent Williams, and we will call him by that name for the rest of the story.

I ran directly into Williams, so closely that he had to push me back in order to strike me, and he gave me one blow with his right fist beside my nose, broke my nose and glasses and nearly floored me. Then I saw there was still another person whom I have identified, to the best of my knowledge and belief, as James Leslie. The three of them overcame me in a very few minutes and pushed me into an automobile which was standing out in the middle of the street with no driver and with the door open. They put me on the floor board in the back of this coach. Williams followed immediately and sat down in the seat directly over my head, which was the left rear seat. Leslie stopped and gathered up the papers I had dropped, which were the remaining portions of these papers that I have previously described, and, evidently, Hanna drove the car.

They continued to club me—especially, Williams did —for the first portion of the ride, until I lay perfectly quiet for a few minutes, and the conversation that passed between them indicated that they believed me to be unconscious, whereupon they stopped beating me and stopped kicking me, and I lay, pretending unconsciousness, for the entire rest of the ride.

As we drove along Williams took out a flashlight and started reading from the documents that I had had; and he was reading particularly from the Scottsboro case, because he would read a passage which his mind would consider lewd—after all, it is a rape case and there is medical testimony in it—and then he would nudge his companion, show him the line, read a few lines aloud, laugh boisterously, and kick me most ferociously.

SENATOR LA FOLLETTE: This occurred at night?

MR. GELDERS: This attack took place about 11:30 at night, on the night of September 23, 1936.

SENATOR LA FOLLETTE: How were they able to read?

MR. GELDERS: They had a little flashlight that Williams had and held the paper quite close to his face, and by the flashlight I was able to get a better picture of his face than I had gotten at the moment of the original attack, and this aided me in his identification. He did not pass the paper and the flashlight to the man sitting on his right, however. He would show him a passage, but he would do the reading, so that I was never able to get quite as good a look at the man identified as Leslie as I was able to get of Williams and Hanna.

He searched me for firearms and found none and later searched me and took all the papers I had on me —little notes I had in my pocket. Then he searched me again and took my wallet, which contained $59, and took my watch and money out of my pants pockets—my watch and a few $1 bills. When he looked into my wallet, he said, "This one has lots of money," with the distinct intonation that there were others who had less. When they first started off he said, "You nearly let him get away, didn't you?" and the driver answered, "I could not get a good lick in at him." Then the driver or one of them said, "He thought he was smart. He did not get off at Eleventh Avenue," and then they laughed about that. It seemed that I had gone slightly past my station and they were under the impression I was really dodging and was conscious this would throw them off the track. As a matter of fact, I carelessly ran past the station and got off the first time I became cognizant of my whereabouts.

We drove about half an hour and stopped and Hanna got out and came back in a few minutes and said, "Could you hear what we were saying?" Williams answered "No." We drove off about a mile and stopped again. Williams and Hanna got out, were gone 10 minutes, maybe, came back and when they got into the car Leslie said, "What are they going to do with him?" Williams answered, "Kill him, I reckon," and Leslie said, "Where are we going to throw him?" Williams answered, "In the river."

Then we drove about a mile or two and Williams and Hanna got out again. This seemed to be a filling station. The smell of gasoline was very strong and I heard the noises that one hears when you take on gasoline. Just a moment before we left, after we had been there about 10 minutes, Williams opened the door very wide and removed a straw hat which he had, just before getting there, placed upon my face, and called someone and said: "Look ahere; ain't that a hell of a mess?" and the person who answered answered with a very nervous laugh and did not seem very happy about it and I thought I noticed a great deal of haste on their part in leaving the station.

Then we rode about half an hour and this time Williams very carefully prepared for this stop by holding the hat as tightly as he could over my face and taking a handkerchief and doubling it up and placing it close to my mouth evidently to be used as a gag if necessary, and Hanna got out. We stayed there a very short time and when they got back in there was another man. They had picked up an additional person whom I now believe drove the car the rest of the way with Hanna sitting in the right front seat.

As we drove away from that place, Leslie handed the person in the right front seat the papers he had been holding and that person busied himself turning through those papers, making almost inaudible comments or comments which could not be well understood, but making comments about the papers—"Uh, huh; yes"; et cetera.

We drove this time about 2 hours and pulled into a road and stopped. One of them said, "This is not the right place." Then they backed out and drove half a mile, maybe, pulled into another road and went about half a mile down a lonely country road. As we were going down that road Williams, who was sitting just above me, pulled out a long leather strap that he had doubled up in his clothing. It was a strap about 2½ inches wide, three-eighths of an inch thick, and perhaps 3½ feet long—black leather with a handle carved into the strap.

They stopped the car and turned out the lights. The man in the right front seat, who I believe to be Hanna —I know Hanna was the man who first attacked me, but I believe this man also to be Hanna—they walked up in the direction of the front of the car. Williams grabbed hold of me and started to pull me out, thinking I was unconscious, but I saw the place he was pulling me through and I came to quickly and wiggled out. It was a space between the back of the seat and the door jamb and I was afraid I would lose an arm coming out and so I wiggled out and, as I did, he burst into a fit of rage because I had successfully feigned unconsciousness all this time. He grabbed me by the collar and struck the back of my head up against the running board of the car and left me lying there. Then Hanna gave me a lecture, saying, among other things, "You are down here meddling with our business." That was one of the things he said. "You were warned last April to get out of here and, at that time you did get out but you came back. We are telling you now that if you do not get out and stay out you will be loaded with lead." Then there was something else that I do not remember and he said, "If you tell anybody what happened tonight, you will be loaded with lead." Then he gave some orders—"Strip" and they stripped all my clothing off, cut my tie and threw it aside, ripping the pants into two pieces and left me in my trunks and socks and then gave the order to flog me, whereupon Williams threw me over on my face and started flogging me with this strap that I had seen him with.

Well, I became unconscious after a few of the licks. I counted about 15 licks. They struck me one very severe blow across the small of the back and rolled me over. When I was in that position one hit me in the mouth with a blackjack and another kicked me in my stomach, rolled me over and started in again and in quite a few moments I became unconscious.

When I regained consciousness I was alone. I tried to rise but could not. The pain through my middle where I had been kicked was too severe and I could not pull myself up. Then I tried to turn over on my stomach and my head started swimming and I was afraid I would lose consciousness again and so I lay there about an hour and a half, probably. When I first saw the daybreak commencing I tried again and this time I could not get up, pulling myself up from the position I was in on my back, but I did succeed in getting on my hands and knees and was able, finally, to stand. I walked down the road and I noticed which way the tracks came in; so I walked the other way, preferring not to meet with the same people, and walked about a quarter of a mile and found the road ended. So, I had to turn around come past the same place. I walked about half a mile to the main road and to a dwelling I saw there.

In the meantime I had put on what was left of my coat and wrapped one-half of my trousers around me and I went up and knocked on the door, dressed in this fashion, which was rather embarrassing. A lady came to the door and I told her, in a few words, what was the matter, and she started telling me something about somebody who lived down the road whose brother was a detective for the Tennessee Coal & Iron Co., but her husband called her and she went into the back room and he came out then and he loaned me a pair of trousers and said there would be a truck coming for him in half an hour to take him to work and he would take me to the nearest town, which he did. He took me to Maplesville, Ala. That is about 80 miles from Birmingham. That was the first time I really knew where I was, when I got to Maplesville.

I tried there to get some assistance. I tried to find a telephone. I found one and tried to phone Birmingham but the telephone would not work, and there was only one telephone in the town. I tried to get people to take me in an automobile to the next town after the one doctor there refused to treat me. I went to the doctor's home and he took one look at me and he said, "Oh, my, you would not ask an old man to fool with a mess there like you." So I left there and finally got to the next town, which is Clanton, Ala., and got admitted to the hospital there. . . .

I told my story to the officers and a little while after

that Officer J. W. McClung, of the State Highway Patrol, came back with one of the officers—I do not remember whether it was Waites or Henley—and asked me if I had recollected any further details and I had. I had recollected, by that time, what Hanna was talking about when he said I had been warned last April.

When I was down there last April, on the Scottsboro work, I was asked by David Solomon to come to a meeting which he had arranged. It was not exactly that way. He called me on the phone and said he had some information which it was important for me to have and would I meet him that afternoon. I did meet him and found that he had also there with him Leo K. Steiner, Sr., a banker, and Milton Fies, a vice president, I think, of the Debardeleben Coal Co., who, together, tried to convince me that I should leave Birmingham.

A few days after that I finished the business for which I had come to Birmingham and I did leave Birmingham and I do not doubt that one of them threw out his chest and said, "Well, we got rid of him."

Hanna was seen to be throwing away the weapon used in the attack, a sawed-off baseball bat. He was seen to be throwing away Gelders' torn-up papers. His car was identified. Gelders identified him. Various other witnesses including two state officers on the stand were sure enough of the facts obtained in a variety of ways that their testimony coincided with deadly certitude. Yet twice the grand jury returned no bill. Hanna's telephone, unlisted, is in the offices of the Tennessee Coal, Iron and Railroad Company which pays for it monthly. The witness who had been unfortunate enough to tell that he had seen Hanna dispose of the ball bat and Gelders' papers was said to have bought a gun for his protection, taken to drink, and received at last visits from a Major Harry Smith of the National Guard, after which his nervousness became less apparent and he told his employer that he expected to be offered a position, or might even take a vacation. The same Major Harry Smith said that fifteen of the seventeen National Guard officers of the Birmingham district were on the payroll of the Tennessee Coal and Iron Company.

Let us view the phenomenon finally through the eyes of Marshall and Mallie Musick, father and mother of the boy Bennett Musick of Harlan County. Musick is first a minister, and second a miner. His high cheek bones, his aquiline nose and high forehead from which recedes waving reddish hair, seem the traditional cover for the religious temperament within. This he communicated on the stand through his physical sureness, and through his thin but musical voice upon which his words were carried in a given beat, although to be sure, rhythmical intonation characterized the speech of all the mountaineers who gave to a crowded room of breathless spectators the bloody ingredients of employment relations in Harlan County, Kentucky. There, it appears, men who wish to organize for collective bargaining hang onto life with their fingernails, like men dangling from a cliff. Sixty-five labor killings a year has been the employers' stint in the recent past. The government of Harlan County is first owned by the coal operators and then delegated to a high sheriff. At a profit for their depredation which has netted him over $100,000 in three years, this sheriff has deputized a staff of nearly 400 drunken hoodlums whose killings of an evening would seem to be nothing but the merry nightcap of a round of whiskies, if they were not remunerated so handsomely for the results by the coal operators' association.

One Sunday afternoon in January, 1937, Mr. and Mrs. Musick decided to make a church call up the hill. During the organization drive of the mine workers for which Mr. Musick had been active in soliciting membership, a meningitis quarantine had been thrown over the county, and in Mr. Musick's words "while all of the doors of our sacred meeting places were closed, the doors were wide open for all of the road houses and beer gardens that were owned and controlled by Mr. Middleton [the sheriff] and his friends, and we often met to discuss the problem of having this meningitis ban lifted from the churches that we might have a chance or the right to continue our church service."

I shall try to contract the long story of the Musicks' Sunday afternoon pilgrimage. Their goal was the house of Deacon Brewer, but they decided to give up this visit because two cars of deputy sheriffs which they saw at the saloon kept passing and repassing them on the highway, and out of them, pointing at Musick, leaned Tom Holmes, coal operator and manager of the mine in which Brewer worked. Fearing that a visit to Brother Brewer's home would cause him to be discharged, the Musicks abandoned the idea of seeing him and went instead to the home of Brother Atkins. At about three-thirty, after much counseling among the friends and neighbors as to whether it was safe for the Musicks to start home at all, since the deputy cars were seen lying in wait for them, the Musicks set forth to try to get home before dark. A rain of bullets shot at them from moving cars but did not injure them. Mr. Musick tells it: "My wife said, 'Let us wait here for the bus,' and I told her I did not think it was best, but let us walk on. She apparently could not—she was so nervous she was not able to walk, and we rested for possibly a minute until she rather come to her composure, and we walked down the pike for a short distance, down the crossing where we left the highway, possibly a thousand feet to where this bus that we was expecting overtook us, and we loaded up on that bus."

At about this point Senator La Follette asked Musick if he reported the incident to the county officials. Mr. Musick's reason for his not doing so was magnificently simple. "Mr. Middleton, the high sheriff of the county, by word of mouth in his own office in the fall of 1934 advised me that so long as I had anything to do with the racketeering labor organization, that I would never get any protection, and regardless of what might happen to me or my family it would be useless for me to call on the sheriff's office, and for that reason, Senator, I did not deem it worth while, as it was the sheriff's deputies that had trailed me, and I think that they were the ones that was firing the guns."

Ten days later two friends of Mr. Musick advised him to leave the town. Their words were, "They are going to kill you," the word "they" being commonly used to denote the sheriff's gun force. Musick went home and talked things over with his wife. They recalled that she had often said she felt the children were safer with him away than at home, since he was so constantly threatened and followed. "This," said Mr. Musick, "was along possibly 3 o'clock in the afternoon. I stayed home and sat around with my wife until very late, and the train that went up the head of the hollow and back generally went out about 7 o'clock. I called my boy Bennett just before I started to the train after dark, and I related to him the warning that we had had, and when I started to leave the house I said, 'Bennett, I want you to stay here tonight and try to take care and watch and take care of your mother and the other children.' And he said, 'Pop, I will do that.' And that is the last words I ever heard him speak. I left on the train and when I got off that train at Pineville there was a message in the hotel that my boy was killed in the home."

SENATOR LA FOLLETTE: About what time did you arrive at Pineville?

MR. MUSICK: About 9 o'clock.

SENATOR LA FOLLETTE: When did you receive word that your son had been killed?

MR. MUSICK: As soon as I came in the lobby of the hotel, Mr. Arnett was in there and he came over from the clerk's office and he said, "Brother Musick, I have some sad news for you. Your son is killed in your home up at Everetts." He called Sheriff Ridings, and Sheriff Ridings and a number of deputies came over to the hotel, and I asked the sheriff to take me home, and Sheriff Ridings said, "Mr. Musick, I cannot afford to do that. Possibly you and me both would be killed," and he said, "I will do this. I will get some of my deputies" —he told me of some brave men he had, deputy sheriffs in that county, that he would gather them up and get a couple of cars and go to an undertaker and get the ambulance, and the two cars, and they would bring my wife and the other children out, and the undertaker would bring the corpse out. I talked to a number of men there, and they all told me that they could not afford to take me up there, that possibly they would be killed. Sheriff Ridings left, and I waited until late in the night, possibly 4 o'clock or approximately 3 o'clock that night, and one of the Ridings' sheriffs, I don't know whether it was the high sheriff or his deputy, came in and told me that he had been up there and told me about how the house was shot full of holes, and that after he went to the home and the condition thereof up there, that it was too dangerous for him to undertake to take my family out, and he was unable to get an undertaker to go in there owing to the fact that they were afraid of being killed, and he told me that the doctors up there would not go to the home, that they were afraid. He told me that my wife had been struck in the chest and in the neck with pieces of—he described it that it was pieces of porcelain from a door knob, and one of the smaller boys was hit in the arm. And he told my family to stay there until daylight and they would come back to Pineville and get the ambulance, and they would return by daylight and bring my family out. And he did that, and my family was brought down to Pineville about 8:30 that morning.

SENATOR LA FOLLETTE: How old was your son who was killed?

MR. MUSICK: He was 19 years old on the first day of July last year.

SENATOR LA FOLLETTE: Had he ever done any work for the United Mine Workers?

MR. MUSICK: No, sir. I believe, too, he went up to Ridgeway on one occasion to take a man that was working for the organization to show him where Mr. Green Cornett lived in the Ridgeway camp. Outside of that I know of nothing else ever that he had done. He had been a member of the organization since he was 15 years old and had worked in the mines at Black Mountain, and another mine there at Verda and Everetts. He had been working in the mines for about a year.

SENATOR LA FOLLETTE: Had he been a law-abiding boy?

MR. MUSICK: Yes, sir. I never knew of him having any trouble with anybody. Very peaceful and sober.

As he told of his boy, Mr. Musick began to weep, but continued his testimony without breaking. Mrs. Musick followed him upon the stand, a competent and pleasant-looking matron who had herself well in hand. Slightly more literal and detailed than her husband she painted in the vivifying items, and through a very lack of imagination, in a world of authors who had failed, she made the ebbing flood of life run hot.

"We were all in the living room, me and the three boys, setting around the fireplace, and the daughter was ironing at the ironing board just behind us, cleaning up just between us and the radio, where the shooting begin on that side of the house.

"I could not tell how many shots, it was so excitable and unexpected. The first shot that I heard, I was reading the paper next to the baby boy who had just come back from Everetts and brought the day's paper and handed it to me, and I was reading the paper, and the first shot, I thought just for a second it was something exploded in the grate. I was setting in front of the grate, and I looked down, and by that time there was another one, and at that time of course I did not remember seeing Bennett go out of the room at that particular time. It was a week before it come to me that I never did think I saw him leave, but in a week I remembered seeing him just kind of crawl to go into the bedroom, and he must have fell. This boy that is fourteen was setting on the studio couch at the end that came around to the door to go into the bedroom, and he said Bennett just rose out of his chair and went in the front room, and just fell into the bedroom, but he had turned. He was lying right around a trunk just to the left of the door. He crawled around and his feet were past the door.

"Well, about the second shot, the first I remember we all raised—Pauline the daughter was the last one getting out, and we all just made for that—you see, we would have had to meet them to go out of the room, and this bedroom did not have a door going out of it. We had to go out of the living room to go into that. I reckon we just moved without a thought, and all went in there. Myself and the baby boy just went and got down with Bennett just behind the trunk. We did not know he was dead until Pauline—she just fell to the floor and crawled in to the dresser and then she said, 'Be quiet, Mamma.' And we hushed for two or three seconds or two or three minutes maybe, and then the shooting stopped, and I thought—well, I said, 'Are any of you shot?' And the baby boy said, 'I am shot in the arm,' and Pauline said, 'I am not shot,' and Virgil went behind the door, the fourteen-year-old boy got behind the door, and two bullets went in just above his head. He just scattered down behind the door that stood open just a little, and I took Bennett by the shoulder. I was right over him and I thought my leg was bleeding. I had varicose veins and had an operation, and I felt my ankle was hot there, and I thought I probably was shot in the ankle, and I said to Pauline, 'I believe my ankle was stinging, and I must have bumped it against the trunk or something.'

"And she said, 'Ma, come here.' And I shook Bennett, and he was dead. We did not have a light in the room, and Pauline and I just drug him to the door where that light shined in from the living room and seen he was dead. She unbuttoned the clothes and felt his chest, and he was already dead."

x. The Proud Have Hid Snares

INDUSTRIAL management has been on the whole a glum respondent to the Senate query. Even Radio Corporation of America, whose manners on the stand were unexceptionable and who handed over their complete dossier without visible reluctance, conveyed chagrin, in their instance apparently not so much at the publication of their strikebreaking activities, as at being compelled to review them in a cold afterlight. This company was, to be sure, comforted by a sense of deep injury sustained with dignity. Their costly strike had been settled in favor of the union on a point of law which to them had seemed amazing, although its logic was later sustained in another case by the Supreme Court. The National Labor Relations Board, in the first case of its kind, deemed a majority to be a majority not of all the workers, but of all the workers voting in the election. The election had been boycotted by such means as these:

NO VOTING

Tomorrow the UERWA—according to Mitton—will attempt an "old fashioned" election. RCA workers know what this means.

It means violence, bloodshed and perhaps loss of life.

It means rioting, street fighting and general disorder.

To Avoid this, we Advise You to Refrain from Voting.

The arbitrary action of NLRB in changing to Saturday has worked in our favor.

We will now have available all our officers, representing every floor in the factory, to help as counters and to identify those voting.

THE PROUD HAVE HID SNARES

The ECU [the company union] is absolutely confident that less than 1,000 genuine bona fide ballots will be cast Saturday. A plant-wide survey proves that thousands of indignant workers, angered at the unfair regulations and the unseen but obvious political pressure being used in Washington, will refuse to become involved by voting.

NON-VOTING OUR ONLY COURSE

NLRB has acted in a dictatorial manner since this controversy started. We have not the money nor time to appeal to the courts.

NON-PARTICIPATION IS THE ONLY FORM OF APPEAL WE HAVE.

RCA workers know this and we are grateful for the thousands of pledges they have given us.

We have fought and won the strike, which was called to FOIST A RACKET on us whereby we would all pay $7.00 initiation fee and $2.00 monthly dues to the UERWA.

NON-PARTICIPATION WILL KILL THIS RACKET FOREVER!

NO MORE STRIKES

The UERWA is still making wild promises. All of us know that if they get 4,904 votes tomorrow IT MEANS ANOTHER STRIKE.

A VOTE TOMORROW IS TO VOTE A STRIKE IN SEPTEMBER.

A VOTE TOMORROW MEANS LESS JOBS FOR US IN CAMDEN.

A VOTE TOMORROW MEANS EVERY THIRD WORKER WILL HAVE TO BE FIRED TO MAKE ROOM FOR A STRIKER.

PROTECT YOUR JOB AND YOUR FAMILY BY NOT VOTING.

Not many industrialists were called to the stand; chiefly Goodyear Rubber Company, General Motors, Chrysler Corporation, Tennessee Coal and Iron Company. But the attitudes and activities of thousands of others were stated in invoice, ledger, and correspondence. One got the impression from most of those who were so unfortunate as to be called on the tapis that such matters were none of the public's business. Contemporaneous management, as we have heard, is done by instrument largely; is in fact itself an instrument, its nice adjustments responsive to distant controls. It is not a thing to be taken apart rudely. One cannot assume that because we are accustomed to looking within a man for the seat of his judgment, the spring of his practicality, or the animation of his moral life, that the corporate person may be so searched. The corporate person has repudiated the stronger virtues and the softer weaknesses of man in whose image it was made.

The public, of course, is entirely the creator of the super-myth with which big business leaders are surrounded. The leaders themselves, removed to an eminence of infallibility will, for the first lease of their habitation upon that awful hill, feel little better, little smarter than many of the jolly fellows whom they left below them. After a while, it would seem that the very act of sequestration had done its work, and the holy distance had served equally to impress the remover and removed. During the early days of the depression, the public watched management being stripped of its holy vestments. Taught to believe in the inspired intelligence of business leaders, they were at first shocked at the profane suggestion that the priests beneath their tonsures had heads no harder than those which graced the shoulders of the laity. Soon they began to dance around the vandalized altar like small boys drunk with new irreverence. But again the magic worked both ways. When recovery set in, and business leaders began once more to believe in the authenticity of their revelations, or in other words to believe in themselves, once more the chastened congregation was in the fold.

Through this investigation the public, like irreligious boys, has had another chance to peep behind the mystery. No one, not even the corporate person, can be all things to all men, and since we render to Caesar those things which are Caesar's and do not look to business for moral leadership, though why I cannot tell you, it being the theory that in America business attracts all the best available talent, what shall we look for? Is it not for leadership in shrewdness, thrift, and efficiency that we look to businessmen? Is not what we sanctify in businessmen their common sense? We know we have reason to do so. The cost accounting systems of business are marvels of pure mind. Business measures values without romance. Whereas government is known to throw its money away in delusions of grandeur, in business each dollar is regarded like a pea out of season.

Thus if it is with unfeigned gloating that the public has watched the spy's employer taken for a ride by the spy, his childish glee has nothing to do with morals or revenge. It has nothing to do really with the eternal fitness of things. It is purely an emotion of the theater and rises from a low sense of humor.

A prime necessity of the drama of espionage is that someone should play the sucker. Unmistakably a character part, its lines written for labor and supposed to build up to an ignominious exit, it is curious to watch the actors vying with each other for the role. As time goes on, labor grows more skittish, less easy to coach. Made up for the moment as understudy, the spy himself is taken across the boards. Then to our delight we watch the agency drift out of the wings, dressed to the teeth for a dupe. But who is prepared for that matchless sensation of the season, the star herself speaking the humblest lines?

Again and again the record reveals that employers did not know for what they were handing out their money, on what basis they were being charged and what profit was being made out of their accounts. The swollen expense sheets; the built-up report, so edited that it would give the manager an inflamed picture of conditions in his plant; the graft between finks; the lying of spy to agency; the police records of men brought in to act as police; the spying on clients for other clients and the likelihood therefore that one was himself paying for being spied upon. This was the bill of goods for which those same employers who would be considered derelict in their obligations to director and stockholder if they did not know to the last cent the weight and standard of the goods they were purchasing, not only paid for through the nose, but —on unitemized accounts—sometimes paid the bill twice over. The murders, the broken backs, the corrupted police and courts which they would find to be wanting in justice sometime when they themselves really desired it; the miserable little interpretations of events by miserable little men who find it worth their while to report as a charge of sabotage such observations as "the truck driver rested his elbow on the side of the car. I think he was sleepy": These are items tossed into the invoice for good measure.

Nevertheless, there is a fine line to draw between their gullibility and their fear of knowing too much. About

THE PROUD HAVE HID SNARES

the real issue they were not deceived. There was no pig-in-the-poke about the original agreement to purchase spies, gas, guns, or strikebreakers. The customer knew he was buying betrayal, violence, and potentiality to destroy. No matter how great the provocation, and it cannot be denied that many employers with the best intentions in the world have found themselves sorely tried in their efforts to deal with their workers, or more especially with the kind of leadership which too often foists itself upon them, there is no getting around the fact that the aim of the spy is to learn through pretext and inform through betrayal. The aim of the strikebreaker, and the objective in hiring him, is to break strikes by first provoking violence and then crushing it with superior violence. The chief objective of the gunmaker, and later of the gun's possessor, is that it should go off with the purpose of destruction. Even a curator of museum firearms would not deny you that, although it is a fact almost universally overlooked.

That having ordered these things, employers got them, would be no indication that they are swindled. That employers were overcharged and underserved must be at least in part attributed to their secret knowledge that overcharge and underservice were conditions of delivery. The very act of lulling themselves into an ignorance of what they were doing, induced also a prodigal spell. They handed out money as if under the voice of Svengali. Under this stupor even money values, the ones to which they were professionally trained, became distorted into ludicrous proportions.

Witness the American Bridge Company, a subsidiary of the United States Steel Corporation. The local police called upon to protect the overhanging and picketed operations of the Pulaski Highway through New Jersey were concededly in favor of the workers. It was hot. The police had been unhappily removed from their accustomed posts and beats to do a job with which they were not in sympathy. Wanting to keep their good will, or to gain it, as you please, American Bridge allowed them to run up a bill for soft drinks to keep them cool and contented. This bill, a little less than $600, looked high, also intrinsically it was not very pretty. The engineer, known as General Manager of Erection, in charge of a two-million-dollar job, in a labor difficulty that cost the company $290,000 to resist a demand for union wages which would have increased the labor cost by $100,000, took his mind off the problem of safe and complicated construction long enough to write this extraordinary letter.

"Mr. J. B. Gemberling,
Division Erecting Manager,
Philadelphia, Pennsylvania

"Dear Sir: We have your memorandum of the 19th, in reply to ours of the 18th relating to Foster's drink bill for $562.60. We are going to have to overcome a good deal of severe criticism on account of these bills, which I do not like. We would have been much better off and the policemen would have been healthier if we had purchased a small Frigidaire and have something left over in which there would be a salvage. I note that since you have talked to Captain Foster [of the Foster Detective Agency] there has been a drastic reduction and I wish you would let me know approximately how much per day is being spent for these drinks now.

"Captain Foster's opinion in regard to furnishing these drinks may be like his opinion in connection with some other phases of his work and probably our opinion is equally as good as his. In other words, would it not be better for the policemen to have good, cold water?

"I wish you would take this matter into your own hands and work the supply of soft drinks down to nothing just as quickly as it can be done.

"Yours truly,
"C. S. G.
"*Gen. Mgr. of Erection.*"

Finding the United States Steel Corporation, through its subsidiary, American Bridge, struggling with the salvage value of an ice box in the unquestioned expenditure of $290,000, we are able to sustain our amazement at its $4,000 estimate of Bergin's physical injury.

The desire to remain in ignorance of the true nature of such details of the transaction as can be avoided is bleakly clear even when it is not explicit. The head of the elevator union in New York testified that the hiring custom employed by apartment management in taking on elevator operators is to go back into the childhood of an applicant to learn his fitness for a job whose nature gives him access to the dwellings of defenseless people. Yet we have seen how, during a strike, the thugs of New York were signed on as elevator operators in droves, and how they got into a wholesale brawl which landed some in jail and the rest in the hospital when their hiring agency displayed the not overweening if uncomplimentary scruple of asking for their fingerprints. We have seen employers all over the country deliberately close their eyes to the nature of the men whom they wished to have deputized, and indeed make their deputization the sole condition of their being taken on. In receipt of the warm recommendation by Governor Hoffman of Sherwood's Detective Agency in New York, RCA Manufacturing Company hired first twenty-five missionaries to range public opinion on the side of the company, and in addition, between two and three hundred guards at $1.20 an hour to fight the physical fight on the basic assumption that these guards were state detectives. But let us read in words of the contractors of the engagement, the history of those days. I am inserting the record at length because it deals more authoritatively than can a commentator upon two matters of sequential interest in any study of employer's purposes or psychology. The Mr. Cunningham who is speaking is vice-president of RCA Manufacturing Company.

MR. CUNNINGHAM: A Mr. Williams, who was an officer of the Sherwood Detective Agency, called at Camden about a week or 10 days prior to the strike and said there was to be a general strike, that we were going to have a strike at that time. He asked to see me, but saw Mr. Throckmorton, the executive vice president, and presented a letter of introduction to me from Governor Hoffman of New Jersey, and made a selling talk as to the type of service that his agency could render along these lines and that the old methods of strikebreaking were passed and no longer desirable and that the thing to do was to organize the community sentiment; that they had handled that situation for a number of industrial concerns. Mr. Throckmorton called me in New York that day saying he felt in view of the credentials and in view of this explanation of the new character of service to be rendered, that I should go and see them and give it serious consideration. I delayed, still feeling that we were in negotiation and that there would not be a strike, but I called at their office in New York a few days prior to the strike and I met Captain Sherwood and Mr. Williams. They explained their plan of operation to me and I told them I would give it serious thought and if we had a strike I would get in touch with them.

The strike started on June 24 and that night I phoned Sherwood in New York and asked him to come to Camden and see me, and he came down that night and I engaged his service at that time.

The proposal which I approved was, he wanted authority to engage 25 men in the Camden area. . . . As I previously stated, both Sherwood and Williams stated that the old method of using strikebreakers and violence and things of that kind to win or combat a strike were things of the past; that the way to win a strike was to organize community sentiment; that they had been very successful in handling plans of that sort. They showed me enrollment slips—I cannot recall the exact title, but it was something like "Citizens Welfare Committee" of such and such a city. They showed me a large full-page ad, I believe from an Akron newspaper, in connection with a strike. They said they handled that. They sent men from door to door to get citizens to sign these membership slips, and if possible to get them to contribute to advertisements which would be run over the name of the so-called citizens' welfare organization, saying good things about the company and endeavoring in that way to promote a friendly public attitude to support the company. The details were a little more than that, but in substance that was the plan.

SENATOR LA FOLLETTE: Did he say, or did you gather from the newspaper advertisements and the blanks that he showed you, just what the citizens committee was to do?

MR. CUNNINGHAM: Well, it was not clear, other than the

favorable public reaction, throwing the weight to one side as against the other; that is the only—
SENATOR LA FOLLETTE: Did this Akron newspaper ad, as you remember, was it signed by a citizens' committee?
MR. CUNNINGHAM: Citizens' welfare committee, or something like that.
SENATOR LA FOLLETTE: Was the general effect of the advertisement to create the impression on the reader that the citizens' committee was taking the company side of the affair in Akron, so to speak?
MR. CUNNINGHAM: Yes; and without any apparent identity with the company; it was to appear as an independent proposal as far as the public was concerned.
SENATOR THOMAS: Did he show you any editorials that he thought he could have printed in the newspapers as a result of this advertising?
MR. CUNNINGHAM: There was something on that. My memory is not very good on just what he did show me, and I would not want to say exactly, but there was that impression, that editorials and news articles would be developed but that the citizens would be organized to take the lead in the interest of the company and employment and they would organize that and the company apparently was not having anything to do with it.
SENATOR THOMAS: You apparently got the impression his big job was to mold public sentiment?
MR. CUNNINGHAM: That was the impression. At the time, the strike was something new to me and I thought it was worth trying.
SENATOR THOMAS: He was to use the radio, newspapers, and house-to-house methods?
MR. CUNNINGHAM: Yes, sir.
SENATOR THOMAS: That is what they call missionary work in spy terminology; to take advantage of any oppor-

tunity to build public sentiment, feeling that pressure from without would probably do more good than work from within.

MR. CUNNINGHAM: Yes, sir; that was substantially my understanding.

SENATOR LA FOLLETTE: Mr. Cunningham, at this conference did they mention the fact that this might also be referred to as a law and order league, or something like that?

MR. CUNNINGHAM: Yes, sir. That was the main theme, now that you remind me; yes.

SENATOR LA FOLLETTE: Mr. Cunningham, did anyone representing the Sherwood Agency inform you what type of men they would employ for the work when you were conferring with them?

MR. CUNNINGHAM: Just the general assurances that they had regular men that they knew and were available to them and were thoroughly reliable for that work; just general assurance.

SENATOR LA FOLLETTE: Did you discuss with the Sherwood Agency the question of supplying guards or strikebreakers in addition to this community organization work?

MR. CUNNINGHAM: I did not handle that additional detail direct, and Mr. Shannon can give that additional detail, but I can state this is what happened:

There were serious riots, fighting between the workers, that is, those remaining in employment and those on strike, the Tuesday night after the strike was called, and Wednesday morning, either Sherwood or Williams came in and stated—

SENATOR LA FOLLETTE: We will get that from Mr. Shannon, if you please, because he was the one who knew about it.

MR. CUNNINGHAM: I did not arrange the hiring of the State deputies through Sherwood.

SENATOR LA FOLLETTE: Did you discuss with the Sherwood agency, yourself, the question of what their charges might be for any service rendered to you?

MR. CUNNINGHAM: On the initial 25 men; yes, sir, I did.

SENATOR LA FOLLETTE: Can you recall what was said about what it would cost you, approximately, per week or per month?

MR. CUNNINGHAM: As I recall, it was $10 per day per man.

SENATOR LA FOLLETTE: Including expenses?

MR. CUNNINGHAM: Yes; plus expenses, plus the hire of three automobiles, and there was a larger amount for three supervisors. . . .

Mr. Robert Shannon, vice-president in charge of manufacturing, was then called to the stand.

 .   .   .   .

SENATOR LA FOLLETTE: Do you remember how many men, approximately, they said would be required for this missionary work?

MR. SHANNON: I think an outside of 25.

SENATOR LA FOLLETTE: Did you discuss with them the number of guards they were to furnish?

MR. SHANNON: Not at that time.

SENATOR LA FOLLETTE: Well, at some later time did you discuss with them the number of guards?

MR. SHANNON: I did.

SENATOR LA FOLLETTE: How many were to be furnished?

MR. SHANNON: We discussed 200.

SENATOR LA FOLLETTE: Now, what services were the guards to perform?

MR. SHANNON: They were exclusively guards; they were supposed to be State detectives.
SENATOR LA FOLLETTE: State detectives?
MR. SHANNON: Correct.
SENATOR LA FOLLETTE: That is they were to be deputized, you mean?
MR. SHANNON: As he explained it, they would be State officers, State detectives.
SENATOR LA FOLLETTE: Did he explain how he could furnish detectives connected with the State?
MR. SHANNON: No; he did not explain; he said he could furnish them.
SENATOR LA FOLLETTE: And what was the nature of the service that these 200 were to perform?
MR. SHANNON: At that time we had considerable riots and what appeared to be inadequate police protection. These people would be State detectives with full authority to maintain law and order.
SENATOR LA FOLLETTE: Do you remember what rate of pay was to be given to the guards?
MR. SHANNON: I believe it was about $15 a day.
SENATOR LA FOLLETTE: And were they also to have their expenses paid?
MR. SHANNON: I think that was the outside figure.
SENATOR LA FOLLETTE: The inclusive figure?
MR. SHANNON: Yes.
SENATOR LA FOLLETTE: Was there any written agreement entered into at any time between the company and the Sherwood agency or any of its officials?
MR. SHANNON: Not to my knowledge. . . .
SENATOR LA FOLLETTE: And when did the men come to Camden; that is, in relation to the time that the strike broke?
MR. SHANNON: Two or three days later.

SENATOR LA FOLLETTE: Did you know at the time, or after the Sherwood men arrived in Camden, where they came from?

MR. SHANNON: Not exactly; no.

SENATOR LA FOLLETTE: Did you know in a general way?

MR. SHANNON: Yes; some were from Atlantic City, as I recall.

SENATOR LA FOLLETTE: And from any other place?

MR. SHANNON: Trenton.

SENATOR LA FOLLETTE: Did you know whether any of them came from New York at that time?

MR. SHANNON: I did not know.

SENATOR LA FOLLETTE: Who was in direct charge of the men?

MR. SHANNON: Mr. Williams.

SENATOR LA FOLLETTE: And how many were there?

MR. SHANNON: The plan was to get 200.

SENATOR LA FOLLETTE: Did you make any check as to how many actually were brought in by the Sherwood Agency?

MR. SHANNON: I did not.

SENATOR LA FOLLETTE: Were the missionaries or the community organizational men also brought in?

MR. SHANNON: I believe so.

SENATOR LA FOLLETTE: Do you know how many of those there were actually?

MR. SHANNON: No.

SENATOR LA FOLLETTE: Did you make any effort to ascertain?

MR. SHANNON: I did not.

SENATOR LA FOLLETTE: And how long were the Sherwood Agency employees in Camden in connection with this strike situation?

MR. SHANNON: You are referring to the State officers?

SENATOR LA FOLLETTE: Well, I am referring to the men that Sherwood furnished.

MR. SHANNON: The first group of approximately 25 men, I think, were there about 3 days.

SENATOR LA FOLLETTE: Those were the ones that were to work on this citizens' organization?

MR. SHANNON: Yes, sir.

SENATOR LA FOLLETTE: And how long did the guards or deputies remain?

MR. SHANNON: Part of 1 day.

SENATOR LA FOLLETTE: Now, you say that the men who were to work on the citizens' organization activities stayed 3 days?

MR. SHANNON: Yes.

SENATOR LA FOLLETTE: Did they succeed in forming any committee?

MR. SHANNON: I think so.

SENATOR LA FOLLETTE: Did you talk with Mr. Williams, the day the men came in?

MR. SHANNON: The day the State officers came in?

SENATOR LA FOLLETTE: Yes.

MR. SHANNON: Yes.

SENATOR LA FOLLETTE: When you say State officers you are referring to these approximately 200 men?

MR. SHANNON: So-called State officers.

SENATOR LA FOLLETTE: Yes. Well, on the day that you saw Mr. Williams, did you discuss the question of deputizing the guards?

MR. SHANNON: He came to see me the morning that the men came to town. I again questioned him as to whether or not they were State officers. I asked our counsel, who was in my office at the time, to check with the local authorities and to make sure that they were State officers.

SENATOR LA FOLLETTE: Did he make such an investigation?
MR. SHANNON: He did.
SENATOR LA FOLLETTE: And what did he report to you?
MR. SHANNON: He advised me later in the day that they were not State officers.
SENATOR LA FOLLETTE: Did he give you any other information?
MR. SHANNON: Yes; to the effect that Mr. Williams was attempting to have the men deputized locally.
SENATOR LA FOLLETTE: By the city authorities?
MR. SHANNON: The city authorities.
SENATOR LA FOLLETTE: Were they so deputized?
MR. SHANNON: They were not.
SENATOR LA FOLLETTE: Did you learn why they were not deputized?
MR. SHANNON: The police department objected to them and would not deputize them.
SENATOR LA FOLLETTE: Did they give any grounds for their refusal?
MR. SHANNON: Not exactly that I can recall.
SENATOR LA FOLLETTE: Well, to refresh your recollection, did you learn at that time that the reason for the refusal of the authorities of the city to deputize them was because of the type of men who sought to be deputized?
MR. SHANNON: Yes; I believe there was some question; some of them were recognized in the party as undesirable characters.
SENATOR LA FOLLETTE: Now, when you learned that the men were not deputized, did you take any action?
MR. SHANNON: I did.
SENATOR LA FOLLETTE: What did you do?

MR. SHANNON: I went to see Mr. Williams in his hotel room.

SENATOR LA FOLLETTE: On the same day?

MR. SHANNON: On this same day, as far as I remember, yes; I told him he had misrepresented the set-up and to take the men out of town immediately; that we would have nothing to do with them.

SENATOR LA FOLLETTE: You felt he had misrepresented the character of the men he would furnish?

MR. SHANNON: He misrepresented the fact they were supposed to be State officers, and they were not.

SENATOR LA FOLLETTE: Did you feel some responsibility for the character of the men who might be employed for this work?

MR. SHANNON: Not if they were State officers.

SENATOR LA FOLLETTE: You mean if these men had been deputized, the fact you had learned that some of them had undesirable characters or reputations would not have influenced you in any way?

MR. SHANNON: Oh, yes; if I knew that.

SENATOR LA FOLLETTE: You did know that by the time you saw Williams, did you not?

MR. SHANNON: I knew it the evening when I went to see him; not in the morning.

SENATOR LA FOLLETTE: Did you give as one of the reasons why you were requesting him to remove the men, that some of his men had bad reputations or characters?

MR. SHANNON: No. I asked him to have them removed because they were not State officers; he had misrepresented it.

SENATOR LA FOLLETTE: Had you ever had any knowledge prior to the time that the Sherwood Agency was employed, of the general nature and service that detective and strikebreaking agencies render?

MR. SHANNON: I did not.

SENATOR LA FOLLETTE: Did you know anything about the character of the men that agencies of this type sometimes employ?

MR. SHANNON: I had had no experience of that kind.

SENATOR LA FOLLETTE: Did the men perform any service for the company?

MR. SHANNON: I do not think so.

SENATOR LA FOLLETTE: What did you pay the Sherwood Agency, if anything?

MR. SHANNON: Two thousand-and-some-odd dollars.

SENATOR LA FOLLETTE: You paid them the money notwithstanding the fact they had misrepresented the type of men they were to furnish and that they performed no service?

MR. SHANNON: That is right.

SENATOR LA FOLLETTE: I offer for the record a photostat copy of a handwritten paper—please show Mr. Shannon a copy of it. It is dated Camden, N. J., on a blank sheet of paper, that is, it is blank in the sense that it has no letterhead, June 26, 1936, to RCA from M. Sherwood:

```
200 men at $10................ $2,000
Transportation at $1.50........   300
                                ------
Total ....................     $2,300
```

It is signed "O.K. R. Shannon." It is marked, "Charge account 8612-08."

That is the bill you received from the Sherwood Agency?

MR. SHANNON: That is right.

SENATOR LA FOLLETTE: Despite the fact that this man had misrepresented the kind of men he would furnish, and despite the fact that he had not performed any

THE PROUD HAVE HID SNARES

service for the company, did you make any effort to find out whether he actually had 200 men in Camden?

MR. SHANNON: I did not.

SENATOR LA FOLLETTE: Well, at the time you paid him, you were already on notice, were you not, that you could not rely on his statement.

MR. SHANNON: I personally declined to pay him. Our counsel who was present at that meeting with Mr. Sherwood and myself, advised we had better pay it and clear it up.

SENATOR LA FOLLETTE: Did he give any reason for it?

MR. SHANNON: No particular reason, except we wanted to get these people away; we did not want to have any dealings with them.

SENATOR LA FOLLETTE: Mr. Shannon, how did you figure out that the Sherwood Agency, a New York concern, could furnish what you thought were to be State officers in New Jersey?

MR. SHANNON: Because of the recommendation from Governor Hoffman, personal contact with Governor Hoffman.

SENATOR LA FOLLETTE: Did you have any personal contact with Governor Hoffman?

MR. SHANNON: No; but because of their contact with Governor Hoffman.

SENATOR LA FOLLETTE: It was really his letter which gave credence in your mind to Mr. Sherwood and Mr. Williams' statements they could furnish State officers?

MR. SHANNON: That is right.

SENATOR LA FOLLETTE: Otherwise, if you had wanted State officers, you would naturally have gone to the State officials, would you not?

MR. SHANNON: That is right.

SENATOR LA FOLLETTE: I take it you would regard a transaction of this character, where you made so little investigation or inquiry as to whether or not this service had actually delivered 200 men, as unusual in your business practice?

MR. SHANNON: We had a most unusual condition at that moment.

SENATOR LA FOLLETTE: I understand that, but I assume, for example, even though you had a very unusual condition during the strike, you were not paying for merchandise or supplies or material without finding out if it was delivered, were you?

MR. SHANNON: That is right. . . .

SENATOR LA FOLLETTE: Did you make any further payment to the Sherwood Agency in connection with this matter, Mr. Shannon?

MR. SHANNON: I did not.

SENATOR LA FOLLETTE: Did anybody that you know of for the company?

MR. SHANNON: Yes; I understand an additional payment was made.

SENATOR LA FOLLETTE: Who made the additional payment?

MR. SHANNON: I think it was Mr. Cook.

SENATOR LA FOLLETTE: Would Mr. Schneider know?

MR. CUNNINGHAM: I authorized the additional payment and the payment was actually made in New York in cash to Mr. Sherwood by Mr. Cook, the treasurer, on direct instructions from Mr. Throckmorton, our executive vice president. Mr. Shannon believed he had terminated finally with Sherwood the night he discharged them, but then Sherwood came in with an additional bill to Mr. Throckmorton, claiming Shannon had only taken care of one transaction, namely, the 200 guards, and there were these other 25 men. I was chagrined about the situation and said, "Clean it up and get rid of them; I do not want anything more to do with them." I wanted to make those payments and wash the situation up immediately. That is why there were the two payments, because there was a group of 25 men that were to do this missionary work and also the supplemental proposition where they claimed they could bring in 200 State officers.

SENATOR LA FOLLETTE: The Committee is in possession of a copy of a letter which it obtained under subpoena from the Sherwood Agency, dated July 8, 1936, addressed to you, Mr. Cunningham:

"We were engaged by your company to do propaganda work in bringing your employees back to work to give them courage and to enlighten them in reference to the union's reasons for agitation. You put us in the hands of Mr. Shannon, informing us that we were to work under his instructions and that he would give us a list of all the employees who did not report for work. The only list he gave us was one with 14 or 15 names that he obviously did not want. We were told to return the next morning for an additional list, but never received it.

"WHY AFTER WAITING FOUR DAYS FOR THE LIST OF MEN AND WOMEN WHO HAD NOT REPORTED FOR WORK WERE WE LAID OFF?

"We feel that if given a proper opportunity without molestation, and that if favoritism is not shown, but honest efforts made to solve your difficulties, we will be able to fulfill our promises to you.

"Very truly yours,
"SHERWOOD'S DETECTIVE BUREAU."

Meanwhile, undiscouraged, RCA continued negotiations which they had begun with Manning's Agency to supply them with guard service for the plants. These men, some 100 of them, it was put forth, would be ex-soldiers and marines.

SENATOR LA FOLLETTE: Did you discuss with Mr. Manning the question of deputizing guards?

MR. SHANNON: I do not think so.

SENATOR LA FOLLETTE: Why did you make a distinction between these two services? As I understood you to say, you would not take the services of the Sherwood men unless they were State officers.

MR. SHANNON: That is what was offered.

SENATOR LA FOLLETTE: And when they could not be deputized, as I understood you, you discharged the Sherwood Agency?

MR. SHANNON: That is right.

SENATOR LA FOLLETTE: Why did you make this distinction between the Manning Service and the Sherwood Service men in relation to their being deputized or connected with the State?

MR. SHANNON: The Manning men were hired primarily for guard service, for the protection of the company's property.

SENATOR LA FOLLETTE: That is what I understood you were hiring the Sherwood men for.

MR. SHANNON: No; they were State officers, to enforce law and order on the streets.

SENATOR LA FOLLETTE: Oh, I see. If I get it straight now, your idea was that the Sherwood Agency would furnish men who would be State officers and who would have authority to patrol the streets and maintain law and order?

MR. SHANNON: That is right.

SENATOR LA FOLLETTE: And that the Sherwood men would only act on the company's property; is that correct?

MR. CUNNINGHAM: The Manning men.

More than 300 Manning men were on hand for two months at a cost to the company of approximately $150,000, their actions, according to Mr. Shannon, being such as to bring forth no criticism from him. When the Civil Liberties Committee asked for an itemization of the Manning bill, RCA asked Manning for it and received a statement which Senator La Follette read aloud in part:

STATEMENT

Services rendered and expenses incurred on your labor matter, during the months of June, July, and August, 1936, as follows:

SERVICES

(11) Supervisors June 14 to Aug. 7—447 days—5224 2/3 hrs. @ $1.45 per hr. $7,575.80
(287) Spcl. Watchmen June 15 to Aug. 7— 7903 days—99,776½ hrs. @ $1.20 per hr. $119,731.80

EXPENSES

Compensation Insurance Premium, a/c Watchmen on duty at plant involved in labor difficulty or strike (June 23 to July 21, incl.).

Supervisors . . . . . 318 man-days
Spcl. Watchmen . . 7,247 man-days

7,565 man-days at $1.00 per man-day . . . . $ 7,565.00

Allowance to Supervisors and Spcl. Watchmen (298), for Lodging and Meals (8,350 man-days) .... $ 20,436.45
R. R. & Bus Fares, Newark to Camden & Return (206) 705.60
Office: Newark, Telephone & Toll charges, June 15 to Aug. 7 .... 178.35

Total $156,193.00

Mr. Shannon, will you look at a copy of that exhibit and tell me if that is the most complete itemization of Manning charges to the company that you have ever received?

MR. SHANNON: I believe it is.

SENATOR LA FOLLETTE: And you received that statement only some months after you had paid his bill in full, did you not?

MR. SHANNON: That is true.

SENATOR LA FOLLETTE: And you would not have come into possession of even this meager detailed information unless the Committee had requested it, would you?

MR. SHANNON: I might not.

SENATOR LA FOLLETTE: Well, as a matter of fact you would not, would you?

MR. SHANNON: Probably not.

SENATOR LA FOLLETTE: The transaction, as far as you were concerned, was closed long before the Committee requested this information, was it not?

MR. SHANNON: That is right.

SENATOR LA FOLLETTE: To your knowledge, Mr. Shannon, has the corporation ever before made a single payment for merchandise or service aggregating $150,000 without any itemized invoice or accounting?

MR. SHANNON: I do not know of any.

The grand total cost of the strike charged to the RCA Manufacturing Company was $831,026. This does not include other expenses charged to the Radio Corporation of America, the parent organization. One of these was over $45,000 paid to Hugh S. Johnson for professional services and expenses "in connection with labor troubles at Camden."

For a description of some of the Manning men who were allowed to carry on the work for which Sherwood's men disqualified when they failed to achieve the badge of authority, we are indebted to a Mr. Robinson, formerly chief investigator of thefts and union activities in the plant, now discharged and replaced by a Manning man.

MR. ROBINSON: . . . Mr. Hamilton was present, and he introduced me to Mr. Manning and two of his lieutenants.

SENATOR LA FOLLETTE: Were any of these guards armed?

MR. ROBINSON: Only with clubs.

SENATOR LA FOLLETTE: What did you observe about the effect of these guards, if anything?

MR. ROBINSON: Well, at first, they were very quiet. They were standing in the doorways watching and inspecting people coming in and out of the buildings, and if possible, to stop all employees during working hours from going out, and they had to give a good reason where and why they were going, and when they went out, they left under guard. One or two of Manning's men would take them to the different buildings they were going to.

SENATOR LA FOLLETTE: Of your own personal knowledge, can you tell the Committee who some of these men were?

MR. ROBINSON: The Manning's men?

SENATOR LA FOLLETTE: Yes.

MR. ROBINSON: Well, I knew some of them that I met that

day. Right off the bat, by name—I can refer to my notebook. Andy Maxner—

SENATOR LA FOLLETTE: Was he a Manning guard?

MR. ROBINSON: Yes.

SENATOR LA FOLLETTE: Who was he?

MR. ROBINSON: He is known as a wrestler who comes from New York.

SENATOR LA FOLLETTE: Who else did you know?

MR. ROBINSON: Walter DeBolt.

SENATOR LA FOLLETTE: Where was he from?

MR. ROBINSON: He was from Newark, a former policeman.

SENATOR LA FOLLETTE: Did you know any others?

MR. ROBINSON: DeBolt lived in New York. I knew another one. They called him the Big Swede. He was a wrestler from New York.

SENATOR LA FOLLETTE: He was what?

MR. ROBINSON: A wrestler from New York.

SENATOR LA FOLLETTE: Any others?

MR. ROBINSON: I knew Jack Lynch, the captain of the guards, and Frank Woodring, who I was closely associated with practically during all of the strike.

SENATOR LA FOLLETTE: Where were they from?

MR. ROBINSON: Woodring was from Philadelphia.

SENATOR LA FOLLETTE: Did you know a man by the name of Gray?

MR. ROBINSON: "Peaches" Gray; yes; a Camden local pug or boxer. He has a police record.

SENATOR LA FOLLETTE: Did you make any investigation of these men's records?

MR. ROBINSON: Yes, I have.

SENATOR LA FOLLETTE: Tell us what you know about their record?

MR. ROBINSON: Well, I started this week, on Monday, to

make an investigation of some of their records, and I have not had time to complete it. The only knowledge I have is from a man who is here in Washington with me, a former Manning guard, and he knows of some of these fellows—

SENATOR LA FOLLETTE: If you do not know of your own personal knowledge—

MR. ROBINSON: The only one I know of my own knowledge is "Peaches" Gray, and one other; I cannot recall his name. They both have police records in Camden.

SENATOR LA FOLLETTE: During the first week of the strike, what were your duties, if any, in relation to the strike?

MR. ROBINSON: During the day I would investigate homes that were supposed to have been painted by strikers, and complaints of employees coming to work that would make complaint of being beaten or molested by strikers on entering the plant to work; and I would take them up to the police court, on instructions from Mr. Wilkinson, and have warrants made out for the strikers who molested them. We would then—myself and a city policeman named Jones—would make an effort to arrest these people.

SENATOR LA FOLLETTE: Did you do any other investigating work in connection with the strike?

MR. ROBINSON: Not during the strike.

SENATOR LA FOLLETTE: Did you have anything to do with the picket lines during the strike?

MR. ROBINSON: Only to get the name of every picket that was in the line that would be known to me.

SENATOR LA FOLLETTE: Who gave you those instructions?

MR. ROBINSON: Mr. Hamilton.

SENATOR LA FOLLETTE: What was the attitude of the city police during the first week of the strike toward the strikers and pickets?

MR. ROBINSON: The first week, as I can recall, they were very calm; they were more or less in favor of the strikers.

SENATOR LA FOLLETTE: Did the attitude of the police change during the strike?

MR. ROBINSON: Yes.

SENATOR LA FOLLETTE: And when did that change take place?

MR. ROBINSON: About the third week of the strike.

SENATOR LA FOLLETTE: Do you know of your own knowledge any reason for the change in their attitude?

MR. ROBINSON: There had been a meeting between Hamilton, the chief of police, Collsey, Lieutenant Bakeley, Harry Kline, and the superintendent, J. C. Buzzelli. As I understand, they had a meeting in Mr. Collsey's office at city hall as to the arrests that were being made, and the light manner they were being handled—suspended sentences, and so forth. Mr. Manning was at that meeting, and when he came back in the watch headquarters he said, "Watch now; we will get some action." Beginning the next morning any arrests that were made the fines ranged from $50 to $100, and those who were held for bail for the grand jury were held in high bail. . . .

SENATOR LA FOLLETTE: Were any guards employed by Manning, to your knowledge, who had any previous connection with the city police force?

MR. ROBINSON: There were city detectives named Jones and Weber, and they hired as many Camden County constables as they could get, 20 or 25; also justices of the peace to act as guards; some of them were to guard the homes of officials, and they had those men because they were entitled to carry arms.

SENATOR LA FOLLETTE: Were they on the company's pay roll, or Manning's?

MR. ROBINSON: They were on Manning's pay roll. There was one bridge policeman employed by the bridge that goes from Philadelphia to Camden.

SENATOR LA FOLLETTE: Of your own knowledge do you know what they were paid by Manning?

MR. ROBINSON: The only one that I know of was Jones. He got $10 a day expenses for the use of his car.

SENATOR LA FOLLETTE: Do you know of your own knowledge if they remained on the city pay roll while they were working for and being paid by Manning?

MR. ROBINSON: Yes; they were.

SENATOR LA FOLLETTE: Do you know how these city detectives were paid?

MR. ROBINSON: They were paid the same as I was and all other private guards, in a little white envelope. I was also on Manning's pay roll. It was a little white envelope they would hand us on Tuesdays between 2 and 3 o'clock in the afternoon.

SENATOR LA FOLLETTE: Did you make any arrests during the strike with Jones and Weber?

MR. ROBINSON: Yes; I did.

SENATOR LA FOLLETTE: How many?

MR. ROBINSON: Two.

SENATOR LA FOLLETTE: Describe what happened.

MR. ROBINSON: We were standing at the Camden entrance of the Camden ferry and there were several workers going over on the ferry, and in the last part of the line there were two men who looked at one another and one of them said, "Camden cops, bah." Jones said, "Come on, Robby, let's get 'em." We made a rush for them and I grabbed one and Jones took one. The man I had —I cannot remember who the policemen were, but there were several of them that beat him over the head with clubs. As we were putting him in the patrol wagon another policeman known as "Wilkie the notebook cop" rushed up with a club and hit the man a final crack, and that caused him to bleed pretty bad. When the patrol wagon came there were two or three other people in it, and one of them was a woman and she said, "Please let us take this man to the hospital; he is bleeding terribly." Whoever the policeman was, he said, "Shut up or you will get the same dose."

There were a dozen arrests made at that point, and that particular arrest created the arrest of the other 10 or 12, and each was charged with rioting and inciting to riot, but someone made a complaint about the brutality of the police and the minute they opened their mouth they were arrested.

They did not go to the hospital with this man but drove to the city hall and discharged the other prisoners and then finally took him to the hospital. I know that because I followed the patrol in a car.

I must resist the temptation to carry this testimony further. It is not unique but typical. The employer's disavowal of responsibility for public safety is frequently made by the simple expediency of closing two eyes, or, failing that feat, one. The badness of RCA's record, that which makes it so clear, is that it is honestly and fully given, no mean compliment in a Senate investigation. Mr. Paul Litchfield, president of Goodyear Company, less compliant a witness than Mr. Cunningham or Mr. Shannon, short and apparently resentful in his answers, gave evidence of ocular acrobatics amounting to virtuoso performance over a period of years in which, as president of Goodyear Rubber Company, he could forget that the

THE PROUD HAVE HID SNARES

Akron Employers' Association whose membership was composed of representatives from the Akron rubber companies spent most of its money for undercover men from Corporations Auxiliary, although before his elevation to the presidency, he had served as a delegate member to that association from his company. He said he did not know that Corporations Auxiliary had undercover men within his plant. Ward of the Harlan County Coal Operators' Association, which subsidized the hoodlum government of that county, testified that he refrained from asking what was being done with the money he was handing out.

Mr. Herman Weckler of De Soto Corporation made perhaps the blanket answer for all his colleagues, inside and outside his corporation, when he answered La Follette's question:

SENATOR LA FOLLETTE: Just speaking as a human being, Mr. Weckler, and not as an official of the Chrysler Corporation, or of the De Soto Corporation, how can you justify the corruption of men and the use of these undercover operatives who spy upon their fellow workers?

MR. WECKLER: The only way it can be justified is from the fact that we do have and have had proper employee relations.

SENATOR LA FOLLETTE: But I am speaking now from the ethical and moral standpoint. You look to me like a very decent human being, Mr. Weckler.

MR. WECKLER: Thank you.

SENATOR LA FOLLETTE: How do you justify this practice?

MR. WECKLER: It has been a practice that has been in existence for years. It is a practice we have grown up with.

SENATOR LA FOLLETTE: You do not think that just because an industry has lost from thefts for years that you would be justified in continuing, would you?

MR. WECKLER: No, sir.

SENATOR LA FOLLETTE: How do you justify it? Just as one member of this Committee I would be very anxious to know how you justify it on moral and ethical grounds?

MR. WECKLER: Well, the justification for it is that in order to have the information which you require to build permanently for better organization, it is necessary that you have a lot of information as to what is going on in your plants and in the minds of your employees.

SENATOR LA FOLLETTE: Just as an individual now, and as a human being, what would be your reaction, what would be your judgment that you would inevitably pass on one of your executive associates if he should, for hire, be willing to divulge the industrial secrets of the Chrysler Corporation to one of your competitors?

MR. WECKLER: I think it would be terrible.

SENATOR LA FOLLETTE: And yet you think it is all right to do the same thing so far as the men who work in your plant are concerned, and who, as a matter of fact, do contribute to the success of the Chrysler Corporation?

MR. WECKLER: I do not think we are buying secrets of the same type, Mr. Senator.

SENATOR LA FOLLETTE: What is the difference between the secret of a labor union which is founded, at least, on the theory or upon the principle of advancing the welfare of its members and which, at least in theory, is officered and its membership is composed of people who are interested in the advancement of the welfare of themselves and their fellow employees, what difference, on ethical and moral grounds, now, Mr. Weckler, is there between the purchase through surreptitious undercover methods of those secrets and the divulging of the industrial secrets of the corporation by some man who was employed in an executive capacity, secretly, for pay, or for hire, to a competitor?

MR. WECKLER: I think that there seems to be an undue stress on the information that had been passed. In one case it is stressed as secret information. There is a lot of this information that is mentioned in these reports, particularly the two reports that you called my attention to here a few minutes ago, that the members of the unions themselves would have been very glad to give to me, in fact have given to me at different times when I have talked to them at meetings.

SENATOR LA FOLLETTE: We will go into that in just a minute. I do not want you to get away from the moral and ethical aspects of this problem because it is the responsibility of this Committee to inquire into it. I am trying to elicit from you, not for the purpose of embarrassment, but I am giving you a full and free opportunity; I want to elicit if there is any justification for this undercover and surreptitious and corrupt practice that seems to prevail so widely in industry, as far as this Committee has been able to go with its limited funds. Now, if you do not desire to take advantage of that opportunity, I am not going to press you on it.

MR. WECKLER: I think it would take quite some time to express it, and evidently, we do not see the thing in exactly the same way.

SENATOR LA FOLLETTE: Well, you said it was reprehensible, didn't you?

Although in Mr. Weckler's opinion to spy on one's peers may be reprehensible, Chrysler Corporation nevertheless did have reports made to them by Corporations Auxiliary upon 499 of their suppliers, unbeknownst to the supplying company. Fifty-eight of these spied upon vendors are or have been regular clients of Corporations Auxiliary, as for instance, the Electric AutoLite Company of Toledo and Firestone Tire and Rubber Company.

It is a false method, if the only one available, to single out the instance. To do so is to ignore and almost to deny by ignoring, the great prevalence of each practice described and the wide adherence to the doctrines exposed by this inquiry. It is as if we had a wide bolt of fabric before us with a repeated design newly visible on each length of the material unrolled. Only as it is all spread before us to great length, and viewed at a distance, can we be convinced as to the effectiveness of the pattern in its full coverage. Yet if I were to list, as the testimony would permit, the 952 members, for instance, of the Metal Trades Association; were to attempt to give the geographical spread of Burns by naming the employers in far ends of the country whom they service; were to give the range in size of plants by identifying the big and small customers of Pinkerton's or of National Corporations Service, the facts would be precise but tedious to the point of dulling comprehension.

Furthermore, to stress the single instance is to be misleading in another respect. It puts emphasis upon the moral question involved, and implies that choices are set before the participating individuals as if they operated in a world of free selection. These matters of rubbing out a man's life, or the taking away of his livelihood, the acceptance or giving of a bribe for betrayal; they are not matters for chiding. Granted that a widely revivified moral

THE PROUD HAVE HID SNARES

sense can make or break an economic system, just as a revivified moral sense can overthrow tyrants, by the same token that our two greatest statesmen have been great moral philosophers, even so the moral approach to these habits of industry is callow and sophomoric. Men who appear at the hearings for their boards of directors are merely men taking the rap. Some of them look like vestrymen and perhaps are. Some of them perhaps serve very well on school boards and public library committees.

If moral safeguards are no good, so also shall we be foolishly misguided if in the future we put our trust to keep us free of the results of such greed in attempts to secure enforcement of the constitutional guarantee of the rights of free speech and assemblage or the legal rights of labor to bargain collectively. Great labor events occurred while this book has been in the process of being written. The labor upsurge amounting almost to a resurrection that began to occur under NRA kept its impetus, with small losses, until we saw a changed status for labor. The first successful attempt to organize industries swept the labor world before it. United States Steel, which resisted organization for thirty-seven years, has given in to union acknowledgment. The automobile industry and the textile industry have faced a world made of younger men, jovial, but grim for salvation. All sorts of odd units of American business waked up one morning to find a union button on every worker in the place. The decision that the Wagner Labor Disputes Act is constitutional almost created a new industry. The Labor Boards grind night and day. Trade Association leaders are busy as beavers getting out printed matter to explain to their members how to abide by the law. The workers themselves by literal tens of thousands are swamping the Works Progress Administration with requests for workers' education classes. The papers are full of the changed temper of employers. During the first winter of the Civil Liberties inquiry, Corporations Auxiliary, according to testimony of one of their old clients, has closed up shop. One would think the Golden Age was at hand—if he knew no labor history, and if he saw no significance in the equally contemporaneous public disposition to roll the juggernaut over the unemployed.

This happy external collaboration indicates no change in the fundamentals over which the struggle goes on and on. No one in his right mind will rest more easily on his pillow at these assurances. General Motors has set up the nucleus of its own investigative system, according to one of the witnesses. One detective agency man speculates as to whether he might not be better off to take a few of his best men with him, and see if he couldn't go off on his own on industry's pay roll. Another, by the last reports, heads up RCA's investigations, hired since the strike was over. National Metal Trades has shown one way. Tennessee Coal and Iron has shown another.

The quickest distance between two points may no longer be the raveling route of spy between the organizing workers and the employer who wishes to keep them unorganized. But not even the Supreme Court has put labor espionage into past tense, passive form. To regard the story of spying in this country as past history is to be either sanguine or sentimental. These hearings were occurring at a most critical point of America's labor history, at a moment when it was impossible to keep the outside world from intruding upon them. Yet there was no evidence on the stand of changed employers' temper.

Spying is an adaptable business. It has no face to lose. It has no standards to which it must publicly adhere. It spies for one purpose only, to make money. It is hired for one purpose, to save it. These purposes have not changed. The same old task is there for the executive. The man who turns to espionage to save money for him by reducing to impotence the demands of his workers for a larger share in his business can and must, for the purposes of that transaction, adhere to the moral standards of the purveyors. His best attempts to rationalize into any personal ethical system of his own, practiced in the daily conduct of his perhaps unimpeachable life, do not succeed, so he gives up the effort and, like the engineer of the Pulaski Highway, says he is not lawyer enough to pass upon it.

Their course is determined by forces so overwhelming that most of these executives can no more seriously resist the implicit turn things take than can the most miserable man on the hook. The employers who testified were not the owners. They were, as has been said before, the instruments of business navigation in America, subject to the control of the bridge. They are hired neither to make nor save money, really, but as stewards to keep it intact and improve it for the sequestrator. For they find themselves in the tight situation by which their most flexible money cost is that of labor, and labor is not inanimate, as I have said before, but gets notions. Pay more for iron, and iron will not get your money away from you: You still own the iron. Pay more for the worker and it has gone like breath to his diaphragm and he breathes a stouter man: It is his.

We must look behind these spokesmen to see if the effort to tighten the forces of American life will be relaxed. Let us hear Mr. Harry Anderson, personnel director of the General Motors Corporation, and Merle Hale, formerly director of labor relations, on the subject:

SENATOR LA FOLLETTE: Are you a member of the special conference committee?

MR. ANDERSON: Yes, sir.

SENATOR LA FOLLETTE: Do you represent the General Motors Corporation on this committee?

MR. ANDERSON: Yes, sir.

SENATOR LA FOLLETTE: Mr. Hale, during the time you were director of labor relations, did you represent General Motors Corporation upon this committee?

MR. HALE: Yes, sir. . . .

SENATOR LA FOLLETTE: Now, Mr. Anderson, will you tell us generally what this special conference committee is?

MR. ANDERSON: The special conference committee is composed of a number of personnel men that make a practice of meeting once a month, at which time the general discussion of labor conditions and business conditions and their respective operations are discussed.

SENATOR LA FOLLETTE: And where does this committee usually meet?

MR. ANDERSON: In New York.

SENATOR LA FOLLETTE: Where?

MR. ANDERSON: In Radio City.

SENATOR LA FOLLETTE: Well, do you have any usual place of meeting there?

MR. ANDERSON: Yes, sir. It is on the twenty-fourth floor; I think it is the twenty-fourth floor.

SENATOR LA FOLLETTE: Now, is that an office?

MR. ANDERSON: Yes, sir.

SENATOR LA FOLLETTE: Whose office is that?

MR. ANDERSON: Mr. Cowdrick's. . . .

SENATOR LA FOLLETTE: Who is he?

MR. ANDERSON: He is the secretary of the special conference committee.

THE PROUD HAVE HID SNARES 347

SENATOR LA FOLLETTE: Does he maintain offices there?
MR. ANDERSON: Yes, sir.
SENATOR LA FOLLETTE: Does he have any other position or occupation?
MR. ANDERSON: None that I know of.
SENATOR LA FOLLETTE: And are there any other officers of this special conference committee?
MR. ANDERSON: They have a chairman of the committee.
SENATOR LA FOLLETTE: And how often is he selected?
MR. ANDERSON: I believe once a year.
SENATOR LA FOLLETTE: Do they have any others?
MR. ANDERSON: That is all that I know of.
SENATOR LA FOLLETTE: Is this office of Mr. Cowdrick's the office of the special conference committee?
MR. ANDERSON: Yes, sir.
SENATOR LA FOLLETTE: Is it in connection with any other office?
MR. ANDERSON: Standard Oil Co. of New Jersey offices are there also.
SENATOR LA FOLLETTE: And is this a part of those offices?
MR. ANDERSON: Senator, I do not know the set-up, how they rent them around there.
SENATOR LA FOLLETTE: I mean, is it a part of the suite?
MR. ANDERSON: I would say it was; yes, sir.
SENATOR LA FOLLETTE: Now, Mr. Anderson, can you tell us what corporations have representatives on the special conference committee?
MR. ANDERSON: I believe I can.
SENATOR LA FOLLETTE: Name the representatives, please.
MR. ANDERSON: Mr. Pierce, who represents the Standard Oil Co. of New Jersey.
SENATOR LA FOLLETTE: Where you can remember their initials, give them, please, too. Mr. Hale will help you.

MR. ANDERSON: Frank Pierce. Then there is Si Ching of the United States Rubber Co.
SENATOR LA FOLLETTE: Si what?
MR. ANDERSON: Si Ching.
SENATOR LA FOLLETTE: C-h-i-n-g?
MR. ANDERSON: That is right.
SENATOR LA FOLLETTE: Who is he?
MR. ANDERSON: He is the personnel director of the United States Rubber Co. Then there is Art Young, of the United States Steel Corporation. There is Joe Larkin of the Bethlehem Steel.
SENATOR LA FOLLETTE: How do you spell that?
MR. ANDERSON: L-a-r-k-i-n. There is George Kelday, of the International Harvester.
SENATOR LA FOLLETTE: How do you spell that?
MR. ANDERSON: K-e-l-d-a-y. There is Art Griffith.
MR. HALE: It is Griffin, of the A. T. & T. Co.
MR. ANDERSON: And there is Fred Climes, of the Goodyear Tire & Rubber Co. There is John Holbrook, of the Irving Trust. There is Frank Evans, of the du Pont Co. George Pfeiffe, of the General Electric. Mr. Marshall, of Westinghouse. . . . I think that is all. . . .
SENATOR THOMAS: Do you have any representatives from one of these companies that come from as far as the Pacific coast?
MR. HALE: Chicago is the farthest away. George Kelday comes from Chicago.
SENATOR THOMAS: Nothing west of Chicago?
MR. HALE: No.
SENATOR THOMAS: And nothing south of Chicago?
MR. HALE: Nothing south; no, sir. . . .
SENATOR LA FOLLETTE: Now, Mr. Anderson, do you know about when the special conference committee was formed?

MR. ANDERSON: No, sir; I do not.
SENATOR LA FOLLETTE: Do you, Mr. Hale?
MR. HALE: It was probably 20 years ago. It was way, way back.
SENATOR THOMAS: Did Ivy Lee have anything to do with the organization?
MR. HALE: No, sir. It was formed, if I remember, by a get-together of Mr. Schwab and the man in the Standard Oil Co., I believe Mr. Teagle. He is a sort of sponsor of it. It started out with a few companies. The membership of the committee is about as it has been for a great many years. I think the U. S. Steel was taken into membership about 3 years ago, when Art Young went to U. S. Steel. Before that I think the membership was practically constant over a period of 10 or 12 years. . . . The principal order of business was for each man to give a sort of a résumé of business conditions of his company, and the outlook for business conditions, and then anything unusual in the—well, I will not say labor, because it is much broader than that. The broader situation—for instance, one of the problems that we discussed considerably at the time I was going there was this Social Security and Unemployment Insurance. We worked on a recommendation for our principals—that is, speaking of our superiors we always referred to them as principals—we worked on an unemployment insurance program, or the principles of unemployment insurance. But, as I say, the principal discussion was for each man to tell monthly the story about his affairs. Naturally when the NRA came up that was a point of a great deal of discussion, the NRA phase of it.
SENATOR LA FOLLETTE: When NRA was discussed did you discuss 7(a) any?

MR. HALE: Yes, sir; yes, sir, we certainly did.
SENATOR LA FOLLETTE: Did you find that there was a sort of a meeting of the minds about how you felt about 7(a)?
MR. HALE: No; there was not. That is the beauty of the committee, that there is some good hot discussion. We had our liberals and our conservatives in that group just the same.
SENATOR LA FOLLETTE: Would you say the conservatives outnumbered the liberals, or otherwise?
MR. HALE: Well, I suppose that would be a definition of the term.
SENATOR LA FOLLETTE: I am letting you use your own definition.
MR. HALE: I would say it was pretty equally divided.
SENATOR LA FOLLETTE: Were there any there that thought that under 7(a) it would be a good idea for the corporations to have outside unions?
MR. HALE: I remember the question of outside unions as a method of representation was discussed, and I think there were quite a few that felt that if—not quite a few—I remember the discussions on outside unions hinged around the point as to the responsibility of the unions, and that if unions could be responsible it might be a good thing.
SENATOR LA FOLLETTE: Were there any there who thought they could or would be?
MR. HALE: No; I think we felt that if we could get something of the English picture of a financial responsibility, or something of that kind.
SENATOR THOMAS: You would make the unions incorporate?
MR. HALE: That was the question I answered; that was

Senator La Follette's question, did we discuss outside unions.

SENATOR THOMAS: Did you discuss that question?

MR. HALE: I think we did, and, as I remember it, someone cited or discussed Justice Brandeis' comment on that. I am not certain. I remember there was quite a lot of discussion from time to time about it.

SENATOR LA FOLLETTE: In view of the fact that the English picture was not in the situation, what was the feeling of most of those there?

MR. HALE: Well, you see, Senator, most of those companies were what you might call the pioneers, or there were a great many who pioneered the work in employee representation which has since become known as the works council.

SENATOR LA FOLLETTE: It is also known as the company union?

MR. HALE: I think so, erroneously, it is now; but the original idea of employee representation of the Standard Oil Co. and the International Harvester Co., the Bethlehem Steel Co., the telephone company, the Goodyear and the United States Rubber, if my memory serves me correctly, they started employee representation some 15 or 18 years ago, and, naturally, the men that had had experience with them were very strong in their belief that that was providing the solution to the objectives set forth under 7(a).

The union is legalized beyond the reach of even the Liberty League lawyers. A man can no longer be fired because he joins it. But a union is a means to an end, not an end in itself. It must frame a course and that course can be changed. It must negotiate agreements, and those agreements can be weakened. It must choose officers, and it can be led into choosing traitors.

Nothing is changed. The proud are there, the snare and the will to hide it. The rules for the trapper are changed, but the game is as good as ever, and the bounty on it just as high.

Most Americans love the Republic with the same preoccupation with which a busy man loves a faithful wife: Only when they feel her virtue to be in danger does their ardor become young and jealous. We do not love free speech and free movement until we see them threatened. We will not die for them until they are taken away. With considerable horror we watch men of other nations allow themselves to be robbed of their right to their opinions, or, more insidious, accept dictated predications which they are told to use in coming to conclusions.

We Americans are well-practiced in having our minds made up for us. We clean our teeth, eat our breakfast, and go to war on propaganda. We continue to believe in the individuality of our judgment because we hope that counter-waves of propaganda will wash upon us, leaving us unmoved on our island of integrity, and that the right of free speech itself will thus enable us to hold honest opinions, independently arrived at.

We forget that effective propaganda costs money, and that when its superior effectiveness is demonstrated in maintaining a status desired by those who have money to spend for it, money will be used without stint. In the changing strategy of the war against collective bargaining, we find expensive propaganda displacing more primitive methods. Less visible than spying, more blinding than gas, it should render them both less necessary. Strikebreakers may cease to look and smell like finks; they may look and smell like public relations men instead.

The *New York Times* of July 3, 1937, carried an article by F. Raymond Daniell under the caption " 'Johnstown Plan' Wins Wide Backing." This is a story of how John Price Jones, a specialist in raising funds and creating public opinion, and a native son of Johnstown, had been persuaded to eschew a Harvard reunion to help out the home chamber of commerce. Although the article deserves full reading I shall quote it in part only.

By F. RAYMOND DANIELL

JOHNSTOWN, Pa., July 2.—A national chain of citizens committees to defend the right of loyal workers to continue at their jobs under the protection of elected officials in spite of strikes is being organized from this city with the financial backing of a group of industrialists under the guidance of a nationally known publicity and fund-raising firm. . . .

The representatives of the local chamber of commerce declared that, with Governor George H. Earle openly on the side of the strikers and President Roosevelt at least tacitly supporting them, they did not know which way to turn for help in maintaining law and order.

Mr. Jones said over the telephone tonight that he told the leading citizens of Johnstown that their problem was not local but national in scope. What was happening here, he said, was happening everywhere else. What they should do, he informed the local folk, was to broadcast the story of Johnstown's terror and try to effect an interstate organization to impress upon States and local legislators and Congressmen that American workmen never would be slaves to organization.

There followed conferences in Pittsburgh about two weeks ago between local business leaders and representatives of some of the country's leading industrialists. Soon afterward there arrived in Johnstown a representative of the National Manufacturers Association and a member of the firm of Ketcham & McLeod, the agency which handles the advertising for the Weirton Steel Company, headed by Ernest L. Weir.

Correspondents covering the steel strike developments here have been under the impression that Mr. Weir was underwriting the costs of organization and advertising, but through a spokesman at Pittsburgh this afternoon he denied that he had contributed "either to the local or national campaign for organizations of citizens' committees."

However, the day after the representative of the agency handling the Weirton account was in Johnstown, full-page advertisements appeared in forty newspapers at an estimated cost of about $50,000. These advertisements contained this paragraph which defines the thesis on which all the vigilante groups are acting in the Middle West, where C. I. O. is conducting a vigorous drive for members:

"Let us make two things perfectly clear at the outset. We are not arguing for or against the unions. We are not arguing for or against the steel company. We take our stand in defense of two fundamental American liberties—the right of local self-government and the right of every worker to pursue his occupation peaceably and within the law."

Majority Held Against Strike

The advertisements also declared: "The present strike was called by the C. I. O. in spite of the fact that an overwhelming majority of Cambria workers did not want it. There was no dispute about wages, hours or working conditions."

Asserting that "if this can happen in Johnstown, it can happen anywhere," the advertisements concluded with an appeal for funds. Funds poured in from thirty States to the amount of about $30,000, with the bulk of the contributions coming from neighboring communities, New York City and industrial centers of Michigan, principally Detroit.

The response was so gratifying to the local citizens' committee, the organization of which was inspired by an employee of John Price Jones, that the following telegram was sent eight days ago to upward of 200 chambers of commerce, civic organizations and leading business men in as many cities:

"Your offer of cooperation to the Citizens' Committee of Johnstown has encouraged our intensive efforts. Our problem goes beyond Johnstown's boundaries, for what has happened here can happen anywhere unless we are alert in guarding constitutional rights. A national plan for protecting the rights of individuals at work must be initiated. The Citizens' Committee of Johnstown desires to know if your community or group will send representatives to an organization meeting at a time and place to be decided for launching a national movement. Loyal Americans will not fail in protecting the right to work for all who want to work."

Telegram Signed by Banker

This telegram was signed by Francis C. Martin as chairman of the committee. He is an officer of the United States National Bank, from which the union has threatened to withdraw its funds. . . .

Did Hitler or Mussolini have more of a beginning? Beside this tool, the strap which flogged Joseph Gelders was a teething rattle. Our hallucinations of independent judgment can be charged to labor overhead.

Nothing about liberty, either the goal or the reality, is fixed. None of its gains is safe for a moment. Men mill around the principle of freedom like sailors trying to lash themselves to a mast in shipwreck. But even the mast is subject to hygroscopic change, its absorptive power susceptible to the influences of the century in which it is trying to keep afloat. Those who were first in the lifeboat try to row away from the contemporaneous scene into the past. Sometimes they cannot overcome the suspicion that history will overtake them. This fear is what gives to the struggle its persistent character; management, or rather, that part of it concerning whom this book is written, fights not to win, but to defer defeat; to postpone the day when it must recognize that all sides must fight for a common cause. The reluctance of the die-hard is what renders his role almost a humorous one: one David with one small stone and a stiff upper lip, mistaking for Goliath the Giant Time.

INDEX

Abt, John, 17, 28
Addressograph Multigraph Co., correspondence, 250
A. F. of L. *See* American Federation of Labor
Ailes, A. S., 169-179, 187-192, 216, 218
Akron Employers Association, 57
Aliases, use of, 27, 84, 85, 140
Allen Company, S. L., 259
Allied Corporation Service, Inc., 48, 149
Amalgamated Ass'n of Iron, Steel & Tin Workers, 44
Amalgamated Clothing Workers of America, 104
American Bridge Co., 141, 150, 276-278, 313, 314
American Hawaiian Steamship Co., 194
American Federation of Labor, 6, 70, 99, 113, 258, 259, 292
Amoskeag Mills, 66
Anaconda Copper Co., 205
Anderson, Harry, testimony of, 345-348
Andrews, Johnnie, 55, 56
Anthracite Institute, 219
Auxiliary Company of Canada, 51

Bambrick, James, 141-144
Bank of America, 168, 170, 195

Barker, B. H., testimony of, 192-198
Barton, Jack, testimony of, 277-289
Bergin, Edward, 141, 276-278
Bergoff, Pearl, 133, 143, 145, 146
Bethlehem Steel Co., 215
Black and Decker, 211, 250-257
Blacklist, 23, 233-237, 268
Blaiser, Robert D., 26, 33, 34
Blankenhorn, Heber, 18, 45, 46
Boycott, 12
Brady, Sam, 26, 79, 83, 84, 97
Braidwood, Illinois, strike, 44
Bromley, Bruce, 26, 34, 36, 37
Brotherhood of Railway Clerks, 84
Burns' International Detective Agency, 24, 25, 36, 59, 64, 131, 149; clients of, 62, 63; correspondence of, 66-69, 104-113
Burns, Raymond J., testimony of, 59-62
Burns, W. Sherman, testimony of, 59-62
Burnside, Ray L., 27
Burr, Borden, 154; testimony of, 155-157, 289, 290
Business Week, 11
Byrnes Law, 145

INDEX

California Hawaiian Sugar Refinery, 186
Camden Police Department, 215
Carnegie Illinois Steel Company, 44, 80, 81
Casey, Michael, 132-136, 149, 153
Central Industrial Service, 46, 47
Chevrolet Motor Car Co., 86, 94, 206
Child Labor Amendment, 9
Chinese coolies, 9
C.I.O. *See* Committee for Industrial Organization
Civil Liberties Committee. *See* U. S. Senate.
Chrysler Co., 45, 51, 55, 56, 310, 340
Chrysler, Walter J., 57
Class struggle, 6-15
Coates, William, 104-112
Cohen, Chowderhead, 140, 141, 149
Cole, John, 244-247
Committee for Industrial Organization, 8, 113, 117, 119
Commons, John R., 10
Communism, 68-70, 89, 105, 183, 278, 282, 284, 292
Company union, 8, 308, 309
Corporations Auxiliary Co., 23, 45, 46, 50-57, 248, 344; instructions to salesmen, 70-72
Cravath, De Gersdorff, Swaine, and Wood, 26, 36
Crawford County, Iowa, 220-222

Cunningham, E. T., 158; testimony of, 316-320

Daily Worker, The, 68, 112, 279
Davidson, John, 128
Davison, E. C., testimony of, 233-236, 241
DeGersdorff, Carl, 26
Delco Remy Co., 240
Deming, George E., 258-260
Deputizing, 153-158, 315-329
DeSoto Motor Corporation, 55, 339
Detective agencies, 21-24, 45-63; clients of, 48, 50, 62, 63; obstructionist tactics of, 24-38
Detective business, estimated volume of, 45-63; solicitation of, 39, 42-44, 64-77
Dinius, C. B., 205
Dubuc, Frenchy, 84, 86
Dudley, Ralph, 36
Duplicate Transfer Rebate Co., 46

Eastern Engineering Corp., 47
Eddy, J. H., 69
Eckhardt, Carl, 237-239
Education and Labor, Subcommittee of. *See* U. S. Senate
Erie Chemical Co. *See* Lake Erie Chemical Co.
Equitable Auditing and Publishing Co., 51

Federal Laboratories, Inc., 24, 168-192, 211, 213, 214; cli-

INDEX

ents of, 215; testimony of, 192-201, 206-211
Fink, 132-136, 140-153
Fisher, Jack, 136, 162; testimony of, 166, 167
Foote, Herrick, correspondence, 201, 218
Frankensteen, Richard, 54-57, 85, 131
Frick Coal Co., H. C., 44, 83, 139, 215
Frigidaire strike, 149

Gadd, Charles A., testimony of, 250-257
Gas, 23, 168-222; alleged humanitarian effects of, 215-222; known volume of sales, 215
Gelders, Joseph, 154, 265, 288-291; testimony of, 291-300
General Motors, 24, 28, 29, 32, 37, 45, 51, 57, 73, 86, 100, 206, 310, 344; testimony, 345-351
Golden, Clinton S., 118
Golden, Ralph, 141, 276
Goodyear Tire & Rubber Co., 202-204, 228, 310, 338
Goss, Col. B. C., 179-187
Gray, William, 72, 76, 137, 153
Groves, W. B., 47
Groves, W. W., 47

Hale, Merle, testimony of, 349-351
Hampton Roads Ship Repair Co., 234
Hanna, Walter J., 293-300

Harlan County, 154, 166, 212, 339; Hearings, 18, 225, 301-307
Hemphill, William Earl, 113-119
Hoffman, Governor, 158
Holman, Joseph, 237-239
Homestead strike, 44
Hooking, 77-86, 236-240

I Break Strikes, 146, 147
Industry, migration of, 11, 12; see Management
Internal Revenue, Bureau of, 212
International Ass'n of Machinists, 233, 241, 243
International Auxiliary Co., 51, 52
International Labor Bureau, 47
International Labor Defense, 293
International Library Service, 47
Ivey, Eugene P., 72, 153, 212

Jackson, Gardner, 21
Johnson, Hugh S., 333
Johnston, Col. J. J., 213, 214
Jones & Laughlin, 206, 215
Justice, Department of, 4, 40, 170, 176, 188

Kaul Lumber Co., 69
Kuhl, Red, 79, 85, 86, 95, 128, 137, 138, 140, 147-149
Kilian, Paul, 206

Labor in the United States, History of, 10

Labor Statistics, Bureau of, 150
La Follette, Senator, 17, 20, 26, 29, 37; examination of witnesses, 30-34, 40, 41, 60-62, 101-103, 114-118, 133-136, 147-149, 159-162, 192-198, 203, 204, 229, 233, 236, 243-248, 250-257, 270-275, 293-300, 303-305, 317-338, 339-341, 346-351
Lake Erie Chemical Co., 24, 216-218; correspondence, 168-192, 201, 213, 214
Lamb, W. J., 256, 257
Lawson, A. E., 48, 49, 97, 137
LeMay, L. D., 69
Letteer, Lyle, 37, 98-103
Lewis, Harold, 86, 94, 95
Litchfield, Paul, testimony of, 202-204, 338
Labor movement, 8

MacGuffin, E. E., 48, 49, 147, 148, 213
McCarty, Ignatius, 211; correspondence, 168-192, 199
McDade, E. J., 146, 154; testimony of, 159-165
McDuff, Milton, 279
McParlan, James, 40
Maddox, A. D., 281
Management, attitude of, 8, 9, 11, 258, 259, 306-351
Manning's Agency, 330-338
Manville Manufacturing Co., 24, 168, 201, 202
Marshall, Alfred, 206
Master Bakers Association, 106-112

Matles, James, testimony of, 243-248
Middleton, Sheriff Theodore R., 302, 303
Miners, Western Federation of, 11
Missionary, 136-138, 315, 317-319, 322
Molly McGuires, 40
Money, political power of, 7, 10, 12
Moyer, Charles H., 11
Mullen, John T., 80-82
Munitions, industrial, 168-222; collusion with government authorities, 211, 213; how to turn plant into fort, 207-211; merchandising methods of, 168-201; secrecy of transactions, 202-206
Munitions Committee. *See* U. S. Senate
Murphy, Senator, 17
Musick, Bennett, 266, 301
Musick, Mallie, 301; testimony of, 306, 307
Musick, Marshall, testimony of, 301-306

National Corporation Service, 24, 46, 48-50; list of clients, 50; list of operatives, 120-127
National Dairy Strike, 162
National Labor Relations Board, 18, 21, 83, 257, 308, 309
National Metal Trades Association, 24, 46, 221-262, 342; constitution of, 227, 232; correspondence, 233,

INDEX

240-243, 260, 261; definition of operative, 232; how it works, 225-229; witnesses: Davison, E. C., 233-236; Gadd, Charles A., 250-257; Sayre, Homer, 229-231, 248, 249
New Jersey Engineering Corp., 47, 145
New Orleans Public Service Strike, 62, 131, 142-144
Newport News Shipbuilding & Drydock Co., 234, 235
N.L.R.B. *See* National Labor Relations Board
Noble, 132-146
NRA, 14, 65, 67, 104, 343, 349

Patterson, George A., 81-83
Pendleton, Forrest C., 48, 49
Pendleton, Inc., Forrest C., 47
Pennsylvania Industrial Service, 46; correspondence, 212, 213
Peterson, Robert H., 30-32
Pfohman, Lawrence, 249, 250
Picketing, 8
Pinkerton National Detective Agency, 24-38, 44-46, 57, 64, 73, 79, 86, 94, 98, 119, 131, 145, 278; correspondence, 74, 79, 96, 97; witnesses: Blasier, Robert D., 26, 33, 34; Bromley, Bruce, 26, 34, 36, 37; Dudley, Ralph, 36; Peterson, Robert H., 30-32; Pinkerton, Robert A., 36; Pugmire, Arthur L., 40; Rossetter, Asher, 32-35, 50, 63; Whitney, William D., 26-28

Pinkerton, Allen, 40, 44
Pinkerton, Robert A., 27, 58, 59
Propaganda (*see* Missionary), 8, 269, 315, 317-319, 322, 352-355
Pugmire, Arthur L., 40

R. A. & I. *See* Railway Audit and Inspection Co.
Radio Corporation of America, 150, 158, 214, 308, 315, 344; strike, 270-275; testimony, 316-338
Railway Audit and Inspection Co., 24, 25, 46-48, 72, 73, 131, 141, 149, 151, 204, 212; contract with strikebreaker, 151, 162; correspondence, 72-76, 89-93, 95; list of clients, 48; witness, Hemphill, W. E., 113-119
R.C.A. *See* Radio Corporation of America
Remington-Rand Strike, 62, 131-136, 145, 211
Republic Rubber Co., 80
Rice, L. D., 47, 77, 95
Robinson, John T., testimony of, 333-338
Ross, Dan G., 54, 131-136
Rossetter, Asher, 32-35, 59, 63
Roush, Joseph M., correspondence, 199-201
Rowan, Richard Wilmer, 39-41

Sayre, Homer, 224; testimony, 229-231, 248, 249
Secret Service, U. S., 44
Securities and Exchange Commission, 51

INDEX

Senate Munitions Committee, 18, 183, 204
Senate, United States, Civil Liberties, Committee of (Education and Labor Subcommittee), 3, 4, 16-21; funds of, 20-22; methods used in examination of witnesses, 22-38, 52, 53; Resolution 266, 19
Shannon, Robert, 320-332
Sherwood Detective Agency, 158, 317, 320, 325-329
Shults, Frank, 240-243
Smith, James H., 51-54, 131, 248
Smith and Weber, 51
Social Security Act, 25, 260, 261
Souder, Jesse W., 270-275
Special Conference Committee, 345-351
Spying, nature of, 39-45, 53-57, 87-130, 240-248, 344, 345
Standard Oil Company of N. J., 347, 349
Steel Workers Organizing Committee, 118
Stettinius, Jr., Edward R., 11
Strike, 9, 12, 37; first recorded American, 5; government dealing with, 12-14; hardship of, 14, 15; weapon of, 12
Strikebreaking, characteristics of, 128-167, 250-257
Stringham, L. A., 237, 240
Stow, Ashfield, 193, 194, 197
Swope, Gerard, 259, 260

T.C.I. *See* Tennessee Coal and Iron Railroad Company
Teapot Dome, 19
Tennessee Coal and Iron Railroad Co., 69, 114, 154-157, 166, 265, 278, 281, 282, 290-300, 310
Thomas, Senator, 17, 20, 26, 27, 53, 230; examination of witnesses, 155-157, 162-167, 231, 248, 249, 278-289, 318

United Automobile Workers, 55
United Mine Workers, 305
United States Rubber Co., 348
United Electrical and Radio Workers, 270

Vigilante, 8, 21, 315, 317, 319, 322, 352, 353
Violence, 3, 4, 19, 28, 44, 152, 153, 158-167, 250-257, 265; purpose of inciting, 138-144; effects of, 266-307

Wage-earner, 4-8
Wagner Disputes Act, 65, 260, 261
Walsh-Healy Act, 261
Webster, Timothy, 40
Weckler, Herman L., 55, 57, 85; testimony of, 339-349
West Point Manufacturing Co., 212
Whitney, William D., 26-28
Williams, Dent, 294-300
Wilson, G. H., 238
Winstead, Ralph, 129

INDEX

Wisconsin Light & Power Co., 146-159, 160
Wisconsin Strikebreaking Statute, 229
Wohlforth, Robert, 17, 18, 26
Woodward Iron Company, 91-93, 114
Young John, 206-211
Ziegler, Phil, 84, 97

American Labor: From Conspiracy to Collective Bargaining

AN ARNO PRESS/NEW YORK TIMES COLLECTION

SERIES I

Abbott, Edith.
Women in Industry. 1913.

Aveling, Edward B. and Eleanor M. Aveling.
Working Class Movement in America. 1891.

Beard, Mary.
The American Labor Movement. 1939.

Blankenhorn, Heber.
The Strike for Union. 1924.

Blum, Solomon.
Labor Economics. 1925.

Brandeis, Louis D. and Josephine Goldmark.
Women in Industry. 1907. New introduction by Leon Stein and Philip Taft.

Brooks, John Graham.
American Syndicalism. 1913.

Butler, Elizabeth Beardsley.
Women and the Trades. 1909.

Byington, Margaret Frances.
Homestead: The Household of A Mill Town. 1910.

Carroll, Mollie Ray.
Labor and Politics. 1923.

Coleman, McAlister.
Men and Coal. 1943.

Coleman, J. Walter.
The Molly Maguire Riots: Industrial Conflict in the Pennsylvania Coal Region. 1936.

Commons, John R.
Industrial Goodwill. 1919.

Commons, John R.
Industrial Government. 1921.

Dacus, Joseph A.
Annals of the Great Strikes. 1877.

Dealtry, William.
The Laborer: A Remedy for his Wrongs. 1869.

Douglas, Paul H., Curtis N. Hitchcock and Willard E. Atkins, editors.
The Worker in Modern Economic Society. 1923.

Eastman, Crystal.
Work Accidents and the Law. 1910.

Ely, Richard T.
The Labor Movement in America. 1890. New Introduction by Leon Stein and Philip Taft.

Feldman, Herman.
Problems in Labor Relations. 1937.

Fitch, John Andrew.
The Steel Worker. 1910.

Furniss, Edgar S. and Laurence Guild.
Labor Problems. 1925.

Gladden, Washington.
Working People and Their Employers. 1885.

Gompers, Samuel.
Labor and the Common Welfare. 1919.

Hardman, J. B. S., editor.
American Labor Dynamics. 1928.

Higgins, George G.
Voluntarism in Organized Labor, 1930-40. 1944.

Hiller, Ernest T.
The Strike. 1928.

Hollander, Jacob S. and George E. Barnett.
Studies in American Trade Unionism. 1906. New Introduction by Leon Stein and Philip Taft.

Jelley, Symmes M.
The Voice of Labor. 1888.

Jones, Mary.
Autobiography of Mother Jones. 1925.

Kelley, Florence.
Some Ethical Gains Through Legislation. 1905.

LaFollette, Robert M., editor.
The Making of America: Labor. 1906.

Lane, Winthrop D.
Civil War in West Virginia. 1921.

Lauck, W. Jett and Edgar Sydenstricker.
Conditions of Labor in American Industries. 1917.

Leiserson, William M.
Adjusting Immigrant and Industry. 1924.

Lescohier, Don D.
Knights of St. Crispin. 1910.

Levinson, Edward.
I Break Strikes. The Technique of Pearl L. Bergoff. 1935.

Lloyd, Henry Demarest.
Men, The Workers. Compiled by Anne Whithington and Caroline Stallbohen. 1909. New Introduction by Leon Stein and Philip Taft.

Lorwin, Louis (Louis Levine).
The Women's Garment Workers. 1924.

Markham, Edwin, Ben B. Lindsay and George Creel.
Children in Bondage. 1914.

Marot, Helen.
American Labor Unions. 1914.

Mason, Alpheus T.
Organized Labor and the Law. 1925.

Newcomb, Simon.
A Plain Man's Talk on the Labor Question. 1886. New Introduction by Leon Stein and Philip Taft.

Price, George Moses.
The Modern Factory: Safety, Sanitation and Welfare. 1914.

Randall, John Herman Jr.
Problem of Group Responsibility to Society. 1922.

Rubinow, I. M.
Social Insurance. 1913.

Saposs, David, editor.
Readings in Trade Unionism. 1926.

Slichter, Sumner H.
Union Policies and Industrial Management. 1941.

Socialist Publishing Society.
The Accused and the Accusers. 1887.

Stein, Leon and Philip Taft, editors.
The Pullman Strike. 1894-1913. New Introduction by the editors.

Stein, Leon and Philip Taft, editors.
Religion, Reform, and Revolution: Labor Panaceas in the Nineteenth Century. 1969. New Introduction by the editors.

Stein, Leon and Philip Taft, editors.
Wages, Hours, and Strikes: Labor Panaceas in the Twentieth Century. 1969. New introduction by the editors.

Swinton, John.
A Momentous Question: The Respective Attitudes of Labor and Capital. 1895. New Introduction by Leon Stein and Philip Taft.

Tannenbaum, Frank.
The Labor Movement. 1921.

Tead, Ordway.
Instincts in Industry. 1918.

Vorse, Mary Heaton.
Labor's New Millions. 1938.

Witte, Edwin Emil.
The Government in Labor Disputes. 1932.

Wright, Carroll D.
The Working Girls of Boston. 1889.

Wyckoff, Veitrees J.
Wage Policies of Labor Organizations in a Period of Industrial Depression. 1926.

Yellen, Samuel.
American Labor Struggles. 1936.

SERIES II

Allen, Henry J.
The Party of the Third Part: The Story of the Kansas Industrial Relations Court. 1921. *Including* **The Kansas Court of Industrial Relations Law** (1920) by Samuel Gompers.

Baker, Ray Stannard.
The New Industrial Unrest. 1920.

Barnett, George E. & David A. McCabe.
Mediation, Investigation and Arbitration in Industrial Disputes. 1916.

Barns, William E., editor.
The Labor Problem. 1886.

Bing, Alexander M.
War-Time Strikes and Their Adjustment. 1921.

Brooks, Robert R. R.
When Labor Organizes. 1937.

Calkins, Clinch.
Spy Overhead: The Story of Industrial Espionage. 1937.

Cooke, Morris Llewellyn & Philip Murray.
Organized Labor and Production. 1940.

Creamer, Daniel & Charles W. Coulter.
Labor and the Shut-Down of the Amoskeag Textile Mills. 1939.

Glocker, Theodore W.
The Government of American Trade Unions. 1913.

Gompers, Samuel.
Labor and the Employer. 1920.

Grant, Luke.
The National Erectors' Association and the International Association of Bridge and Structural Ironworkers. 1915.

Haber, William.
Industrial Relations in the Building Industry. 1930.

Henry, Alice.
Women and the Labor Movement. 1923.

Herbst, Alma.
The Negro in the Slaughtering and Meat-Packing Industry in Chicago. 1932.

[Hicks, Obediah.]
Life of Richard F. Trevellick. 1896.

Hillquit, Morris, Samuel Gompers & Max J. Hayes.
The Double Edge of Labor's Sword: Discussion and Testimony on Socialism and Trade-Unionism Before the Commission on Industrial Relations. 1914. New Introduction by Leon Stein and Philip Taft.

Jensen, Vernon H.
Lumber and Labor. 1945.

Kampelman, Max M.
The Communist Party vs. the C.I.O. 1957.

Kingsbury, Susan M., editor.
Labor Laws and Their Enforcement. By Charles E. Persons, Mabel Parton, Mabelle Moses & Three "Fellows." 1911.

McCabe, David A.
The Standard Rate in American Trade Unions. 1912.

Mangold, George Benjamin.
Labor Argument in the American Protective Tariff Discussion. 1908.

Millis, Harry A., editor.
How Collective Bargaining Works. 1942.

Montgomery, Royal E.
Industrial Relations in the Chicago Building Trades. 1927.

Oneal, James.
The Workers in American History. 3rd edition, 1912.

Palmer, Gladys L.
Union Tactics and Economic Change: A Case Study of Three Philadelphia Textile Unions. 1932.

Penny, Virginia.
How Women Can Make Money: Married or Single, In all Branches of the Arts and Sciences, Professions, Trades, Agricultural and Mechanical Pursuits. 1870. New Introduction by Leon Stein and Philip Taft.

Penny, Virginia.
Think and Act: A Series of Articles Pertaining to Men and Women, Work and Wages. 1869.

Pickering, John.
The Working Man's Political Economy. 1847.

Ryan, John A.
A Living Wage. 1906.

Savage, Marion Dutton.
Industrial Unionism in America. 1922.

Simkhovitch, Mary Kingsbury.
The City Worker's World in America. 1917.

Spero, Sterling Denhard.
The Labor Movement in a Government Industry: A Study of Employee Organization in the Postal Service. 1927.

Stein, Leon and Philip Taft, editors.
Labor Politics: Collected Pamphlets. 2 vols. 1836-1932. New Introduction by the editors.

Stein, Leon and Philip Taft, editors.
The Management of Workers: Selected Arguments. 1917-1956. New Introduction by the editors.

Stein, Leon and Philip Taft, editors.
Massacre at Ludlow: Four Reports. 1914-1915. New Introduction by the editors.

Stein, Leon and Philip Taft, editors.
Workers Speak: Self-Portraits. 1902-1906. New Introduction by the editors.

Stolberg, Benjamin.
The Story of the CIO. 1938.

Taylor, Paul S.
The Sailors' Union of the Pacific. 1923.

U.S. Commission on Industrial Relations.
Efficiency Systems and Labor. 1916. New Introduction by Leon Stein and Philip Taft.

Walker, Charles Rumford.
American City: A Rank-and-File History. 1937.

Walling, William English.
American Labor and American Democracy. 1926.

Williams, Whiting.
What's on the Worker's Mind: By One Who Put on Overalls to Find Out. 1920.

Wolman, Leo.
The Boycott in American Trade Unions. 1916.

Ziskind, David.
One Thousand Strikes of Government Employees. 1940.